Richard Restak, M.D., is a neurologist who teaches at Georgetown University School of medicine. His first book, *Premeditated Man,* was selected by The New York *Times* as one of the Notable Books of 1975. His second book was the critically acclaimed *The Brain: The Last Frontier;* it was selected by *Psychology Today* as one of the Best Behavior Books in 1979.

PHOTO BY CAROLYN RESTAK

The Self Seekers

The Self Seekers

RICHARD M. RESTAK, M.D.

Doubleday & Company, Inc.
Garden City, New York
1982

Grateful acknowledgment is made to the following for permission to reprint their copyrighted material.

Excerpt reprinted by permission of Grosset & Dunlap, Inc. from *Catch Me If You Can* by Frank W. Abagnale, Jr., copyright © 1980 by Frank W. Abagnale, Jr.

Excerpt from *The Borderline Syndromes* by Michael Stone, copyright © 1980 by McGraw-Hill, Inc. Reprinted with permission of the publisher.

Excerpt from *Looking for Mr. Goodbar*, copyright © 1975 by Judith Rossner. Reprinted by permission of Simon & Schuster, a Division of Gulf & Western Corporation, and Jonathan Cape Ltd.

"True Love at Last" and selections from "Behaviour" and "Sphinx" from *The Collected Poems of D. H. Lawrence*, collected and edited with an Introduction and Notes by Vivian de Sola Pinto and F. Warren Roberts. Copyright © 1964, 1971 by Angelo Ravagli and C. M. Weekley, Executors of the Estate of Frieda Lawrence Ravagli. Reprinted by permission of Viking Penguin, Inc., and Laurence Pollinger Ltd.

Library of Congress Cataloging in Publication Data

Restak, Richard M., 1942–
   The self seekers.

   Bibliography.
   Includes index.
   1. Identity (Psychology) 2. Self. I. Title.
      BF697.R42   616.85′82
      ISBN 0-385-15976-5   AACR2
Library of Congress Catalog Card Number 81-43417

In memory of Heinz Kohut, M.D., who, in a period of failing health and diminished physical resources, generously found time to teach me his concepts about the self.

Acknowledgments

This book would not have been possible without the cooperation and direction of many people who have thought and written about the self.

I'm particularly grateful for the opportunity over the past three years for fruitful discussions, conversations and interviews with Otto Kernberg, M.D.; Heinz Kohut, M.D.; James Grotstein, M.D.; Gordon Pask; R. D. Laing, M.D.; Frank W. Abagnale, Jr.; Joseph Lichtenberg, M.D.; Vamik Volkan, M.D.; Daniel Stern, M.D.; Joel Swerdlow; W. W. Meissner, M.D., S.J.

I am particularly grateful to Ben Bursten, M.D., who first brought to my attention that self disorders inevitably lead to various forms of manipulation. Finally, I'm indebted to Carolyn Restak for research, typing and wise counsel.

Contents

I. INTRODUCTION

II. THE SELF

III. BEYOND FREUD

IV. THE NARCISSIST

V. CROSSING THE BORDER

VI. THE PSYCHOPATH

VII. THE DESTROYERS

VIII. THE MANIPULATOR

I

Introduction

"I have some ambivalent feelings about him. The guy is likable. The only problem is that he is a manipulator; he uses people."

Chief Deputy U. S. Marshal Robert Christman after arresting convicted spy Christopher Boyce

Contemporary American society is currently overrun with a personality that I call the manipulator. He exists at all levels of society, from the boardrooms of our nation's industries to the maximum-security wards of our prisons. Manipulators are numbered among our employers and spouses; many of our heroes are manipulators. So widespread is the manipulator, in fact, that manipulation has become a life-style which threatens to change the very fabric of American society.

Basically, the manipulator suffers from a deficiency in the sense of self: what we usually refer to as a sense of identity. This disturbance exists along a continuum beginning with innocent and commonly encountered difficulties in the regulation of self-esteem which we all experience from time to time and extending, at the other extreme of the continuum, toward dangerous psychopathic murderers. Along this continuum are encountered different kinds of manipulators: narcissists, borderline personality disorders, impostors and, finally, psychopaths. This book explores each of these different personalities and illustrates how they all share a basic disturbance in the self. To this extent, the book is about the importance of self in modern life.

In the first part of this book, I take up what a self really is. How do we establish a self? How early in life does it first appear? How can a person suffer from a disturbance in the self? Why does a disturbance in the sense of self create a manipulator? The remainder of the book will try to answer these questions by examining the different guises under which the manipulator is commonly encountered.

At the lower level of the continuum of manipulation, we find the narcissistic personality. This is a person whose sense of self-esteem is based on the maintenance of a grandiose self: lavishingly wealthy or an intellectual giant, or perhaps a legendary lover. The exact details may vary but the grandiose self exists as an inner ideal which is usually beyond the capabilities of ordinary mortals. Coupled with this grandiose self there exists within the narcissistic personality an alternative devalued self-image of helplessness and impotence. The manipulation of the narcissist consists in turning the tables on the rest of us so that we have to acknowledge his superiority as well as help him to ignore the existence of his devalued self. He wants to be a superman and manipulates the rest of us into helping him realize this ambition.

Further along the continuum we encounter the borderline personality who suffers from an even more serious split within the core of his identity. Some experts consider the borderline to exist midway between neurosis and psychosis, inhabiting a kind of no-man's-land between mild emotional distress and outright insanity. In the borderline individual, the self disturbance is serious. He suffers from explosive feelings of rage, pervasive alienation, loss of the sense of personal integration. Based on the view of psychological development known as Object Relations Theory, which we will describe later in the book, the borderline individual is now thought to be reliving in the present past frustrations and failures dating from early in life, sometimes even as far back as infancy. He manipulates the rest of us into providing the love and attention that he missed earlier in life. Further, he doesn't want and can't accept our love when it's offered. He rejects it and tosses it back into our face, only to move on to yet another person who can be exploited and manipulated into loving him.

With the psychopath we approach the outer limit of disturbances within the self. He lacks all sense of community. He's a rebel without any sense of commitment to anything other than himself. He is cold, calculating and totally ruthless. But he also shares with his less disturbed counterpart, the narcissistic personality, the ability to charm, beguile and win us totally over to his side. Many murderers and major criminals possess the ability, when the occasion demands, of evoking the sympathy of others. Psychopaths count on our feeling sorry for them, so they can manipulate us once again.

A particularly interesting and increasingly encountered variety of psychopath is the impostor who makes up for his lack of personal integration and identity by taking on a series of assumed roles. This is a form of real-life playacting with masks. We are fooled into believing the psychopathic impostor is someone he isn't. We buy a product from him, introduce him into our offices or homes and, all the while, he laughs to himself at how well his clever imposturing is working. If caught in this deception, the impostor typically plays the role of the aggrieved martyr until, once again, we feel sorry enough for him or begin to doubt our own correct suspicions, that the impostor is pretending to be someone else. We are "stung," in a word *manipulated* in our perceptions and judgments.

All of these different personalities are united by their tendency to manipulate. Whatever else they may do and for whatever reason they may do it, they are, above all, manipulators. And the manipulator is a man (or woman; I vary the gender designation freely throughout the book both to avoid sexism and to underscore the fact that neither sex has a monopoly on manipulation) of many faces and many roles. He revels, in fact, in his chameleon-like talents. Since he is a consummate actor (even capable of fooling himself) I think of the manipulator as wearing a mask. I've arrived at this image by way of a dream.

Over my lifetime I've experienced a repetitive dream in which a mysterious figure is standing alone and barely perceptible in the mist surrounding the top of a mountain such as one might encounter somewhere in the Himalayas. As I look closer I notice the dream figure is wearing a mask. At my request he removes the mask only to reveal yet another mask. At my urging this too is surrendered, but once again with the same result. Finally, after the appearance and disappearance of a varying number and variety of masks (in some of the dreams the masks seem to go on forever), the figure stands revealed: a creature without face or identity.

At this point I've often awakened with a start at the realization that I've encountered in my dream a kind of prototypic mask: a seeming human who, at heart, isn't a human at all but a series of changing and unpredictable unsubstantialities.

Later, during my waking moments, I've often considered that this dream may account for my lifelong interest in masquerade, masks, magic and "drag" as well as in the lives of people I've personally encountered or, in many cases, only learned about second-hand who resemble my dream figure, the possessors of an unending series of identities.

Psychiatrists and others concerned with human personality have commented over the years upon certain people who are distinctly masklike. To the casual observer the people in question appear perfectly normal. They are often charming and friendly and fail to express or display even the usual quota of behavioral peculiarities possessed by us all. Such people seem so "normal," in fact, that almost everyone is surprised when, suddenly and without warning and just at the moment when all observers feel they've gotten a "fix" on their personalities, they metamorphize into an alternative, often strikingly, in fact almost terrifyingly different, being.

Within the last half century, particularly the past twenty-five years, psychiatrists throughout the world have been encountering an increasing number of such patients whose personalities are as elusive as the figure in my dream. These people suffer, in fact, from identity disturbances so fundamental and profound that the psychiatrists who encounter them have had to revolutionize some of their most basic concepts concerning mental health and illness.

Character disorders is the technical term usually applied to these patients, who include borderline disorders, narcissistic personalities and psychopaths. Together they have puzzled, frustrated and intrigued their psychiatrists.

Although a character disorder is a form of mental illness, it's not at all like your everyday idea of craziness. Character disorders are also more ubiquitous than any form of emotional disturbance. For one thing, the character disorder is often indistinguishable from his normal counterpart. He is like all the rest of us, in fact *is* all the rest of us: we're all character disorders of one sort or another. That's what makes the whole issue so important.

I think of character disorders as people who wear masks like my dream figure, only in this case they're not only fooling other people with their multiple masquerades but, most importantly, deceiving themselves.

In *Being and Nothingness*, the French philosopher Jean-Paul Sartre wrote of "bad faith": a lie to oneself within the unity of a single consciousness. According to Sartre's formulation, the person in bad faith denies the obvious implications of his actions. Sartre's example is that of a woman who seeks to deny the implications of a man's taking her hand while they sit together in a café. The act, according to Sartre, calls for an immediate decision: "To leave the hand there is to consent within herself to flirt, to engage herself. To withdraw it is to break the troubled and unstable harmony which gives the hour its charm. The aim is to postpone the moment of decision as long as possible. We know what happens next: the young woman leaves her hand there, but she *does not notice* that she is leaving it."

In such a situation, comments Sartre, the woman may begin speaking of sentimental or lofty subjects, all the while ignoring the bond that has been formed without words or explicit intentions. By conversing while at the same time continuing to ignore the intimacy implied in the act of hand holding, the woman engages, according to Sartre, in "bad faith": "While sensing profoundly the presence of her own body—to the point of being aroused, perhaps—she realizes herself as *not being* her own body, and she contemplates it as though from above as a passive object to which events can *happen* but which can neither provoke them nor avoid them because all its possibilities are outside of it."

At the time when Sartre first described it, bad faith was little more than a curious phenomenon which, although pivotal to existential philosophy, had little relevance to everyday life. But in the ensuing years, bad faith has become a life-style. The character disorder lives a life of bad faith, deceiving others but, most of all, deceiving himself. In fact, at the basis of his disturbance is a disruption in the sense of the self. Rather than an integrated self, the character disorder is many selves, many "I's" which have little knowledge of each other. The "I's" are isolated from one another by a process (splitting) which causes a defect in emotional integration.

Imagine a clock in which all the parts are together and correctly aligned but the clock still won't run. The character disorder is a personality that "won't run," can't be depended on, is inconsistent and has problems with intimacy as well as other areas of emotional life which we'll say more about later. The reason for these difficulties? The character disorder lacks the emotional integration necessary to experience that sense of wholeness which lies at the root of a healthy identity. To this extent, the character disorder suffers from a disturbance in the sense of self.

At first glance such disturbances of the self would seem restricted to instances of extreme emotional illness. But it's the theme of this book that such disorders of the self are not rare. Further, there are large numbers of people—and I think the numbers are growing, as I'll show later—who suffer from an impoverishment of their sense of self, a basic insecurity about who they are. Out of this insecurity arise certain attitudes and behaviors which are aimed at restoring the sense of self.

The character disorder is like a country which is renamed every few years and therefore never has time to develop a history. The character disorder exists in the here and now and experiences himself as basically at odds with his surroundings. His conflicts are with other people in the environment rather than with himself. As a result of his inner fragmentation, the character disorder doesn't feel many ordinary human emotions such as guilt or remorse. For these emotions require the achievement of an inner standard against which present behavior can be compared (the superego of Freudian psychology). But the character disorder lacks this internal standard since he doesn't experience himself as a person with a past or a future. There is only the present. The character disorder's experiential myopia results in specific behaviors. The most pivotal of these is manipulation.

Within a technological society such as ours, it was probably inevitable that some people would begin to interact with others in ways similar to their interactions with machines. Machines are manipulated in order to bring about an effect. People, too, can be manipulated in order to get something out of them. They can be persuaded, threatened, cajoled, seduced, implored, intimidated—the verbs may change but the process is similar in each instance: treat the other individual as a "thing" little different from a complicated piece of machinery.

My experience with individuals afflicted with the split within their selves referred to above has taught me that character disorders can be recognized with uncanny accuracy by their tendency to manipulate those around them. Uncertain from one moment to another who they "really are," they cannot risk revealing themselves to the other person lest their own lack of integration be detected.

Naturally, the person who is unsure of who he is remains perpetually at risk when dealing with other people. Since he neither knows nor can trust himself due to his lack of inner continuity and consistency he can't trust other people either. Thus, human relationships shift from what philosopher Martin Buber called I-Thou relationships to I-It relationships: people are to be manipulated like objects for the purpose of control. This change in attitude ushers in new "techniques" of interpersonal relationships.

The very word "technique" when applied to human interactions already implies a dehumanized exploitive orientation to human affairs. Further, certain currents and trends within our society lead to an increase in the employment of manipulation as a means of dealing with others: increased fragmentation; the playing out of multiple and varied social "roles"; increased social mobility; loss of a sense of community; the disruption of authority; the disappearance of ethics and morality as important forces in many people's lives—each of these developments has brought about a deterioration in the "quality" of interpersonal relations. It's also resulted in increasing numbers of people who fail to experience any sense of personal integration. What they do now and how they feel about something on one day has nothing to do with their actions and feelings a day later. Not unexpectedly, such feelings of personal lack of integration are distressful. But most distressful of all, our present society has elevated fragmented, makeshift emotional approaches to human relationships to the level of a cultural norm.

"The people who will live successfully in tomorrow's world are those who can accept and enjoy temporary systems," psychologist Richard Farson wrote several years ago. The world of tomorrow that Farson referred to is already upon us. As a result of our individual and collective sense of fragmentation, new value systems have arisen based on the development of techniques for the manipulation of other people. And behind this need to manipulate is the loss of the sense of self. If hysteria was the psychological malady of sexually repressed nineteenth-century Europe, disorders of the self are the expressions of twentieth-century malaise.

Now for a few words concerning how this book came about. My interest in the self and its disturbances began as a result of encountering patients in my neuropsychiatric practice who complained of a lack of "integration" or "cohesion" in their lives. A review of the literature on the subject revealed that such complaints, formerly almost unheard of, have become commonplace among people presenting themselves for professional help. But the most important contribution to my present conviction on the ubiquity of self disorders came not from patients but from my contact with colleagues and acquaintances and even intimate friends who, when asked about the matter, volunteered that they experienced a multiplicity of selves or identities. And when saying this, they weren't speaking in a metaphorical sense. Nor were they talking about playing a series of roles. They felt, in fact, that they were multiple selves without any vital connecting link. It's important, at this point, to emphasize that I'm not talking about the phenomenon of multiple personalities: the "Three Faces of Eve" phenomenon. A few points will make this clear.

In most instances, multiple personalities—so-called split personalities—involve dramatic, hysterical phenomena: sudden blindness, paralysis, trancelike states, automatic writing or singing and so on.

In addition, multiple personalities within a single individual regularly exist in strong opposition to each other. For example, one personality may be saintly, kind and self-effacing while its counterpart is lewd, vicious and angrily explosive. Or one personality may represent all that is childlike while the other is a strong and resolute adult.

As another point of difference, the occurrence of multiplicity often has a dramatic onset: a traumatic event such as a death in the family; a period of prolonged unconsciousness; or perhaps head injury from which the patient is aroused only with difficulty. (The alterations within a true multiple personality are typically associated with irregularities in the sleep-waking cycle.)

In addition, the multiple personalities have a distinct appearance and "style" which can be readily recognized and identified. Finally, each of the multiple personalities frequently possesses knowledge of the others, in fact, may comment disparagingly of the others or speak of being influenced by the others such as through dreams.

This pattern of multiplicity is distinctly different from the splitting within the personality to which I refer. Rather than a disruption of the continuity of memory, the individuals I speak about display a lack of continuity within the *emotional sphere*. They remember their actions, sometimes with photographic clarity, but somehow lack the feeling tone that accompanies the actions. Thus they complain of being "cut off" from their pasts, as if looking at a video of themselves absent the emotional coloring which could bring their past experiences "to life." In response to this split within the emotional sphere, they begin to feel as if they are, in fact, a string of separate individuals, a series of multiple selves. While each separate identification is reasonably consistent, there is no overall integration or, in many cases, even coherence, between one self and the other. This absence of emotional continuity is often described as a sense of inner fragmentation, a feeling of utter meaninglessness.

Frequently, this division within the self is so far-reaching that the individual experiences a gnawing internal conviction that something is "missing" or incomplete within his personality. Such feelings may induce in the individual the desire to merge with another person, interact with his identity for the purpose of extracting from the experience a firm identification of his own. Or the individual with a disturbance in the sense of self to which I refer may go to the opposite extreme: resist any intimacy with another person lest his own fragile sense of self be swallowed up within the vastness of the other. In each instance, the sense of self is precarious and must be maintained by the process of manipulation.

This book examines the manipulator as he or she exists along a continuum of increasing disturbance. Starting with individuals who fit well within the "normal range" we progress toward people with serious self disturbances. But all share similar conflicts in regard to forming an enduring, consistent self. As a result of these conflicts, the various character disturbances emerge which are the subject of this book: narcissists, borderline personalities and psychopaths. In recent years, psychiatrists have noted that each of these distinct personalities shares the common tendency to manipulate others in order to make up for the difficulties they experience in regard to the formation of an integrated self.

In the first and second portions of this book I take up what we really mean when we speak about a "self." Defining the self is actually more difficult than it initially appears.

Sections III, IV, V and VI describe the manipulator as narcissist, borderline and psychopath.

In the last portion of the book I show how manipulation and our present culture exert mutually supportive influences on each other: the society is presently greatly influenced, almost dominated, by manipulators.

Finally, in the last section I describe a new proposal for decreasing manipulation and self disorders within our society.

A word is in order at this point concerning the profiles contained in this book. They are all "real" people either encountered by me or, in most instances where I've learned about them secondhand, drawn from other people's recorded impressions. Many psychiatrists and psychoanalysts have helped by generously allowing me to quote from their notes or published writings. None of the portraits are composites, nor are they fictionalized, although, of course, suitable alterations have been made in order to preserve anonymity. Nor—with few exceptions—are the subjects representative of extremely "sick" or pathological characters. In most instances, the people I'm writing about would be readily accepted as fitting within the broad range of "normal" personalities. But they've all been selected as representative of those disorders of the self—the manipulators—who are the subjects, if not necessarily the "heroes," of the book.

This book is, admittedly, a highly personalized interpretation written from the position of a neurologist with a lifetime interest in disorders of the self. My viewpoint has been principally shaped by the diagnosis and treatment of patients. While this has the advantage of personal encounter, it also has the liability of perhaps a too limited vantage from which to view vast and complex social phenomena. For this reason, I've tried whenever possible to broaden my view by interview and personal discussion with others outside of the treatment situation who have been interested in and have written on the psychology of the self.

Since the development of our modern ideas on narcissists, borderline personalities and psychopaths (all included under the general heading of character disorders) represents the work of numerous psychiatrists over the years, I've tried to maintain—within the limitations of a book intended for the general nonspecialist reader—the historical continuity involved in this denouement. In my view, we can usefully understand these varied and complex personalities by concentrating on their shared tendency to *manipulate* their fellow man. I take particular responsibility for the not terribly flattering view that we are all manipulators to a certain degree.

As further inroads are made into the cohesiveness of our individual selves—a process that, to all intents and purposes, can be expected to increase even further over the next several decades—manipulation can be anticipated to occur with even greater frequency. Our awareness of the process, particularly of the insidious inroads manipulation is already making in our personal relationships, may help to restore a true communality wherein people can react to each other in less dehumanizing and less alienating ways. If *The Self Seekers* can contribute to this process, it will have served its purpose.

II

The Self

"For a man cannot change, that is to say become
another person, while continuing to obey the dictates of the self which he has ceased to be."

Marcel Proust, *Swann's Way*

R. D. Laing, Where Are You?

On a misty, muggy, uncomfortably warm August morning I walked out of the Chalk Farm tube stop in London and began the two-block uphill climb to my meeting with R. D. Laing. Among experts on the self, Laing must be considered a pioneer. His book *The Divided Self*—rejected by the first six publishers Laing sent it to—has gone on over the two decades since its publication to become a virtual classic in the field of psychiatry. In it, Laing first formulated the then unconventional proposal that the self isn't at all the unitary structure most of us conceive it as but, rather, in many instances our selves are divided, much as an apartment building may be divided, into essentially uncommunicating units existing in physical contiguity but nonetheless functionally cut off from each other. My familiarity with Laing had begun twelve years earlier during my psychiatry residency and I was now curious to see if and in what direction Laing's ideas had changed since the publication of *The Divided Self*.

Laing's office-residence at 2 Eton Place is a tall, imposing white stucco structure dating from the Regency Period. A private kind of dwelling on a quiet street: a perfectly fitting setting for explorations into the interstices of personal identity. As I opened the gate into a small yard, I caught sight of Laing from the second floor peering out at me through gold pince-nez glasses from his position at a book-cluttered desk pressed against three bay windows which overlook the yard and street below. I rang the bell and waited.

Almost instantaneously my presence was announced by the deep barking of a dog and, seconds later, I encountered a huge Labrador held in check by a middle-sized thin man dressed in a

dark-green corduroy suit. At first I was surprised that Laing wasn't
taller than he is (no doubt a symptom of hero worship he would
be capable of exploring with cunning and perspicacity!), and I
was even more surprised as well as curious about the thick
Scottish brogue which seemed little affected by many years spent
in London, a brogue interrupted periodically by a nervous stam-
mer. After a few words of greeting, Laing led me into a study
where, after motioning me to a wicker chair, he lit a cigarette and
stretched out on a comfortable divan while propping himself lan-
guidly against a pillow.

Laing's study is a testament to the diversity of his interests: wall
on wall of books spill onto the floor, over the piano, even trickling
perilously close to the fireside. Six tennis rackets in various states
of repair; a guitar; several small paintings and pieces of sculpture—
all compete for space and the visitor's attention with books ranging from art history to Zen Buddhism. Laing's conversation, too,
is sprinkled with wide-ranging allusions gathered with equal frequency and appropriateness from Thucydides to Charles Schulz.
While sitting there perfectly relaxed and staring over my shoulder
in the direction of the far end of the room, toward the window
which perfectly conveyed the cloudy, cheerless day outside, Laing
began: "Not sure exactly what you had in mind when you wrote
me. Searching for something new about our ideas on the self, I
take it?"

Over the next hour, Laing developed for me the directions his
thinking has taken over the years on the subject of the self. Since
he gently forbade the use of a tape recorder ("We're much more
paranoid about that kind of device here than you are in America,"
he commented with a thin smile) and since I'm gifted with talents for neither shorthand nor "photographic verbal recall," I can
only present a précis of some of his arguments freely and interpre-
tively intermixed with sentiments on the self Laing has expressed
over the past twenty years on various occasions and in multiple
media.

First of all, Laing has given up totally on any theory which pur-
ports to "explain" the self via analogies drawn from the theater.
Roles, masks and various forms of playacting not only provide an

incomplete vista from which to construct a viable concept of the self but are, according to Laing, simply wrong.

Consider, for instance, the metamorphoses (Laing's word) that we all undergo in a typical day. At various moments we are parent, employer, employee, lover, spouse, customer, citizen, consumer and so on. "There are not simply roles," Laing asserts. "Each is a whole past and present and future, offering differing options and constraints, different degrees of change or inertia, different kinds of closeness and distance, different sets of rights and obligations, different pledges and promises."

But most importantly, these various selves can never be separated entirely from the other people who surround us. Even basic human emotions and experiences become meaningless outside the social situation. "There are no 'basic' emotional instincts or personality outside of the relationships a person has within one or other social context," Laing has written. Thus love, hate and fear exist only because something or someone excites these experiences within us. In a sense, we are not a self at all unless engaged in an interplay with others in the formation of a kind of collective self.

Laing's ideas on the social origin of the self, like Freud's, originated in the psychiatric consulting room. But this, in turn, creates its own kinds of problems. To what extent are the lessons learned from the "mentally ill" applicable to the wider majority who—though perhaps they should—never come to the attention of psychiatrists at all? I posed the question to Laing during a lull in our conversation.

"In a technological society, particularly such an alienating one as we now experience, we can't help but implicitly ask ourselves who we are. It's not necessarily restricted to patients or those suffering from a mental illness, whatever that supposedly means. Rather, everyday people today tend to express themselves and somehow split. I don't know the reason for this and I don't know if we can ever really get to the bottom of the question."

"Do you think it has something to do with the multiple social identities people are called upon to enact?" I asked.

Laing sat back, pulled quickly and nervously at a cigarette and stared into the distance, his eyes somewhat glassy, as if searching for an answer in the streams of sunlight which, only moments before, had burst in upon us for the first time. "I'm not really convinced that the situation is terribly different from many occasions in the past," he continued. "I'm thinking particularly of the parental 'role.' A lot of people seem to think that the answer may lie in certain changes—in the way parents approach parenting, particularly the mother's approach to the experience of motherhood. Many women with career plans, for instance, think of children as a trap. But if you look at the attitude of people in the past toward their children you see that many different attitudes, some of which people today would regard with horror, have existed throughout history. There simply isn't any single attitude toward the family that we can confidently declare to be the right one. Therefore, I have no firm conviction about the effects of early experience on the later development of the self."

Although Laing is a card-carrying psychoanalyst, his unorthodox interpretations of Freud and other shakers and movers of modern psychoanalytic thinking—partially the ones conveyed in the above remarks—are both original and provocative. But by stressing the importance of fantasy as a determinant of human experience, he's an acquiescing fundamentalist. To Laing, fantasy is not something having to do with night or daytime dreams, Walter Mitty experiences in which we exhibit awesome intellectual or physical talents which are applauded by an appreciative audience drawn from our day or nighttime imaginations. Rather, fantasy is a specific way of relating to the world, a means of making sense out of the things we do and why we do them.

As an example of this, consider a husband and wife discussing an impending vacation. She wants to go to the seashore, he to the mountains. Over cocktails each puts forth the reasons for choosing one or the other vacation resort. The husband, while listening to his wife, is silently recalling that last year, at her suggestion, they visited friends in Arizona, an experience he hated. He's determined that this time *he* will make the choice of vacation. This, however, is not specifically stated but only vaguely formulated in his mind. The wife, meanwhile, having forgotten completely about her recommendation last year to visit friends, is conscious only of a sudden sharpness and tenseness in her husband's attitude. She therefore bristles and pushes all the harder in her advocacy of the ocean over the mountain resort. Previous to this "perception" of her husband's changed attitude, she really didn't care that much one way or the other about the choice of vacation and would have been willing to settle for either alternative.

In this instance, each person is responding not to the other's actual words but to a fantasied explanation of the other's intentions. He fantasizes a wife who is controlling and manipulative; she responds to a husband who is trying to boss her around. Fantasy rather than the objective facts regarding the merits of seashore versus mountains is the determinant of their behavior. A wide divergence exists between the seeming rationality of their discourse and the spouses' responses to each other. In addition, each person's fantasy of the meaning of the discussion is a more accurate explanation of why the discussion breaks down at a later point into bitter recriminations than any explanation which remains tied down to the specifics of what each person actually said. This, in essence, is fantasy, and obviously it's all around us: we're all steeped in fantasy. The important issue is the extent of our awareness of the pivotal role of fantasy in the shaping of our lives. In those instances where the awareness is minimal or even completely absent, as in the above example of a family quarrel, the participants remain cut off or alienated from each other.

Laing speaks frequently of alienation, a word which originates in modern-day existential philosophy. But the term carries many additional meanings depending on the context. A Marxist, for example, speaks of the typical worker in a mass-production assembly line as alienated from the product of his work: he has little grasp of the part his repetitive, boring contributions have in the creation of the final product. He also has no control over the ownership or control of the product. In both of these ways the worker is alienated from his work.

In a psychological sense, a person can be alienated from others so that he misinterprets what is going on around him. By insisting that a decision about vacation plans concerns only the merits of the seashore versus a mountain retreat, both parties are alienated from each other: both are operating on the basis of misperceptions of the other's intentions.

In all social interactions the behavior of any particular individual is dependent on that person's perceptions of what's going on—his "experiences." We all experience certain feelings about everyday situations, particularly what we believe are other people's attitudes. If we experience them as friendly or open, we respond one way; hostile or seemingly malicious intentions earn yet a different response. And since, on many occasions, our experiences of other people are wrong (initially the wife really did intend to restrict the level of discourse to selecting a mutually pleasing vacation spot), our actions are often inappropriate and tuned to an incorrect reading of the situation. This, in turn, elicits additional behavior from the other person which corresponds to our original misperceptions, compounding them. (As the husband begins to get nasty, the wife becomes even more rigidly determined not to be "pushed around.") But since neither person is correctly experiencing the other's intentions, they remain alienated from each other.

Even more important than the alienation that may exist between two people are the various forms of solitary alienation in which the individual begins constructing what Laing refers to as a "false" self. Laing's perception that the personality may be divided into one or more "false" selves, each of which may be functionally cut off from its fellows, constitutes one of the most innovative and remarkable insights of modern psychiatric thinking on the subject of the self.

To understand what Laing means by a false self, it's helpful to compare it with certain processes we all engage in on a daily basis. On many occasions when we're bored or uninterested we force ourselves to act out parts we feel are expected of us. In fact, a significant amount of time may be devoted to these scenarios. Our boss, for instance, invites us to join him at the opera. We may detest opera but nonetheless choose to pretend otherwise because of the opportunity the invitation provides for "advancement." On such occasions, we take on a mask, if you will, present a false self to the other person in order to further the ends of the "real" self, which, in this instance, is concerned with climbing the corporate ladder. We all engage from time to time in these momentary constructions of false selves and are able, at the appropriate moment, to take off the "mask," discard the false self and express our true feelings. "Christ, wasn't that boring! But at the dinner prior to the opera I think I made some good points with the old man. So I guess the evening was a success after all."

But on occasion the individual isn't sure how he really feels. Laing has described a student who, after attending a performance of Shakespeare's *Twelfth Night*, was asked to write an essay about his reactions to the play. At the time, the student was majoring in mathematics and "hated" English literature. But by "pretending" that he enjoyed the play and "imagining" what his teacher expected of him, the student composed a marvelous piece that actually went on to win a prize. "Not one word of it was the expression of how I felt. It was all how I felt I was expected to feel," he told Laing. Thus far, the experience is similar to our executive who pretended enjoyment of the opera in order to win his "prize" of an evening with the boss. In this case, however, the student, at a later point, began reflecting in a serious way about his feelings toward English literature. After a time he came to the conclusion that the feelings expressed in the essay represented his true attitudes while his "hatred" of literature had been the false one. As a mathematics major he had felt that it was expected of him to be uninterested in literature. "But he had not dared to admit this possibility to himself because it would have precipitated his going into a violent conflict with all the values that had been inculcated into him and entirely disrupted his own idea of who he was," said Laing.

The executive and the student share a capacity for disengaging from their "false" selves, fully realizing their pretentions and resuming—or, in the case of the student, rediscovering—their *real* attitudes. In these instances, the self momentarily creates a false self and later discards it as an actor takes on and later discards a mask. This process may involve forms of playacting or even impersonation and imposturing, as we will see later. But in each instance there exist simultaneously two opposing attitudes, one emanating from a "false" self (the executive who pretends a liking for opera) and one from a "true" self (an ambitious junior corporate executive). But what happens if the "false" self takes over—as it did momentarily with the mathematics student—and the individual is left confused as to which is his "real self"?

"Some people are given to the feeling that their expressions and actions towards other people are false," Laing told me. "They perpetually feel as if they're phony. After a while they may begin to feel controlled by these feelings of phoniness, by the inauthenticity of their lives. Some even go on to the point of expressing themselves as persecuted by this inner autonomous existence, this 'false' self."

As an example of a firmly entrenched and deeply pathological "false" self, Laing pointed to the case of David, who at eighteen was referred to him because of bizarre and dramatic behavior. Laing recalls David as "a most fantastic-looking character—an adolescent Kierkegaard played by Danny Kaye." Long hair, a capacious collar, short trousers, big shoes, a cape and a cane—all comprised the outfit of the young man Laing suspected was "*playing at being eccentric.*"

Discussion with David revealed that he had developed early in life a split between what he knew himself to be and the "personality" he revealed to others. Shy and self-conscious, he had discovered early on that by playing a part he could overcome these feelings and even go on to impress others with his self-confidence and overall competence. At all times he secretly reveled in the fact that only he was aware of his "real" self, a self that was deeply hidden away in an area of his mind into which others could never hope to penetrate. This process, it seemed, had started with his earliest relations with his mother.

"*His* self was never directly revealed in and through his actions," Laing has written. "It seemed to be the case that he emerged from his infancy with his '*own self*' on the one hand and 'what his mother wanted him to be,' his 'personality' on the other; he had started from there and made it his aim and ideal to make the split between his own self (which only he knew) and what other people could see of him, as complete as possible."

David's attitude toward social relations was a theatrical one in every sense of the word. Not only was his speech and dress melodramatic in the extreme, but he considered everyone in the world to be playing a role. His view of human nature in general, and himself in particular, was that everyone, without exception, was an actor. Furthermore, the best way of getting on in the world was to play life's different roles as skillfully as possible in order to avoid "giving oneself away."

Although David's emphasis on role playing superficially resembles many of the temporary "roles" each of us takes on in the course of a day, there are distinct and important differences. The donning of social masks is generally a voluntary one (the opera-shy executive was free to pass up the evening by pleading illness, for example). In addition, the occasions for taking on and removing the mask can usually be fairly sharply defined (when returning home all pretentions about loving the opera can be discarded and the whole episode remembered with amusement and even ridicule). But in David's case his masks soon began threatening to overwhelm his "real" self. David's outlandish dress, it turned out, provided not only a means of concealing his "real" self from others but a means of primary identification with his mother. Partly as a means of consoling himself for his mother's death, which occurred when he was ten, and partly for more complex reasons having to do with his father which do not concern us here, David took to dressing himself before a mirror and acting out the parts of women. While dressing as a woman, he often rehearsed female parts from plays, mouthing the words in female accents. Soon these aspects of David's "false" self began to take over. "He caught himself compulsively walking like a woman, talking like a woman, even seeing and thinking as a woman might see and think," Laing writes. In an attempt to avoid engulfment by this "false" self, David had taken on the bizarre garb of a theatrical character. "For, he said, he found that he was driven to dress up and act in his present manner as the only way to arrest the womanish part that threatened to engulf not only his actions but even his 'own' self as well," concludes Laing.

David's fear of engulfment is a theme that we will hear in many different voices throughout this book. Individuals with a fragile sense of themselves frequently complain of being "overwhelmed," "engulfed" or "absorbed" by another person. It appears that their sense of selfhood is so fragile that movement toward another person, a true relatedness, constitutes a threat to their being, a loss of their self. Commonsense, everyday experience provides little insight into such an attitude, which, when it exists in its fully developed form, as with David, can eventually lead to a schizophrenic breakdown. But such a tenuous grasp on the self can take subtler forms which merge imperceptibly into "types" which are common within our culture and would not, by most criteria, be considered terribly abnormal. Since this fear of the loss of the self is so very important a part of the theme of this book, I'm going to interrupt my discussion with Laing and take a short excursion at this point to present two individuals who suffer from even more subtle disturbances in the self.

An Attorney with Too Much to Lose

Mark, a forty-two-year-old attorney, consulted me several years ago about migraine headaches. After several hours with him it became obvious that his headaches were only a somatic expression of a deep-seated dissatisfaction with life, particularly in regard to his "failure" to achieve a satisfying long-term relationship. On one cold and dreary November afternoon, he came to my office and talked to me about his feelings; this is what he said:

"As long as I can remember I've had problems with loving another person. Often I'd go for long periods of time, sometimes months or, even on a few occasions, several years without any 'romantic interests.' During these periods I'd be happy—perhaps contented or quiescent would be better words. Even so, I'd know something was 'missing.' Sometimes I could even feel it in a vague sort of physical way, perhaps at the end of a weekend when I'd go out for a walk and watch the summer sunset. At such times I'd know that there was something missing in my life, but I couldn't quite put my finger on what it was.

"After a while I'd meet somebody I'd like. I could tell early in the relationship that I was stuck on her. Almost immediately I'd find myself thinking about her all the time. She'd literally become an obsession with me. I'd go through all sorts of imaginary situations in my mind involving me and this new person. Soon she'd come to occupy all my waking moments.

"Sometimes the images were pretty fantastic; other times just day-to-day events that I'd imagine myself experiencing with her. After a while, she would become so important to me that I'd start figuring out ways of getting together with her, dreaming up excuses where I'd be likely to run into her. Then if I was lucky and didn't like her too much, I'd ask her out. If I was unlucky—that is, if I was already in love with her—it was often already too late, I'd feel shy and small around her. My self-esteem, which is usually pretty good, would slip away. She would seem independent and carefree while I, as a result of my feelings toward her, was locked into a cycle of wanting to get to know her better but being unable to do so because of my shyness. I know this sounds sort of crazy, but I'd actually be experiencing a kind of pain.

"I'd find myself imagining situations where she was with other people, usually one or two mutual friends who, as I discovered much later when things were over between us, didn't mean anything at all to her. In other words, I'd guess you'd say that I would be kind of jealous. On those occasions when I did meet her, I'd have trouble looking her in the eye. I would find myself talking too much or saying things that later, when I went over everything in my mind, seemed foolish. This, of course, made me feel even smaller and more foolish and I'd start to get angry with myself. After a while, it would seem to me that she was aware of my discomfort and, in a way, was even enjoying it. At these times the jealousy would get worse and I'd be on the alert for instances where she seemed to be interested in somebody else. I'd often be suspicious that maybe she liked one of my friends. I don't mean I was paranoid or anything like that. In most cases I knew nothing was going on but I still couldn't stop myself from imagining all sorts of things.

"Sexual images would begin to occur and they were pleasurable until I began mentally imagining that she and I were having a sexual relationship. This would fill me with a kind of dread, a sort of accentuation of the low despicable feelings that I was having about myself. I know this sounds odd, but I imagined sex as a kind of *draining experience*: she would become even more independent and alone while I'd be depleted and shrunken somehow. It seemed at such times that I wasn't in complete control of my own self, if you know what I mean. It was almost as if I was losing my identity in this other person, merging with her in a way. I know this sounds silly but it was as if she were becoming the whole center of my life. While she grew in stature and importance I experienced myself less and less as a whole person; rather I was a kind of attachment to her. Although I wasn't exactly afraid of this feeling, it did make me uncomfortable with myself. I guess this feeling corresponded to the feelings of threat which I encountered within myself whenever I was with her. Somehow I always found myself imagining situations where I would become more dependent and involved while she retained the capacity to walk away from the relationship at any time, leaving me traumatized.

"Soon my waking moments were dominated by this other person I was 'in love with.' I was unable to get her out of my mind, and my work soon began to be affected. Usually my work occupied most of my energies but now it became trivial and not worthwhile. I couldn't keep my mind on my clients or the cases I was arguing. After months and months of preparation my arguments seemed empty and lifeless. So what if I was prepared for the case? So what if I won or if I lost? Everything that formerly dominated my life was now becoming somehow not worth the trouble. Only one thing mattered. The only thing I cared about was this woman. But by now the experience wasn't pleasurable at all, in fact it was a veritable torture.

"Soon my sleep would be affected. . . . I'd have a hard time getting to sleep and I'd wake up thinking about her . . . wondering if she were asleep in bed and, if so, with whom? Eventually the pain would become almost excruciating and I'd torture myself with ideas about how somebody else might be having her, usually somebody who really didn't care for her, while I, who loved her so much, was locked up in a state of longing, loneliness and pain.

"Eventually, I'd enter the final stages of what I call my 'love affairs,' although there was rarely any loving or sex. I'd just be too nervous when the time came to do much. Besides, by this time the girl had become so important to me, occupying so many of my waking moments, that I was literally frightened to death of losing her. What if I would be impotent? Somehow didn't please her? The risks of a sexual encounter increased as time went on until I was psychically paralyzed with the conflict between my intense desire to move closer to her and this feeling of losing myself. I know it sounds silly to say but it was almost as if I had reached the point where there was a danger that soon there wouldn't be a *me* and a *her* but only a *her*. I would be sucked up into her personality. In a sense I would no longer *be*.

"When things progressed this far I was absolutely miserable. Impelled and driven, on the one hand, by my love, I was, at the same time, afraid to act on it because of the danger of losing myself. At about this point, in order to save my very existence, I had to begin the agonizing process of breaking off the relationship. In order to resolve the situation, I developed over the years a pattern of behavior which worked, although, I must admit, I'm not proud of it.

"First I'd start up a relationship with somebody I didn't care as much for, someone who was neutral, in other words, who didn't involve me in this feeling of being drained or annihilated. As quickly as possible I'd develop this relationship into a sexual one. And it was amazing how easily and quickly I could accomplish this. Since this new person didn't stimulate in me the feelings of being diminished or somehow destroyed, I could be completely at ease with her. Instead of tension and discomfort, I projected an easy grace which, without any great effort on my part, quickly led to a romantic, sexual relationship. While I was with this second person it would seem that I had resolved my difficulties with the other girl. I'd feel better and the pain of being constantly threatened with the loss of myself would disappear for a few hours: it would seem as if my agonizing was over. I'd know later, however, that I was wrong. I can remember the return of my feelings of longing as I became once again totally absorbed in thoughts and longings for the first girl. The sleep problems would return with a greater relentlessness. I'd go through elaborate explanations in my mind, mentally calling up the girl I loved and tearfully telling her how I really loved her and how the 'one-night stand' with the other person had all been a mistake. But by the next day I'd find I couldn't do it. The same feelings of tremendous inferiority and pain would return and, once again, I would be psychically paralyzed.

"After several weeks or so or, in rare cases, months of this kind of torture, I would decide—usually suddenly and with an exhilarated feeling of relief—that I had to get the loved one out of my life. Almost always, this involved a complete breaking of all ties. I would really go to extremes to avoid any contact with her. It was almost as if she had died. In fact, I recall that on at least one occasion that's what I dreamed had happened. The day after this dream, I had such a strange sensation when I ran into the girl. The ebbing of my sense of losing myself was starting; I felt somewhat more secure. I smiled to myself as I reflected on the fact that the dream was helping me gain the necessary emotional distance from the girl, who wasn't dead but very much alive, in fact, right there in front of me (somewhat puzzled, no doubt, at my altered behavior, the cool sense of ease I was beginning to display).

"But each day the pain would be a little less, almost as if I were withdrawing from alcohol. In some ways I think that my way of going 'cold turkey' on the person was every bit as painful, particularly, as often happened, if the person attempted to reestablish contact. Naturally, she wondered what was happening and would call up on some pretext or other but with the obvious intention of reestablishing contact. But her efforts were to no avail.

"With every passing day my strength was returning and I felt more like myself. I was liberated from the ceaseless scenarios I had been devising. I no longer experienced the fear of being swallowed up or totally absorbed into the girl. She was herself and I was myself again. How glorious it felt! It was a liberating feeling to regain my sense of being a *real solid self*, existing in my own right and not really needing anybody else. The whole process was almost a kind of rebirth, a reestablishment of my own boundaries. And with this rebirth, I was able, once again, to get back to myself. My work took on a renewed importance. I was able to prepare and argue my cases. My law career became, once again, the most important aspect of my life. I could concentrate, plan—in a word, I could function and be myself. Finally, after several weeks of renewed vigor, the 'process would be completed' and I'd be ready for a real test of my strength: I'd call the person or perhaps pay her a surprise visit.

"On these occasions I suppose I seemed relatively unchanged to the girl when, in fact, I had, of course, undergone a profound change. I guess you might say I had 'fallen out of love,' but I can also understand that not everyone would be willing to accept the process I'm describing as an example of love. In any case, this is what I experienced as love and I think it's pretty obvious by now that it was far from a pleasant experience. But to return to my point, I was totally comfortable now with the girl. In fact, I'd experience a kind of high when I realized that I was completely cured of her and was even able to coolly estimate what it was that had attracted me to her in the first place.

"It was almost as if I could stand back and observe the girl in an objective way. By doing this, I noticed lots of things that you might say were highly critical. In fact, after a while it seemed amazing to me why I had ever fallen in love with the girl in the first place. There were so many things about her that I was now able to see in an objective way. For instance, I noticed little things that formerly had escaped my attention. I'd seize on little things such as the way she talked, her absence of makeup, the desultory nature of her conversation. I'd found these observations helped me to support my new attitude. Not only was she now herself and I myself, but the balance was restored whereby I didn't want anymore to be part of her in any way. Not that this led to fights or angry disagreements. In fact, I went out of my way to avoid anything resembling a confrontation. If she became upset about my change in attitude I was even able, for a short period, to take on a tender manner. Since I was no longer threatened with the loss of myself, I could extend myself, so to speak. This usually helped quite a bit. I'm very proud of the fact that, considering all the times that I've fallen in love and repeated this process—and there are many such occasions—things never ended in a fight or any kind of unpleasantness. I always thought of the person as a friend and, in some cases, even continued the friendship for many years.

"After I had been successful in altering my attitudes toward the person, I never again experienced any pain because of her. Things would go along rather well for varying periods of time until, once again, the process would repeat itself with somebody else. I suspect that after a while the loneliness of my life would catch up with me and, in response, I'd fall in love but always with the same agonizing cycle.

"Finally, as I got older I figured out the solution to my dilemma: establish a loving relationship with someone who didn't cause these feelings in me. Naturally this couldn't be done with *just anybody*. But there were many girls I met whose company I enjoyed but whom I could forget about between dates. When I found one who shared a lot of my attitudes about life in general I married her and now enjoy what I think is a pretty nice life. She's never caused me any anguish; I'm never jealous about her and, in fact, she's a good friend, probably the best friend I've ever had.

"Several times since I've been married, I have met women who have stirred up the beginnings of feelings which I've recognized could result in a repetition of my earlier painful experiences. But now as a married man, of course, the solution is much easier. I just avoid them from the beginning and the stirrings just go away. Still, on occasion I have brief paniclike attacks in which I think that I have missed something very important in life. But these feelings, too, pass off and eventually I feel better. After all, I tell myself, nothing is perfect in life and nobody can have everything."

The speaker, a forty-two-year-old lawyer and father of two children, poignantly describes the threatened engulfment of his fragile sense of self whenever he reaches out in a caring way toward another person. To this man, love is a menacing rather than a nurturing experience. It strikes at his sense of wholeness, his very integrity and identity as an independent person.

Freud described such a "love" relationship in a paper written in 1929 entitled "Being in Love and Hypnosis." According to Freud, a person's normal self love can be transferred from the lover to the beloved. When this occurs the "loved one" takes "possession of the entire self-love of the ego, whose self-sacrifice thus follows as a natural consequence. The object has, so to speak, consumed the ego." In its fully developed form, as described above by the attorney, the lover's ego is, in Freud's words, "impoverished, it has surrendered itself to the object, it has substituted the object for its own most important constituent." To such a person, the sense of self is evanescent and mercurial. Suddenly and without any warning it can be snatched away, purloined by the "loved one." To prevent this dreaded loss of the self, defensive maneuvers are engaged in such as indifference, morbid self-absorption and the unwillingness to give of oneself in a mutually sharing relationship. Naturally, aspects of the self cannot be shared if the self isn't possessed in the first place. This pattern, described so accurately by the attorney, is frequently the cause of repetitively unsatisfying "love" relationships. Lacking a firmly integrated sense of self, it's impossible to love—give oneself—to another. Whatever sense of self does exist must be hoarded like a treasure lest it be lost, merged with the other person.

The second speaker is a charming and seductive woman who has achieved occupational success at a very early age. Despite this, she's concerned about the lack of direction her life has taken up until now. Most vexing to her is a sense of incompleteness, a subtle inability to fully realize what she considers her own "potentialities."

Love Life of a Pinup Girl

Sonya remembers the evening of her wedding proposal as a combination of spiritual revelation and worldly disillusionment.

"It happened while I was a graduate student finishing my degree requirements in Greek literature. I was deeply upset at the time and was visiting a nearby Greek church to pray for a favor, the recovery of my sister back in the U.S., who was terribly sick, in fact dying."

As Sonya recalls, the service lasted "three days and three nights" and although, as she admits, she has never been a religious person she thought it not unlikely that if she prayed long enough and hard enough her prayers would be answered and the miracle of her sister's recovery would take place.

As she relates the story now, a trim attractive brunette of twenty-nine dressed in a sumptuous fur coat and with gold jewelry dangling from both wrists, it's difficult, in fact requires a strenuous effort of the imagination, to envision the events that occurred at the conclusion of the service. And even though she's told me the story several times, I'm still not convinced that it isn't a fantasy. But fantasy or not, it has affected her life in countless ways and therefore provides its own kind of truth. Besides, as we shall see throughout this book, what matters most in the search for the self doesn't depend so much on whether or not the experience a person describes corresponds to "objective facts." If memories are laced with fantasy the resulting distortions and inventions are by no means accidental or irrelevant: they tell us as much about the person as any number of verifiable "facts."

"At the end of the service the monks took off their black cowls to reveal, underneath, exquisite white-and-gold robes. At this point, the world seemed to suddenly open up: the Easter bells started ringing, everyone in the church started kissing one another and I was overcome with a profound and deep happiness. Suddenly, just at this very moment of great joy, a man came over to me, took my hand and said, 'It's fated that we should be married.' As foolish as that sounds now, such a proposal at the time seemed the right thing to do. Somehow the proposal blended into the total picture: the long period of prayer which I had just undergone, the beauty of the monks now transformed on the altar into creatures possessing flowing white robes and so on. In fact, the whole experience embodied the miracle I had prayed for. I accepted his proposal."

But the marriage "which seemed fated" was complicated by Sonya's subsequent discovery that she wasn't in love. She recalls telling a friend the night before the marriage, "I suddenly realize I don't like this guy." But when advised against proceeding into a loveless union, she decided to go through with the marriage anyway. "I can always get a divorce later if it comes to it."

And it *did* come to it five years later and following a marital experience which Sonya finds painful to talk about even now, five years removed from any contact with her former husband. But more important than the details of her failed marriage—the husband's alcoholism, his inability to hold a job and finally the physical assaults which she claims completed her husband's transformation from a Dr. Jekyll into a Mr. Hyde—are the changes such experiences seemed to have triggered within Sonya. As she sees it, her marriage was only the most conspicuous example of a deeply hidden vulnerability.

"Ordinarily, I project a nonvulnerable image," she says with a provocative laugh, crossing her legs and sitting back, the model of a strikingly poised, attractive and articulate woman. "But it's camouflaging a very deep vulnerability. For instance, just the other day I went out on a date with a television actor, a guy who spends his whole day before lights and cameras. And you know what he said? 'You make me feel inferior.' And all the while he was talking, I was thinking to myself, 'Be careful, Sonya, be careful, you're going to be wiped out.' "

Sonya's conversation is peppered with oblique references to being "wiped out," "annihilated," "smothered" by other people. Along with this are frequent references to self-development and voyages of self-discovery which, although not associated with any form of treatment (she candidly remarks that she's never met a neurologist before), involve a goal which neurologists and psychiatrists over the past twenty years have become increasingly accustomed to encountering in their patients: a lifelong search for identity.

"It seems my whole life involves a search for new directions, ways of finding out who I am. On occasion I think each person, myself particularly, is a series of selves each of which can be developed. I guess when I married I was trying to develop that part of myself which had to do with the Greek tradition, a cultural thing which isn't really important to the self which I'm now developing. I wouldn't, for instance, think of marrying another Greek—I mean I wouldn't eliminate anybody simply because they were Greek, but the cultural thing isn't important to the self I'm developing now."

On occasion I've remarked to Sonya that such comments on different selves arouse my curiosity about which is her "real" self and how other people and, more particularly, how *she* will know when she has encountered this quintessential self.

"I think it's important to keep one's identity fluid," she remarked recently. "For instance, I never really know what people mean when they talk about a 'meaning' in life. For me, I've only experienced the questions in the form of a series of *isn'ts*. Life *isn't* just financial success, good looks, etc. And this series of *isn'ts* has provided me with quite a few interesting experiences."

Sonya's interesting experiences are as far-ranging and diverse as posing for the centerfold of a men's magazine and, at a later date, helping to negotiate a government contract. Presently she identifies herself as president of a small architectural firm. But such wide-ranging accomplishments have also involved her in embarrassing, occasionally hurtful experiences.

"One of the local gossip columnists picked up on my posing in the nude for the men's magazine stint and did a story on me in the newspaper. How could a female architect be the same person who, a few years earlier, posed in the nude for a men's magazine? I can still recall her remark when I asked her not to run the story: 'Honey . . . you're vulnerable.'"

"That scandalmonger didn't realize that the girl who posed in the nude was really another person, another self than the person I am today. I don't mean that literally, of course—I mean I *did* pose—but to tell you the truth, I'm not in contact with that self anymore. I think the whole thing had a lot to do with my need for attention. . . . I remember how flattered I was that the photographer was willing to take several hundred pictures of me and how happy I thought I'd be when people would start recognizing me as a person they had seen in a national magazine. Of course, I'm ashamed of all that now . . . the embarrassment to my family . . . things like that. But I feel I can deny that self now, that other self. It's simply not me."

Worse than the embarrassment, however, were the peculiar distortions which resulted in Sonya's perceptions of other people. On occasion, she speaks of being "disoriented" by the way strangers would look at her after her appearance in the men's magazine.

Other people's opinions have always been important to Sonya. "Being seen and recognized is important to me. I guess I'd make a poor ghost writer," she laughs. "One's peers are witnesses. When I accomplish something, I can point to these witnesses and say, 'See, I did that.' At that point I can go on and take up something entirely different."

But behind the search for "different" accomplishments lies, Sonya believes, the potential for an "incredible growth." To Sonya, the self is not something so much perceived and experienced as something planned and created. Although on occasion her personality undergoes "extraordinary periods of vacillation," this seems appropriate, even inevitable, to her since "every day is a growth experience." But along with this potential for "growth," and perhaps as an intrinsic part of it, there persists within her deeply seated fears of annihilation, the vulnerability which she has experienced all of her life.

"I admit there are certain things I'm bad at. Close personal relationships, for instance. Perhaps my emotions have never really recovered from my marriage. I'm no longer capable of saying, 'My life is going to become this person.' I'm no longer capable of doing that. There's somebody I've been in love with for five years now, but still it's a safe thing. He's living with another woman. Besides, I know nothing will ever come of my love for him. But even so, at least I can always say, 'Hey, I'm really in love.'"

Sonya recalls an experience which she suspects may have something to do with her present dependence on other people's approval.

She remembers playing in a sandbox at about five or six with another child who, in a fit of fury, threw sand in her face and ripped a spoon out of her hand at the very moment she was molding the finishing touches on a sand castle she had worked on over the space of what seemed at the time an endless and beautiful summer afternoon. Rather than retaliating in kind to this childish rudeness, Sonya appears to have shrugged the whole thing off, much to the dismay of her aunt. Sonya's words: "My aunt actually cried when she saw how easily I gave up and refused to fight for what was clearly mine. Above all, she wanted me to be a fighter. But after she saw that I wasn't capable of outright aggression, she encouraged me to fight in subtler ways rather than simply giving up. Developing methods of doing this has provided the principal challenge that I've tried to meet during my whole lifetime."

By her own admission, Sonya is not any more aggressive today. In fact, she's downright frightened now because of a recent multimillion-dollar contract she says a group of West Coast architects has offered for her architectural firm. Rather than pleasing her, however, the offer has stirred up a series of unanswerable questions, at once exciting and threatening. Should she accept the offer? And are they actually making the offer or merely inquiring in order to determine how low a price she would be willing to settle for? Is someone now really offering to buy her spoon? Or is it merely another instance of somebody throwing sand in her face?

Sonya's plans over the next few years remain, as she puts it, "in a creative flux." But whatever her future may hold, she remains confident that "new options will always arise, new opportunities for growth and the forging of new identities."

"It's important to me to always be trying something different." She repeats, "Even though I have been involved in a lot of totally different projects—and some of them don't seem to make much sense—I know they are all somehow interconnected. The important thing is to always keep my identity fluid. Someday I know I will find out who I am."

Sonya's need to keep her identity "fluid" highlights the difficulties some people experience in regard to achieving a sense of self. Unsure of who she really is, Sonya speculates that she may, in fact, be "a series of selves, each of whom can be developed." But since her basic identity is "fluid" and uncertain, she also must tread carefully lest the self of the moment be ensnared, "wiped out" or "annihilated" by other people. Sonya's uncertainty about her identity, her multiple selves, is similar to that of Hermione Roddice in D. H. Lawrence's *Women in Love*: "She always felt vulnerable, vulnerable, there was always a secret chink in her armour. She did not know herself what it was. It was a lack of robust self, she had no natural sufficiency, there was a terrible void, a lack, a deficiency of being within her."

Sonya's conflicts about identity and her resultant fears of destruction are not necessarily a form of emotional illness. In fact, judged by contemporary standards she is a highly successful person. In many ways her efforts at concentrating on "the self I'm developing now" could even be considered admirable. But behind this veneer of successful adaptation is a lonely, isolated woman who cannot trust or even interact on a one-to-one basis with other people. To Sonya, other people are competitors who must be left in the dust as she trots off to the scene of her next triumph. "One's peers are witnesses. When I accomplish something, I can point to these witnesses and say 'See, I did that.'" She's satisfied with "a safe thing," a man she loves but cannot marry. "But even so," she comforts herself, "at least I can say, 'Hey, I'm really in love!'" Apparently Sonya's vulnerability is so acute that the fantasied experience of "being in love" is preferable to the real thing.

Both Sonya and Mark experience an inability to let go of their own perceptions, thoughts and preoccupations. They are literally "self-conscious," to the extent that the events and persons around them must be experienced at a distance, as it were: they must first retain an intense awareness of themselves and only then can they engage with the objective world surrounding them.

At times, self-preoccupation is perfectly normal, as when we focus our attention on a dance step or the grip on our tennis racket. But, as any dancer or tennis player is well aware, such self-consciousness is an extreme liability when it comes to developing a natural dance or tennis "style." At the extreme of this self-consciousness is a patient of Laing's who described her predicament in the following terms: "I forgot myself at the Ice Carnival the other night. I was so absorbed in looking at it that I forgot what time it was and who and where I was. When I suddenly realized I hadn't been thinking about myself I was frightened to death. The unreality feeling came. I must never forget myself for a single minute. I watch the clock and keep busy, or else I won't know who I am."

The elusiveness of the self is based at least partly on the difficulty inherent in defining it outside of a social situation. We literally depend on others not only for our physical well-being, but also for our very identity. "There is no pure zone of integrated self outside of social structures," Laing commented to me at one point in our conversation. He then went on to develop his concept of complementarity.

Me, You and the Others

All identities require other persons. A woman must have a child in order to be a mother. The husband requires a wife. A lover without a beloved is a contradiction in terms. A teacher is not a teacher unless he has students. The students, in turn, derive their identity, their student self, in the relationship to the person who teaches. This process of identity confirmation can even involve aspects of the self that are unwanted or abhorrent. The lawbreaker who gets caught must come to grips with a new identity: the self as criminal. In each instance, the definition of self is conferred by others in a process Laing refers to as complementarity: "that function of personal relations whereby the other fulfills or completes self." In some instances, the "other" may not be precisely defined. My reconstruction of R. D. Laing's theories on the self confirms my identity as a writer even though at this point I have no direct interaction with you, the reader. Nevertheless my relationship with the readers of this book, who presently must remain nameless, confirms my identity, my *self*, as a writer.

This requirement that others contribute to our sense of self results in several paradoxes. We speak frequently of wishing to "find" ourselves and, in order to do so, we may pack up our things and go off to a meditation center or isolated cabin in the woods where, through solitude and communing with nature, we can attempt to "get in touch" with ourselves. Or, we may quit a job because we discover after a while that there is little room for self-advancement or self-development.

Or at times we angrily respond to a frustrating situation, put on a scene and later plead innocence with the remark "I didn't feel like myself; that just wasn't me."

In each instance, the "self" that we allude to as a personal possession is principally an expression of our interaction with others. We're talking in the above examples about our dissatisfaction with the self that the other people in our environment are trying to force upon us. Here's what we're really saying:

"Since I find the present social interactions unfulfilling, I want to get away from the self which is being imposed upon me by the others, hence I'll withdraw to a meditation center or a mountain retreat."

"I'm not happy with the narrow confinement of my job. The self that my boss and coworkers are conferring on me is too trivial; not sufficiently important."

"I lost my temper at those others who tried to degrade and humiliate me. The self they attributed to me is unpleasing and petty."

But the steps that we take in order to redefine ourselves involves a paradox: we withdraw from others into a private world, as if we could construct a self in the manner of a seamstress fashioning a dress. But such efforts are doomed to failure. Identity is always a matter of complementarity: we depend on others to fulfill and complete our self. The self that we construct in our own minds in the isolation of our own imaginations, as it were, is a fantasy identity, a false and grandiose self which seeks to deny the contributions of others to its own development. The price that is paid for this splendid isolation creates divisions within the personality ranging from a sense of alienation to madness—the *divided* self that has occupied R. D. Laing's attention over the past twenty-five years.

"The most significant theoretical and methodological development in the psychiatry of the last two decades is, in my view, the growing dissatisfaction with any theory or study of the individual which isolates him from his context," Laing wrote as far back as 1961. He continues today to subscribe to the importance of other people in forming and maintaining the self. Put at its simplest, as the society changes, people's ideas about each other change and self-concepts are altered accordingly. "In an alienating society one can't assume a constant identity," Laing remarked, a seeming confirmation of the intuition that the modern search for identity is more the logical consequence of the present social order than an indicator of mental instability.

The ways in which the self is altered by other people's responses have been recognized as far back as the early years of this century. The psychologist George Herbert Mead wrote in the 1920s, "We are in possession of selves just in so far as we can and do take the attitudes of others towards ourselves and respond to these attitudes." Subsequent psychological research has confirmed Mead's assertion, particularly in the area of self-esteem—the self's attitude toward itself.

A study carried out by psychologist Kenneth Gergen, professor of psychology at Swarthmore College and author of *The Self in Social Interaction,* measured the influence of social context on self-appraisal. Undergraduate women were interviewed and asked questions aimed at eliciting self-evaluations regarding such things as intelligence, sociability and beauty. Throughout the interview, the interviewer nodded or expressed agreement whenever the students made a positive evaluation. In instances of negative self-appraisal, the interviewers frowned or otherwise indicated their disagreement. Thus, as the interview progressed, the students learned that the interviewers' conception of them was positive. They reacted accordingly: the participants' self-ratings became steadily more positive. No such increase in self-esteem was noted in a control group where the interviewers were careful to suppress any positive or negative reactions to their subjects' responses. Later testing outside of the interview situation using a questionnaire demonstrated that the enhanced self-image endured among those exposed to the interviewer who confirmed their sense of worth. In addition, our evaluation of our own behavior and feelings may be altered according to other people's ideas about how "honest" or "candid" we've been.

A group of college students took part in an interview in which they were asked about future plans, goals and aspirations. After the interview, as part of the experiment, the students were provided the results of the interviewers' attitudes toward them. The interviewers' impressions were carefully constructed so that in 50 percent of the cases the interviewer response conveyed a sense of warmth, admiration and generally positive feelings toward the subject. In the other 50 percent of the cases the interviewer, while not actually hostile, expressed feelings of reservation and guardedness. At this point, the subjects were asked to rate the candor of their responses during the interview. Did they reveal a true picture of themselves? Were they totally honest in their responses? Such measures of subjective interpretation of one's own behavior were strongly influenced by the interviewers' responses, which, it must be remembered, were not related to any actual perceptions of the interviewer, but were arbitrarily positive or negative according to the demands of the experiment. The results?

The students who encountered positive evaluations looked back upon their performance as a totally honest one, while those students who received guarded evaluations thought that perhaps they had been less than candid. In essence, the subjects' later evaluation of their candor could be modified on the basis of other people's responses, suggesting that a person does not know for certain about his own honesty until he is privy to other people's reactions. If others rate him honest and candid he tends to feel that he has been totally straightforward. But any reservations on the part of outside observers lead to reconstructions in which, typically, the performance is rated as less than truthful. Essentially a person must learn from others whether or not he has been candid: self-evaluation is structured and can be changed on the basis of the reactions of the other people in the environment.

At one point I asked Laing about the psychological effects created when people bestow unwanted or unfavorable identities on us. "Shame rather than guilt appears to arise when a person finds himself condemned to an identity as the complement of another he wishes to repudiate but cannot."

If other people's definitions of us are inconsistent or contradictory it seems that we must experience difficulties in reaching a satisfactory definition of self. Laing refers to a collusion between two people whereby one person's identity may depend on inducing certain behavior in others: the self as giver, for instance, requires a collusive identity with another willing to be the re-

ceiver. In those instances where others are not willing to go along
with collusive arrangements, failures may result in the development of the self.

Over the years we've become accustomed to the idea that the
more we get to "know ourselves" the happier and more complete
we will be. Encounter groups, psychotherapy, forms of meditation
—all rest primarily on the assumption that we can acquire self-
knowledge. I want to learn to "control myself," "explore my feelings," "get to know myself," says the explorer in the woodlands
and marshes of the psyche. But to what extent is self-knowledge
possible? Further, will the learning of more "facts" about my personality and my relationship with others lead to an increase in
self-knowledge?

In recent years, psychoanalysts, principally Laing, have pointed
out how an increased inwardness, a concentration on the self
eventually leads not to self-knowledge but to a painful kind of *self-
consciousness* which, continued long enough, leads up to divisions within the self as exemplified by Sonya and Mark. Through
learning how to become an object of our own attentions—"seeing
ourselves as others see us"—we enter into a kind of double-
bookkeeping system: I experience myself in the sense of shutting
out extraneous activity and concentrating, like Descartes, on my
own inner processes: I think, therefore I am. At the same time I
also experience myself as the object of someone else's observation.
Rather than contributing to our search for self-knowledge, such
self-consciousness excludes its very possibility. "We strive continuously," wrote Pascal, "to adorn and preserve our imaginary
self, neglecting the true one."

True insight certainly requires some sensitivity to the impression one is making on others, but an overpreoccupation with "impression management" precludes a true concern and commitment
to the activities we're engaged in from one moment to another. In
essence, sincerity becomes impossible because we've lost our spontaneity: we are no longer free to be "just ourselves." The self becomes divided, split into separate categories of experience, some of

which we are comfortable with, while others result in anguish. Forms of depersonalization become common.

We may act, on occasion, in many ways that are "not like ourselves." Slightly further along the continuum, we may experience a sense of strangeness and discomfort with our bodies. Even further along we encounter the schizoid personality which Laing has described so compellingly.

"The individual in the ordinary circumstances of living may feel more unreal than real; in a literal sense more dead than alive; precariously differentiated from the rest of the world, so that his identity and autonomy are always in question. He may lack the experience of his own temporal continuity. He may not possess an over-riding sense of personal consistency or cohesiveness. He may feel more insubstantial than substantial, and unable to assume that the stuff he is made of is genuine, good, valuable. And he may feel his self as partially divorced from his body. . . . If the individual cannot take the realness, aliveness, autonomy, and identity of himself and others for granted, then he has to become absorbed in contriving ways to be real, of keeping himself or others alive, or preserving his identity, in efforts, as he will often put it, to prevent himself losing his self."

Let us now move on to some of the ways that many of us are losing our "selves."

Ethical Quandaries of a Nymphet

At this point it's obvious we're using *self* here as a synonym for identity. But what is identity? Surely it's more than simply a list of physical features, background characteristics and so on. We can change our hairstyle, shave off our beard, gain or lose twenty-five pounds without losing our identity. Although each of these bodily transformations may result in temporary discomfort, they don't ordinarily produce within us an "identity crisis." In a similar way, removal from our physical surroundings may induce sadness and loneliness but not ordinarily a loss of the sense of who we are. If it did, then all prisoners of war would wind up "brainwashed," when, in fact, brainwashing can be produced only after deliberate efforts directed at altering the prisoner's experiences and evaluations—in a word, his values. Once again, we return to the pivotal insight that a person is, at all times, self-evaluative; in fact, derives his existence from the evaluations he makes.

It's this insight into the nature of identity that explains some of the recent changes in our theory about the nature of the self. Evaluation plays a leading role in the formation of the self and humans can never be adequately understood on the basis of a passive response to a series of drives. At all times, the self is imposing some sort of meaning on its experiences. In fact, it's in situations where events begin to become meaning*less* that we can properly speak of an "identity crisis." People are, at all times, self-interpreting and can be properly understood only when their words and actions are viewed within the context of these self-interpretations. Thus, whatever else an "objective" observer may think, a person is very much what he claims to be.

A woman with an extremely chaotic personal and sexual life

once mentioned to me that her difficulties stemmed from the fact that her parents had beaten and abused her in early life. It would be very easy to "interpret" her statements as rationalizations: she behaves the way she wishes and, when things get beyond her control, she blames her difficulties on earlier experiences in which other people, in this instance the parents, are the villains. But to opt for this "interpretation" of the woman's statements is to discard the most important part of what she's saying. From the point of view of her self-interpretation, events from the past are affecting the ways she's now evaluating her present reality. She experiences herself as still somehow inextricably bound up with people and experiences which, in the objective sense of her being physically and temporally separate from them, have long since passed out of her life. Rather than dismissing her remarks as a surface rationalization and plumbing for something deeper, setting out, as it were, on a sort of archeological exploration of her psyche, it makes a good deal of sense to assume that she really means what she says. Her evaluations of her current situation, the meaning which she is imposing upon it, derive from a self-concept in which her parents are continuing to do her harm. Where others may see a selfish, pleasure-driven woman with little interest in others, she experiences herself as a victim of parental neglect and abuse. Further, this maltreatment has extended even to her present life, accounting, so she feels, for her inability to achieve stability or happiness. These two interpretations of my friend's reality are not just slightly different ways of looking at the same phenomenon but, rather, two mutually exclusive views. If one is true, the other must be false.

She cannot be both a hedonistic seeker of her own pleasure who is, all the while, fully responsible for the choices she makes (the objective viewpoint) and, at the same time, an early victim of other people's cruelty and callousness who has been so transformed by the experience that she is now somehow forced to behave as she does. So which is the true interpretation?

Until recently, most psychiatrists—particularly those trained along Freudian lines—would have rejected this woman's remarks as inadequate. The "real reason" must lie in deeply unconscious forces which, although completely outside of her awareness, are directing her to act in certain ways. They might even, after prolonged interviews, arrive at the very explanation she offers: parental abuse. But, at this point, by a curious twist of logic, the psychiatrists would likely come to a most paradoxical conclusion: this couldn't possibly be the *real* reason for her actions since her memory and awareness of parental abuse, openly avowed, hasn't enabled her to change her behavior. In a word, she lacks insight. Hence, the search must be continued: the psychiatrist must delve deeper until he comes up with an "explanation" which the woman hasn't previously considered.

An alternative explanation places emphasis on what the woman actually says concerning the reasons she acts as she does. Her belief that somehow earlier experiences can "cause" later kinds of behavior—a view which certainly has much to recommend it, as we shall discuss later—affects her present perceptions and experiences in fundamental ways. Thus, her self-evaluation provides meaning to present events and relationships: she is once again the victim of other people's abuse just as she was the victim of parental abuse. This interpretation isn't a deep one which has to be extracted like a precious metal hidden at a great depth; to the contrary, it is an *explicit* part and parcel of herself. The only meaningful way of understanding this woman in the truest sense is to accept her explanations. Her own statements are more "real" than any inferences which ignore or deny her own account of her life. Interestingly, however, such an emphasis on the self turns traditional psychiatry on its head: the most obvious data, a person's own self-descriptions and statements, may turn out to be the most revealing sources of information about the inner realities of her life. It's not necessary or even wise to take the view espoused by traditional psychiatry that the important aspects of a person's life must be somehow hidden.

The psychiatrist is often compared to the detective who searches for clues within the psyche of his patients. To extend and complete the analogy, the psychiatrist who recognizes the pivotal role of the self in a person's reality is like a detective who remains ever mindful that the most helpful clues concerning human personality are often the most obvious ones: the individual's descriptions of his own inner experiences, his self-evaluations. My friend has been exploited and abused because, in her own mind, her self-evaluation has always been that of a person suffering the wounds of abuse. Further, this abuse is not an incidental or trivial aspect of her identity, but its very essence—what she was, is and will be is now inextricably identified with this self: the victim.

Lessons in How to Drive
Another Person Really Crazy

Among the most sensitive indicators of the importance of interpretation in the formation of the self are the various forms of
personal disintegration which may result when one person un-
wittingly or—even more diabolically—deliberately sets out to
confound another's sense of who he is. The psychoanalyst Harold
Searles, in a now-classic paper, "The Effort to Drive the Other
Person Crazy," sets forth a series of maneuvers which, if continued
long enough, may produce madness in another human being.
Searles cites as an example a man who persistently casts doubts on
his sister-in-law's mental stability. In discussions with her, he repeatedly refers to her behavior with comments which suggest that
her behavior is inconsistent and her personality more than slightly
unstable. Since everyone, on occasion, expresses feelings which are
"inconsistent" with previous declarations, it's not too difficult to
find and focus in on examples of seeming contradictions. Indeed,
if this process is continued beyond a certain point, an individual's
self-evaluation becomes threatened. Faced with the force of another person's expression of doubt concerning our adjustment, we
gradually begin to suspect that in fact we are not adjusted at all,
but only pretending at adjustment. This confoundment can be
further increased if the attacker reinterprets examples of our past
adjustment as proof of our unwillingness to face squarely certain
problems, which, unresolved, have stimulated deliberate efforts on
our part to *appear* adjusted. Thus, we are accused simultaneously
of being adjusted and of not being adjusted.

Other examples of similar discrepancies between our self-evaluation and another person's evaluation of us include the deliberate
creation of ambiguous situations in which we are left in doubt

about how to respond. For instance, a person may speak or act in a sexually provocative manner within a setting where sexual interaction is impossible. Or, he may alternate expressions of profound seriousness with playful humor. In this way, we are simultaneously informed that we are both important enough to merit being "taken seriously" and yet ridiculous enough to be the butt of humorous hostility.

Another variation involves the retention of a single emotional tone when discussing both serious and trivial matters. Both of these techniques aim at the confusion and bewilderment of another person's sense of self. Am I *really* the person I consider myself to be or, instead, a kind of humorous figure, a distorted and fragmented self which is both serious and comic, sane and insane, a creature of certitude and yet, at the same time, someone who is irresolute and incomplete?

In general, Searles writes, "[the] initiating of any kind of interpersonal interaction that tends to activate varied areas of his personality in opposition to another, tends to drive him crazy."

Searles's insights into this process are based on his own deeply intense and, by his own admission, often ambivalent and conflictual encounters with the psychotic patients under his care. By carefully monitoring his own responses to the patient's communications—the feelings and emotions which the patient stirs up in him—Searles has grasped what he believes is a fundamental insight: that the patients are enacting in treatment with him a similar process of "driving crazy" or "being driven crazy" that occurred earlier in their lifetime, prior to their mental breakdown.

For example, Searles writes of an unusually attractive hospitalized schizophrenic patient who spent many hours talking with him about political and philosophic matters "in which she was expressing herself with a virile kind of forceful businesslike vigor, while I, though not being given a chance to say much, felt quite strongly urged to argue some of these points with her and did so." The outward behavior which accompanied these dialogues, however, was anything but consistent with the atmosphere one might expect from such encounters: "Stalking about the room or posing herself on her bed in an extremely short-skirted dancing costume in a sexually inflaming way."

Gradually, Searles felt himself caught up in the contradiction between what was actually being discussed and his patient's covertly seductive manner. On the one hand, Searles was being asked to respond to an intellectualized orientation while, simultaneously, he was aware of the stirrings of his own passion. "But how could this be?" he asked himself. "Am I imagining the whole thing?" The patient seemed to think so—in fact, earlier in the session she accused Searles of "lustful, erotic desires." *She* certainly was not contributing to it, and she suggested that any sexual feelings must remain Searles's responsibility.

"I felt no consentual validation (at a conscious level) from her about this more covert interaction; this non-verbal sexual interaction intended to appear as simply a 'crazy' product of my own imagination. Even though I knew there was a reality basis for my responding on these two unrelated levels, I still found it such a strain that I felt, as I say, as though I were losing my mind."

Another patient's efforts to "drive crazy" took on a more deliberate aspect. A hospitalized young male schizophrenic began insisting that Searles, rather than himself, was actually the "crazy" one. His remarks, reiterated over two years of treatment, repeatedly questioned his doctor's mental stability. "You're kind of strange, Dr. Searles—you think peculiarly. . . . You don't express yourself to other people the way you do to me, do you?"

At first glance it seems that such accusations could be managed quite easily. But as Searles indicates, repetitively expressed doubts about one's sanity can create a snowball effect in which disquietude rapidly turns into panic and a painful inner terror that there might be some nugget of truth in the patient's restated accusations that the doctor—presumably the healthier member of the patient-doctor pair—is "slightly or more than slightly cracked."

In any event, Searles's own reactions underscore the power of such a technique if continued with sufficient relentlessness: "He reiterated for years maddeningly bland stereotypes labelling himself as thoroughly healthy and good, and myself as warped and evil, with a kind of eroding tenacity." The process eventually went on and "to such a degree that I could scarcely make myself remain in the room."

"The struggle to drive one another crazy" (Searles's words again) eventually took the form of the patient accusing his doctor of trying to drive *him* crazy. "After my having gone through a number of hours with him in which I had to struggle with unaccustomed effort to maintain my own sanity, it began to occur to me that this oft reiterated accusation of his—that I was trying to drive *him* crazy—might involve some projection"—the patient was trying to drive Searles crazy.

Basically what's being attacked in such situations is the person's inward sense of integration and cohesiveness. To a large extent, most of us feel that we're one self, clearly separated from others in the environment, and that we change relatively little over the span of years. But Searles's experience illustrates that our integrated sense of identity (who I am) can be shaken by experiences involving others close to us whose fragmentation and splitting can lead us to conclude either that they're more than one person or that we are actually multiple selves.

The idea that personality may consist of a series of multiple selves seems, at first glance, frankly preposterous. But to Searles, the majority of patients under his care provide evidence that "the healthy individual's sense of identity is far from being monolithic in nature." Further, on the basis of more than thirty-five years of clinical experience with patients whose psychosis has been serious enough to confine them for many years in a mental institution, Searles has concluded, "I have come to believe that the more healthy a person is, the more consciously does he live in the knowledge that there are myriad 'persons'—internal objects each having some sense-of-identity value—within him."

Searles draws his conclusions from a novel, highly innovative and frequently controversial technique. An immensely serious man of sixty-three, he has, over the years, published as much as any person alive on the psychotherapeutic approach to psychosis. To many psychiatrists, his probing and often shocking barbs into the patient's unconscious are the trademark of a highly original and creative innovator. But to others more accustomed to considering serious mental illness as having physical causes—primarily the result of complex and so far undetermined brain disorders—his methods are sadistic.

"Searles is a wild man," one of his former students confided to me. But whether you consider him a wild man or a genius, you'd have to agree that Searles is a master in the deployment of powerful but nonetheless deeply unsettling explorations into the inner core of insanity.

Imagine fantasizing or dreaming a surrealistic, otherworldly conversation in which you and your conversant are free to verbalize the most bizarre, most outrageous, most disturbing thoughts and you have some idea of the ground rules of a Harold Searles's interview.

One patient who had been in treatment for eighteen years was greeted on a Saturday morning: "Well, did you—just *hear* something—so—clearly that you—assumed I must have heard it, too?"

To psychiatrists trained within the traditional doctor-expert-supercilious-dispenser-of-wisdom-and-health tradition such an immediate engagement with the irrational is profoundly unsettling. Any inquiry about auditory hallucinations would come later and tentatively. But to Searles, the process of interviewing involves an immediate descent into fantasies. For, above all, Searles is a secret sharer in the processes that have driven his patients to madness.

Searles engages his patients within the core of their psychosis, grappling with their insanity within a framework of their delusions and hallucinations. To witness Searles interviewing a schizophrenic leaves one with an increasing and uneasy acquiescence that there really is only a thin line between sanity and insanity. One wishes for a scorecard in order to dispel the bewilderment which accompanies one's efforts to differentiate patient from doctor. "If you get confused and wonder who's who, remember, the doctor is the one wearing the suit." (On occasions when I've witnessed Searles in action, I've never been able to remain in the room for the duration of the interview. Invariably, I've fled into the sunshine or into an adjoining conference room or into a hallway—anywhere I can quiet my racing heart. "It's not true . . . that isn't real . . . I refuse to accept that I, as well as that poor patient, can be capable of experiencing such wildness, such craziness!")

Out of this bizarre combat, Searles has emerged with novel and disturbing ways of interpreting ordinary conversation. Like Freud in *The Psychopathology of Everyday Life*, Searles cautions that his interpretations are culled largely from the psychoanalytic situation and should, most appropriately, be applied to psychoanalytic encounters. But also like Freud, Searles isn't hesitant to suggest that many of his observations can be applied—outside of treatment situations—to many people most of us would have little difficulty in accepting as "normal."

Take the seemingly innocent remark, "I feel terribly uneasy in my family, in my marriage, in my home." Behind the ordinariness of this remark, Searles detects "a feeling tone which reveals the existence, at an unconscious level, of three separate identities in her—one having to do with her family; a second with her marriage, and a third with her home."

Another patient, "a much travelled woman," comments on the feelings she experiences in different countries: "I feel more disturbed in England than I do in other countries. I feel more comfortable in Italy; I feel more comfortable in France; I feel all right in Canada." Most of us would conclude—on the basis of making similar remarks ourselves—that the woman simply prefers some countries over others. To Searles, however, such remarks hint at subtle divisions within the self. "This innocuous-seeming statement is said in a curious manner that conveys the unintended meaning that, at an unconscious level, she is living simultaneously as several different selves, in England and in other countries including Italy and France."

Or consider the kind of remark we all make almost every day in order to excuse ourselves from the consequences of certain of our actions. "Gee, I'm awfully sorry . . . that wasn't like me," or "That wasn't me," or, as with Searles's patient, "It wasn't like me to react as I did." To Searles, such remarks are "an allusion to the presence of another 'me,' this one unconscious, who governed his behavior in the past incident."

Once plugged into the possibility of multiple selves, seemingly casual remarks take on meanings never previously considered. The patient who begins a psychoanalytic session, for instance, with the words, "I don't know where to begin," may be expressing more than mere confoundment about how to bring his analyst up to date. Searles suggests that, in some instances, such remarks may be an unconscious way of saying, "It is not clear which one of my multiple I's will begin verbally reporting its thoughts, its feelings, its free associations during this session."

In such a situation, the patient may be expressing the fact that "there are too many I's which are, at the moment, competing among 'themselves' as to which one shall begin verbalizing." Further along in the analysis, patients may, as an expression of "ego strength," be capable of integrating into their conscious sense of identity "many previously warded off identities." Searles cites as a healthy example a patient who began her session with him, "Now let's see, which one of my several identities will materialize today?"

Searles has written of a patient whose mother was "completely unpredictable in her emotional changeability." She might, for instance, return from the temple with a "beatific expression on her face," as though still immersed in a deeply religious experience, yet, moments later, lash out at her children. Warmth and friendliness could alternate within seconds with verbal and even physical abuse. Out of this unpredictable and chaotic background, there emerged over the years a fully developed paranoid schizophrenia in her son, Searles's patient. At the basis of his delusion was the firmly held and often repeated belief that he was related to not one but many mothers. He objected whenever anyone inquired about "your mother." He explained: "When you use the word 'mother' I see a picture or a parade of women, each one representing a different point of view."

In all cases, the effort to "drive crazy" aims, to use Searles's words, at undermining "the other person's confidence in the reliability of his own emotional reactions and of his own perception of outer reality."

In essence, the person being "driven crazy" is repetitively forced into the position of doubting the reality of his own perceptions.

Like Searles discussing philosophy with the sexually provocative patient, the person who is the object of another's efforts to "drive crazy" begins to suspect that his own perceptions are somehow distorted and unreliable. And to correct for this feeling, he may rely, more and more, on the interpretations offered by the other. "We're only talking about philosophy, aren't we?" Thus a kind of "psychological equivalent of murder" exists in which the selfhood of another person is destroyed, his very being dissipated into a kind of mist, a psychological no-man's-land. This process, although a profoundly disturbing one, may begin with little more than subtly expressed doubts about the rationality of one's own thought processes or emotions: to be sexually aroused during a philosophical discussion is disturbing because, on sober reflection, it seems "crazy."

Haven't we all, on occasion, experienced attenuated versions of such a process? The individual who we're never sure is to be taken seriously; the confidant who laughingly makes a joke in the middle of our recitation about something that is deeply troubling us; the person who transmits a sexual message through a prolonged glance or handshake which takes place is a situation (perhaps in a crowded room, or in the presence of one's spouse) where a sexual response is not only inappropriate but impossible to act upon—in such encounters we are left in doubt concerning what's *really* going on. Am I missing something? Is my imagination overactive? Am I responding in ways that are, well, crazy?

A woman I once knew who was both a good mother and a good wife was the object of her husband's sadistic undermining of her view of herself as a basically well-adjusted, middle-class housewife. He repeatedly pointed out to her how the romantic books and movies she enjoyed were actually the vicarious expression of her own wish for a romantic liaison. Unsure after a while how she "really felt," she had a brief and guilt-ridden affair. This, of course, only further weakened her certitude regarding what was "really going on." Desperate, she confessed to her husband, who used this new knowledge of her behavior as a means of bolstering his relentless insistence that she was "confused." On the verge of a mental breakdown, she shouted at me that I had to help her: "My husband is out to murder my mind."

References to a "murdering" of the mind occur frequently in the conversation of persons on the verge of mental breakdown. While these persons may refer to the destructive and painful process they are expressing as involving my "mind" or my "brain" they're actually saying, "So-and-so is out to murder my sense of who I am—my self." If asked to elaborate on their feelings, they often complain the other person is trying to "control" them or "push them around," somehow displace them from themselves, nay, actually capture their very essence, their self.

Everyday life provides many examples of attenuated versions of this fear of the loss of self: "He's trying to force his opinion down my throat." "She's a very weak character [self]." In any human relationship which is more than merely casual, the selves of the different parties must make some accommodation to each other. Since some people are "stronger" or "deeper" than others, the relationship often takes a form whereby one self surrenders to the other.

We are all familiar with recently married couples whose behavior becomes increasingly that of one of the partners. It's almost as if the less "dominant" partner quietly relinquishes attitudes and behaviors in favor of the attitudes and behaviors of his or her spouse—the other self. While such a process isn't necessarily abnormal—and to a certain extent is probably inevitable whenever two people differ radically enough in certain areas—it can progress to the point where, after a while, the more "passive" person ends up not feeling like a self at all. His identity becomes merged with the dominant partner's, almost as if an identity were being molded or imprinted upon him. In response to this, he may, at times, rant and rave, in a word, become "unreasonable" about his experiences of the loss of his self. These periodic outbursts often take the form of marital quarrels: the partners argue over who is going to modify his "life-style," make concessions, in effect, compromise. In essence, which self is going to have to change and which is going to remain as it is? On occasion, the dilemma terminates in a permanent impasse: both are too rigid (or too "strong," as they might prefer to think of it) and the marriage breaks up.

In other instances, the surrender of the self of one person to that of the other is so total that, in the event of a breakup, the individual no longer feels that he even possesses a self. This self has been taken away from him by the lover, purloined, as it were, along with the china and the sports car. And if this loss of the sense of self is sufficiently acute, the offended person may take measures to get it back. Recently, a West Indian man entered a bank in Toronto and fired five shots into the face of a Canadian girlfriend, a teller who, the day before, had left him after four years of living together. He then turned the pistol on himself. Surely such an extreme reaction requires more in the way of an explanation than simply "hurt feelings." What had the girl taken from him that required that he kill both of them in order to get it back?

Although no one knows for certain about such tragic events, I think it's likely he felt "lost," disoriented, stricken with a sense of loss and yearning, but for whom? The woman? Surely it won't sound too cynical to remind ourselves that there were other women in Toronto whom, perhaps, he could get to know and love and who would also learn to love him. After all, people get over such romantic breakups every day; at least they do so frequently enough that they rarely feel compelled to end the matter forever by means of a pistol. No . . . there must be more to such an irrational act than merely the loss of a lover. I'd suggest that the one thing this unfortunate man had lost and couldn't quite regain was his self: where, indeed, would he find another self?

A similar dilemma about who is going to impose himself upon whom can be found, to some extent, in every marriage. My wife and I have often discussed her feelings that, by helping me in countless ways throughout our marriage—as researcher and critic of my books, to mention only two contributions—she's sacrificed part of her "self." This isn't a statement of anger or resentment but an appropriate and fair request that I at least acknowledge that, on many occasions, when her time and effort could have been devoted to projects dear to either of us, we concentrated on what I wanted. When describing such processes, my wife's quiet statements regarding "sacrifice" are infinitely more than metaphor.

In many other marriages, the issue of how two separate selves can learn to accommodate to each other isn't solved at all. Each person remains incomplete, in fact derives part of his identity from the other, a situation both persons often deeply resent.

Whoever first said, "Familiarity breeds contempt," might wish to revise the statement: "Familiarity, on occasion, breeds not so much contempt as resentment."

Taking the matter a step further, marital partners may supplement certain aspects of each other so as to create a new "self" that's a combination of both partners and yet can't at all be precisely broken down into a strictly additive two-plus-two-equals-four situation. It's almost as if two plus two equaled five: the partners together constitute more of a self than the addition of each person separately. For instance, one partner may be comfortable in situations which demand confrontation and firm resolution. The other partner, in contrast, may agree in principle with the firmness required to attain various goals but nonetheless remain incapable of forging ahead in the face of potential opposition. Such differences in "style" often underlie our comments that two people are "good for each other," an informal way of recognizing that each person somehow makes up for the deficiencies of the other. But what if the collusion, the symbiosis between two marital partners develops to the point that each self is dependent on the other in order to realize any sense of cohesion? What effect could this have on a child, for instance?

An insight into the fragility of the child's sense of identity occurred to Dr. Harold Searles on the occasion of being awakened late at night by a quarreling couple. "As I lay there listening to their shouting at one another—each angry, adamant, tenacious—for a very long time, it dawned on me that they were struggling to demarcate the boundaries between one another. . . . It then occurred to me that one reason the child feels torn apart in hearing his parents' arguing is that neither of the parents is functioning as a separate and well-defined entity. Thus, the child may be affected even more deeply than if he were feeling torn apart by divergent loyalties to well-defined, individual parents: he feels unwhole, through identification with the revealed incompleteness of each of his arguing parents."

A similar situation commonly occurs in the lives of children caught in the breakup of their parents' marriages and, at least partially, explains the destructive effect a divorce may have on children at certain stages of their lives. It's not a matter of whether the child would be better with one parent or the other. Rather, the child's emerging identity is an amalgam of both parents. The loss of either the mother or the father results in a diminishment of the child's self. Aren't we referring to just such a compounding within the child of his parents' attributes when we comment that a child "takes his looks from his father but has his mother's personality and cleverness"? In response to a marital breakup, the child is not so much forced to choose between one parent or the other as he is to truncate his fragile and emerging sense of identity. Perhaps at some point the courts may recognize this situation by appointing not only representatives of parents, but also a guardian of the child's evolving self. "I love them both," a comment frequently made by a child to the judge who is wrestling with the question of the child's custody, is not so much an example of precocious diplomacy in the child as it is a plea for the freedom to develop into a fully integrated self, to be in a sense *both* mother and father.

This incompleteness between a husband and wife can be uncomfortable, even agonizing, erupting periodically into bitter arguments or even, as in the instance of the West Indian man, violence and death. On the other side of it, a couple may bask in the sunshine of mutually conferred identity with both seeming to fall apart when separated from the other. Traditionally, psychiatrists have looked with disdain on such "dependency" relationships. But "dependency" is just another word for a process similar to the symbiosis that exists between a mother and child in which both parties receive and confer benefits on the other. The weakness in a symbiotic relationship, if one exists, often takes the form of an overly intense or prolonged attachment. But there may also occur just the opposite: an inability to form any type of attachment. As we shall see at a later point in this book, this latter failure is currently a much more common source of problems concerning the self. It takes the form of an undue concern about the establishment and maintenance of one's own personal uniqueness. Such people frequently defend their "identity," their role, their sense of "who I am." They are usually sensitive to any encroachment on their time and energies. They keep at a distance and have great difficulty entering into intimate relationships. They are often described as "cool" or "distant"; people complain of never getting to know them. Overall, they are most comfortable in situations where they can work alone and they often choose professions and occupations where they can function as self-starters and can be free, to a certain extent, to choose their own projects. The ordinary work situation of cooperative relatedness is looked upon as threatening, a curtailment of their freedom, a merging into an amorphous organization where other people constantly threaten to swallow them up in a psychic maelstrom. Paradoxically, such individuals are often described as strong characters, individualists, persons who "know their own mind." But the reality of the situation is just the opposite.

Frequently, a person's preoccupation with his or her identity is a tip-off that the sense of self is extremely fragile. Such a person can't get emotionally close to another because, as with Mark and Sonya, the other may impose an aspect of his identity on them. As we'll see later, this fear may develop into madness or a special manner of relatedness to others characteristic of the borderline personality. But we're not now talking of extreme forms of threatened loss of identity. Instead, we speak of more subtle, attenuated fears which result in withdrawal or acute discomfort at the prospect of intimate interrelatedness.

Basically, all human relationships are lived at the symbiotic level of attachment. We give and we receive. We comfort and we're comforted. Through the powers of human imagination and empathy, one human being can react to another's misfortune with a poignancy corresponding to how she would feel if the same thing had happened to her. "Do unto others as you would have them do unto you" implies the achievement of a symbiotic relatedness. You and the others form a psychic unity, almost a separate organism. Hurting the other is felt as a kind of hurting of oneself. Looked at from this vantage, dependency can be seen in a positive light. Psychic interdependence in shared concerns is part of human interrelatedness in its most sensitive and developed form.

But other arguments can also be made for "dependency." Our uniqueness is largely illusory. In fact, we are required to function only rarely as subjectively unique human beings. Almost always our self-image or self-concept is more symbiotic than we realize. At one point, I may relate to my social group and try to act according to the norms that seem "appropriate," while on another occasion I may identify with my family, consciously or unconsciously acting in accordance with, or perhaps even in direct opposition to, what I think they expect of me. Later, while visiting a foreign country I may be conscious of myself as an American. But rarely, if ever, do I consider my situation without some context in which to imbed my momentary impression of just who Richard Restak *really* is. This matter of who one *really* is can vary tremendously, according to the symbiotic relationships that exist at the time: family, nationality, religion, neighborhood, occupation etc. These relationships can also change hundreds of times in a single day and help to explain, I believe, many of the paradoxes and discontinuities of human behavior. For example, symbiotic relatedness—identification, if you prefer—within the family is likely to call for quite a different repertoire of responses than the relatedness established with one's friends. This helps to explain why a child can be an absolute terror at home but behaves as a perfect angel in school. Or how a group of "responsible" citizens can turn into a lynch mob. The expressions of symbiotic relatedness vary in each instance according to the different persons or groups of persons involved.

In addition, many forms of symbiotic relatedness are made outside our immediate awareness and are rarely verbalized. This accounts for the success of brainwashing and various forms of thought reform: a person is physically isolated, exposed to unfamiliar surroundings and forced to form bonds to the captors. From here, the transfer of ideology becomes almost automatic: identification becomes sufficiently strong that beliefs are accepted which ordinarily would be rejected on the strength of other symbiotic relationships to country, family etc. But in the brainwashing situation these earlier symbiotic bonds have been destroyed.

In a sense, symbiotic relatedness is a form of identification, but it's much more difficult to pinpoint since it's preverbal (the symbiotic period of infancy occurs at around five or six months prior to the development of language). We rarely take into account our symbiotic relationships because they are largely outside our awareness—our unconscious, as the psychoanalyst would put it.

It's obvious by now that "normal" individuals may vary greatly in the extent to which they possess a healthy, vigorous and hardy sense of self. Furthermore, the self is exquisitely sensitive to outside influences. Other people can "confirm" our sense of self via complementarity. They can also attack and destroy our sense of self, fractionating it into tiny, separate parts. In order to protect the self against such attacks, some people inwardly withdraw, clutching at their sense of self in the manner of a miser hoarding his gold. But since the self is at least partly socially defined, withdrawal, by a strange paradox, results in a further weakening of the self's structure. In the remainder of this book we're going to examine a series of disturbances of the self which occur along a continuum. At one end of the continuum are mildly disturbed individuals such as Sonya and Mark. At the other extreme are individuals whose inner world is so fractionated, conflicted and disturbed that there is some real question as to whether they possess a self at all.

III

Beyond Freud

". . . to possess a double mental personality has long ceased to be the sort of trick that only lunatics can bring off. On the contrary, at the speed at which we live today the possibility of political understanding, the ability to write a newspaper article, the vigour required to believe in new movements in art and literature, and countless other things, are wholly founded on a talent for being at certain hours convinced against one's own conviction, for splitting a part off from the whole content of one's consciousness and for spreading it out to form a new state of entire conviction."

The Man Without Qualities, Robert Musil

Squeezing a Lemon

Over the past twenty-five years or so, psychiatrists have been encountering in their practices an increasing number of patients whose reasons for entering treatment involve feelings of "emptiness" along with an absence of "goals" or a "life purpose." Often highly successful in their occupations, many of these patients are, in fact, leaders in business, the professions and the arts. Most striking of all, however, is the vast discrepancy between the patients' impressive professional attainments and the absence of any corresponding sense of accomplishment. Many complain that they don't know "who they are," utter expressions of futility and feel, in general, that life doesn't seem worthwhile. In most instances, their existence seems colorless: almost without exception they describe their contacts with other people as devoid of sparkle and zest.

At first, many psychiatrists diagnosed these new patients as "depressed" and initiated treatments aimed at the relief of "depression." But these patients weren't depressed and, after a while, the treatments resulted in failure. In fact, the patients' incapacity to experience depression later emerged as a basic feature of their personality. Eventually, certain other distinguishing features turned up as the number of these puzzling patients increased.

Typically, the patients were in their thirties or early forties, often physically attractive, highly verbal, charming and immensely ambitious. In addition, they exhibited, at first contact, an easy grace in human relations. Closer scrutiny, however, revealed extreme self-absorption accompanied by feelings, often openly expressed, of superiority over other people. One patient described his interpersonal relationships with the analogy of "squeezing a lemon and then dropping the remains." In the words of another patient, the world could be divided into "the famous, the rich and the great," and the "despicable, the worthless and the mediocre." In all cases it was extremely important for these patients to associate themselves with the "winners," and they reacted with rage at any suggestion that success involved factors other than just material possessions and interpersonal domination.

Along with this grandiosity, however, there existed a paradoxical and deeply felt need for approval from other people, even those who were the objects of the patients' ridicule and contempt. A need for external admiration and acclaim turned out, in fact, to be the principal motivation behind most of their actions. While they expressed open contempt for the majority of people they encountered in their day-to-day life (usually including their psychiatrists!), their need for approval and admiration was so great that, in its absence, they developed their symptoms of boredom and emptiness.

Most interesting of all, however, were the kinds of human relationships these patients displayed in their private lives. Manipulative, exploitive and unreasonably demanding, the patients demonstrated a total inability to understand the emotional responses of those around them. Beneath a smooth and socially polished surface lurked a frightening absence of emotional depth combined with a failure to understand, much less respond to, other people's emotions. Convinced of their right to exploit and control others, these patients concealed, behind their charming and engaging manner, a coldness and a ruthlessness that viewed every human interaction as a contest where, in the words of one patient, one is "either screwing or being screwed."

Psychiatrists found little in traditional psychiatry or psychoanalytic theory to explain these paradoxical and enigmatic patients. Further, most attempts at communication and treatment resulted in fierce power struggles with the patients who, on one day, exhibited sudden and intense hatred toward their doctors, followed perhaps the very next day by abject apologies and expressions of esteem, usually accompanied by pleaful repetitions of their request for help in what they, once again, described as an unbeara-

ble sense of emptiness. These mercurial shifts in thought and behavior seemed, in some ways, suggestive of multiple personality,
the "Three Faces of Eve" phenomenon. But, on closer inspection,
the patients failed to resemble any previously encountered instances of multiple personality. For instance, they never developed
amnesias: they were able to recall quite clearly during periods of
quiescence the torrents of abuse they had previously heaped on
their psychiatrists. Nor did they exhibit any of the sudden hysterical losses of such things as the ability to speak or walk which are
often encountered in multiple personalities.

Yet, if these patients weren't instances of multiple personality,
neither did they appear whole and intact. It was almost as if portions of their personalities were somehow *split off*, leading to puzzling and contradictory behaviors. Psychoanalyst Otto Kernberg,
in recalling this period, writes, "The patients were conscious of
the severe contradiction in their behavior; yet they would alternate between opposite strivings with a bland denial of the implications of this contradiction and showed what appeared to be a
striking lack of concern over the 'compartmentalization' of their
mind."

One of Kernberg's patients alternated between periods of intense self-questioning and brooding over her sexual inhibitions
punctuated by episodic impulse-ridden sexual activity. Even more
interesting than the behaviors themselves, however, were the patient's attitudes. Within days, sometimes even hours, diametrically opposed behaviors occurred without any sense of contradiction: sexual scrupulosity gave way to a hedonistic search for
sexual fulfillment.

Another patient went through "binges" of lying during which
almost everything he said was a lie. This alternated with periods
of remorse and guilt over lying accompanied by the confident assertion that lying was no longer a problem but, rather, other people (his psychiatrist included) were lying to him! According to
Kernberg: "What was striking was the complete separation of the
impulsive lying from the time the patient remembered the lying,
but did not feel emotionally connected with it and, on the con-

trary, was strongly convinced that lying was not, or at least was no longer, a part of his psychic reality."

To the casual observer, such puzzling behavior might be labeled *repression*, Freud's pivotal term dating back to his earliest theories on the development of the personality. According to classical Freudian theory, unacceptable impulses of aggression or sexuality are kept out of consciousness—repressed—by an active process aimed at protecting the self from anxiety. The impulse is still present, of course, but camouflaged. The task of psychoanalysis is to remove the camouflage by unraveling the indirect ways that repressed instincts reveal themselves, hence the psychoanalyst's emphasis on slips of the tongue, the symbolization of dreams, the methods of free association and so on. From such indirect expressions, the psychoanalyst is often able to infer the repressed emotions and help his patient gain insight. Thus, to oversimplify terribly, if a patient on the night before her wedding developed a hysterical paralysis owing to repressed fears of sexuality, the cure was likely to come from concentrating less on the paralysis than on uncovering ways to reveal (unrepress) the sexual basis of her fears. Once this was accomplished, the patient, presumably, no longer required her "defense" (the paralysis), which would pass away with the resolution of the sexual fears. In essence, by "making the unconscious conscious" separate parts of the personality could be unified.

Despite superficial similarities with the repressed patients encountered by Freud and the early psychoanalysts, a totally different process seemed to be taking place in the patients encountered by Kernberg and others. The patients didn't repress or deny the contradictory aspects of their behavior. Instead, they described difficulties in experiencing the emotional reality of these separate periods.

One of Kernberg's patients early in his analysis launched into a vicious verbal attack that went on for several weeks and concerned the patient's feelings that his psychiatrist held him in contempt and disgust. After hours of bombastic abuse, the patient's behavior changed into an intense, almost obsequious gratefulness that Kernberg was willing to retain him as a patient. Amid tears and expressions of profound appreciation, the patient expressed his admiration and gratitude. Suddenly, and once again without obvious rhyme or reason, the patient reverted to his former abusive manner. "He then expressed intense hatred towards me, attacked me verbally with a sadistic derogatory attitude, and appeared, at this point, to be completely unable to be aware of any good feelings or opinions he formerly expressed to hold about me," Kernberg has written.

When questioned, the patient admitted the contradictions and discontinuities implied in his different attitudes toward his psychiatrist but, in Kernberg's words, "this memory had no emotional reality at all for him. It was as if there were two selves, equally strong, completely separated from each other in their emotions, although not in the patient's memory, and alternating in his conscious experience."

In order to understand the paradoxes created by such patients, Kernberg relied on an explanation of human personality based on object relations theory. During the past twenty-five years, this has become the most powerful and influential theory explaining human behavior.

Double Bookkeeping

According to object relations theory, the infant, soon after birth, begins to form internal images, mental pictures if you will, resulting from his interaction with the world around him. As a result of his experiences with mother, for instance, the infant builds up images of mother and himself (at the earliest period of development the two are fused: the baby is an inseparable part of mother). At a later stage, the infant begins to appreciate mother as a separate being from himself, an insight which results in two images: an internal *self*-image interacting with the *object* image of mother.

Along with these two images are accompanying feelings which result from the infant's interaction with mother. In those situations of warmth and caring the emotions aroused are pleasurable, leading to the formation of positive internal images (also called representations or introjects of mother). In instances of friction, when warmth and cuddling aren't available, "bad" images result accompanied by feelings of anxiety, frustration and rage. Fortunately, with most infants the pleasurable experiences with mother outnumber the unpleasant ones, thus permitting a buildup of positive images of both self and the other persons in the environment, most notably the mother. Good self-images and good object images resulting from pleasurable and fulfilling early infant-mother interaction lead, in turn, to the infant's ability to gradually differentiate himself from mother. In a phrase, the infant slowly builds up a *sense of self* which is separate from mother.

While most theorists seem clear in their own mind what they mean by "representation," "images" or "introjects," the concepts are far from intuitively obvious to those uninitiated into the arcane world of internal object relations theory. A useful help toward understanding comes from a consideration of how all of us establish and maintain certain "attitudes" toward other people.

Think, for a moment, about the everyday experience of dealing with someone who proves to be "difficult." Let's say the person is a business associate who has an infuriating habit of confronting or resisting us on just about any front. Whatever we decide to do, we can be fairly certain that this individual will somehow have to be dealt with and overcome. After a while, this characteristic of the other person becomes so associated with him in our mind that the mere mention of his name or the prospect of encountering him sometime in the future stirs up an internal image which includes not only our concept of how he appears, but in addition, an emotional "feeling" about him. Attached to our mental picture or schema—the exact terminology isn't important—is an emotional valence.

In a social situation we may meet someone who is acquainted with our "difficult" person, but who doesn't find him difficult at all. Instead, he has formed an internal representation of a friendly, likable, fun-loving person. Accompanying this is quite a different emotional valence, a positive one which stands in stark contrast to the negatively tinged emotions (uneasiness, suspicion, resentment, anger and so on) that we inwardly attach to our representation of the "difficult" person.

In each instance the representation is not just a kind of inner photograph, but rather a symbol of the other person which carries with it emotional overtones. Try as we might, we just can't think of our "difficult" person as being anything other than difficult. Our inner representation is associated with an emotional response, in this instance a negative one, and it's impossible for anyone else to understand our relationship with this person unless they take this emotional valence into account.

In a similar way, object relations theorists postulate that, early in the infant's life, gratifying, pleasurable experiences associated with another person—usually the caretakers—result in the gradual buildup of positive, "good" emotions which form an integral part of the emerging self of the infant. In contrast, frustrating, unfulfilling, painful experiences also attach to these internal representations. Naturally, since only a limited number of people are encountered early in the infant's life, these few people (mother, father) usually wind up, in the infant's mind, as a mixture of positive and negative emotions. This may be the basis for the eventual healthy recognition that no one is perfect and that all human relationships are founded on the capacity of both parties to accept and deal with the "good" and "bad" in every human being.

In instances of extreme stress, however, it's postulated that the developing infant is unable to synthesize these contradictory experiences with others and attempts to make up for this by *splitting* its internal world into tight compartments of all "good" and all "bad." Thus, mother, when she is feeding and caring for the infant, is experienced and anticipated by a positive emotional inner representation. Later, when she doesn't anticipate the baby's needs and fails in what researchers refer to as early "empathic understanding," mother exists as an oppositely charged introject or representation in the baby's mind. In this instance, the infant's "split" object relations are never synthesized. Instead the infant—and later the child and adult—reacts, on some occasions, as if dealing with a positive representation, but later, under the threat or expectation of negative experiences, responds with rage and frustration that would seem appropriate in the face of an enemy—the "bad" internal representation.

The overall result of this "splitting" process is a disruption in the unity of the individual's inner world. People, for instance, may be responded to, on one occasion with positive feelings since the "good" internal object representation of these people is operative at that moment. Later, like a precious stone which has been turned ever so slightly and now reflects light from a different angle, the situation may change toward the predominance of "bad," negatively charged inner representations.

It is important to stress here that nothing "objective" will have changed. Only the subjective interpretation changes and this change is based on alterations in the inner representations of the experiencer. Further, whichever introject happens to be ascendant on any given moment is all-powerful. The individual is convinced, at the moment, that the other person is either a hated enemy or a valuable and loving ally. There is no room for compromise or shades of meaning in this all-or-none world. The split which exists is a total, uncompromising one, with the inner world of introjects divided into the "all good" or "all bad." (All theorists have written, at one time or another, regarding the absence of an appropriate terminology, but for now, metaphorical language will have to do, with "good" and "bad" conveying the polar oppositions along a continuum of experienced emotions in regard to the outer world.)

No one knows for certain why some individuals split their inner worlds. It may depend on the intensity of painful experiences. Supporting this interpretation is the finding that almost all cases of severe borderline personality—the individuals who use this internal splitting most intensely—have experienced frustrating, brutalizing or at least supremely indifferent treatment from their early caretakers. Others postulate a constitutional or genetic defect: the splitting results from inherent deficiency in the synthesizing powers of the developing mind. But whichever explanation is held, one must remember that the whole object relations theory is ultimately a metaphor: none of us carries around in his or her head inner pictures of the world. Rather, the concept of inner representation or introjection provides a coherent and reasonable way of understanding human personality. We do respond *emotionally* to others and these emotions become part and parcel of what these people mean to us, in other words, our inner representation of what they're like.

It's also ultimately a hopeful theory, since the possibility for change is inherent in it. Think back for a moment to our mental picture of the "difficult" person. Imagine a helpful friend who understands the friction between us and the difficult person. He or she may tell us certain things as to why the other person is difficult and lead to a change in our attitude toward him. In this instance, "attitude" is an informal word for inner representation; in this way negative feelings may be neutralized and we may find ourselves reacting less extremely to the prospect of an encounter with the "difficult" person. Thus, we may find the difficult person less difficult since, as the result of our friend's efforts, we are now able to see that he has some positive qualities about him as well. We may come to understand that his "difficulty" may be based on the importance he places on doing the very best job he can within the organization. His theory of how this can best be done may differ from ours, hence his inclination to spar with us, to prove "difficult." Viewing the matter from this perspective, rather than responding as if to a personal attack, makes it easier to get along with the "difficult" person. Eventually, our inner representation of him may change to the extent that, although he still holds different values and goals than our own, we are able to think of him as a competitor rather than an enemy. While we may never reach the point that we will choose him for a friend or an intimate, at least our introjections of him have been altered.

The situation with long-standing or, in some cases, lifelong "bad" internal representations or introjections is, of course, more complicated and less likely to yield to educational techniques or moralistic exhortations. But the principle is the same: alter the individual's inner world toward the "good," less negatively charged representations, and conflicts in the "outer" world of interpersonal relationships will improve.

Object relations theory also explains the origin of certain disturbances of identity. Frustrating and unpleasant experiences exert, it seems, a disruptive effect on the smooth integration of those of our perceptions necessary for the development of a sense of identity. For this reason, positive and negative emotions (or affects, as they're termed by psychiatrists) are kept apart within the developing infant by a kind of *double-bookkeeping system*. Pleasurable and satisfying experiences lead into positive ("good") images of the self and object are combined with previous good self–object relations. Negative or "bad" self–object relations, in turn, which are constructed around negative emotions, such as rage and frustration, are also combined together. At first these "compartments" within the mind are maintained in part because the experiences leading up to them occurred at different times. Later, the separation depends on the disruptive effects such oppositely charged emotional experiences can exert on the developing self. At this early stage of development, conflicts between "good" and "bad" are postulated to result in a particular form of abnormal personality development.

In certain disorders of the self, "good" self- and object images wind up split off from their "bad" counterparts. Most importantly, the "good" and "bad" representations fail to merge. In the absence of integration the "good" and "bad" representations remain separated in the patient, leading, in adulthood, to fragmented and contradictory attitudes to self and object. ("Object," in this instance, refers to other people: the mother is the original "object" encountered by the infant as it begins to differentiate itself from its surroundings.) Later in adulthood, such a person tends to view the world as filled with people who are all "good" or all "bad." In a similar way, contradictory aspects of the self are walled off from each other, precluding the development of a mature self-image which can take both good and bad aspects of the personality into account in the formation of a total self. Thus, a person might harbor both a grandiose conception of himself as an important and powerful person, as well as a coexisting internal representation—totally split off from his conscious awareness—of a weak, inadequate, even defective human being.

In a similar way, other people may, for one reason or another, be considered the possessors of "good" qualities, such as warmth, love and affection—totally ignoring their inevitable shortcomings —while others are just as arbitrarily lumped into a hated, "bad" category which arouses enmity and rage. This type of fragmentation, called by psychoanalyst Erik Erikson "identity diffusion," is met in its pure form in schizophrenia. Dr. Michael Stone, associate clinical professor of psychiatry at Cornell University Medical College, has published a dialogue between a patient and her doctor which illustrates such a fragmentation of the self.

> P: Having self-hate has always been my anger—when I imagine having to control myself and not do the things I want to do. I can't do anything else. I can't enjoy anything else, and I feel incredibly angry. I can appreciate certain songs. Certain music that has notes that I may have once liked . . . might have once pleased me; but I feel completely *controlled* . . .

D: By whom? Or by what?

P: Myself . . .

D: Have you at times felt controlled by people or things *outside* you?

P: They're always *inside* me . . . but it depends on the extent I identify with whatever was controlling me . . . inside of me . . . whether I identified with the controller, or the person being controlled. And what'd happen was, I wouldn't identify with *either* of them, so that . . .

D: The "person being controlled"?

P: In other words . . . *both* of them are *me*: the person controlling and the one controlled are both me, and I didn't identify with *either* of them.

D: Like there's a third "me" in back of both.

P: A "third" me in back of both, yes . . . there's a person who's *controlling*, that I look upon as some sort of stereotype of sterility . . . there's a person who's being controlled, which I look upon as a stereotype of repulsiveness.

D: And then there's a third "real" you in back of all that . . .

P: Um-humm . . .

D: . . . and what is *she* up to?

P: Oh, she dreams, she used to think . . .

D: What sort of stuff?

P: Well, now I dream about complicated scenes with lots of action, many characters, and I always . . . [looks sad, suddenly]

D: You looked sad, I thought, as you talked of this "real" you . . .

P: She never comes out [said sotto voce, and very poignantly].

D: Never!

P: [Pause] No . . . and yet that's the way I could enjoy . . . if I could be the real "me" . . .

Along with the absence of a "real me" such a patient is frequently caught up in an "either/or" dilemma: Both self and others are either good or bad, caring or uncaring, all-powerful or worthless. Thus, shifting attitudes exist without conscious communication with each other, as if they were "split off." In place of continuity and integrity the personality is fragmented and discontinuous. These internal alternations of the self lead to feelings of unreality and emptiness which are combatted by efforts to act in ways which appear to the observer as foreign and strange; thus Dr. Stone's patient feels "straitjacketed."

P: I felt straitjacketed because I felt that a woman had to behave a certain way. She had to be dumb and docile. Either that or she had to be cruel and biting or sharp, and I always felt that if I *were* cruel and sharp . . . and the sharpness was so spread out, I mean this constant idea of a woman as sharp and cruel—was so complete that I wouldn't . . . I refused to buy costume jewelry with pins—pointed objects—because I looked upon them as a *symbol* . . .

D: Of "pointiness"?

P: Yeah.

D: Well, is the real "you"—who hardly ever makes an appearance . . .

P: For you? No! [laughs]

D: . . . witchy or docile or housewifely or what?

P: No she's just . . . *real.* She's just *real,* I don't know how to describe it: I had all the feelings a person is supposed to have . . . uhh . . . I guess I never sat in judgment . . .

D: Well, what is it that makes the coming forward of the "real" you so difficult?

P: Well, when I think about it when I'm awake, I feel that I don't have the strength to bring across the complexity of . . . I feel that I'm too completely sterile and lacking in imagination to get it across . . . I feel that it's so big, I can't get it acr—

D: What's so big?

P: Intricate! The real me. I suppose one way I could get it out would be in speaking of . . . or in dreams . . . The only thing I can say about it is during my entire life I'm constantly faced with a mirror . . .

D: A mirror?

P: Yeah: The way I think other people see me and how I behave as a result . . . it just goes back and forth, back and forth, and . . . I feel I don't have any sense of self. Except for this mirror.

The patient's fragmented self found expression in the contradictory images of being either "dumb or docile" or "cruel and biting." There is no middle path in such a world where self and others are experienced and reacted to in a contradictory either/or fashion. The closest such a person gets to experiencing contradictions is in the form of a need to express the "complexity" (this patient's word) of the "real me." The self, which is never experienced as wholly integrated, comes across in the image of a "mirror." "I feel I don't have any sense of self. Except for this mirror."

Since the individual's thoughts and feelings are "split off" from each other, poorly integrated and often contradictory, the process is known as *splitting*. It's a key to our understanding of modern self disorders.

The Cat Woman

Under the pressure of increased stress, physical abuse or parenting failure, a child may be unable to experience the negative and positive aspects of inner and outer experience. His world remains split, with different aspects of the self emotionally cut off from each other. This primitive mental mechanism may continue into adulthood. Typical of this dilemma is Samantha, the "cat woman," treated by psychoanalyst Vamik Volkan.

According to the history which Volkan obtained over many months of psychoanalytic treatments, Samantha was the oldest child in a family described as both "musically inclined" and "temperamental." The father was a remote, distant man, cold and generally unavailable to his family both physically and emotionally. The mother, despite her best efforts, was unprepared for parenthood and reared Samantha according to the dictates of a book which ordained that babies be largely left alone lest they become "overstimulated." To the mother, Samantha was a lovely doll whom she hoped would grow up to be a concert musician, a career she had fancied for herself prior to her marriage. Despite a generally positive attitude, the mother's practical and intuitive responses to her infant were rudimentary. When Samantha cried for hours on end, a doctor was called who correctly diagnosed that the child was hungry and required more frequent feedings.

During childhood, Samantha and the mother engaged in competitive struggles around music. When the child failed to display the hoped for musical talent, the mother transferred her musical ambitions to her younger daughter, thirteen years Samantha's junior.

Samantha married at seventeen and, several years later, moved to Europe with her husband, an infant daughter and two cats, Maxie, a male, and Marie-Jane, a female. In response to the stress of living away from her mother and the additional stress of settling in a country that she described as one of "the most musical countries in the world," Samantha had a nervous breakdown.

When Volkan first saw her, he recalls, "I was struck by her behavior as a 'cat person.' When she felt gentle she worked her hands like the paws of a kitten kneading its mother's belly while nursing; and she expressed her aggression in clawing gestures."

Investigation revealed that Samantha endowed her two cats with human qualities. Marie-Jane was "playful and gentle"; Maxie was endowed with "strength and power." Her presenting complaints partook of this polarity.

"When I first began seeing Samantha, she complained of having too many selves," wrote Volkan in his highly regarded book *Primitive Internalized Object Relations*. The diverse selves that Samantha described alternated unpredictably, neither remaining for a prolonged period of time. Further, they were under two "main controls"—her left side and her right side. She spoke of these "sides" as separate components of her "double personality." For Samantha, her cats represented the opposite polarities of her own inner experiences. Her "bad self" as well as the "bad" objects and people in the environment were symbolically invested in the cat Maxie. Good self and object representations were identified with the female cat, Marie-Jane. Samantha spoke of herself as divided into a male "right side" and a female "left side." This corresponded with the Maxie and Marie-Jane distinctions she made between her two cats.

Whenever Samantha felt dominated by her right side, she was harsh, aggressive and, on occasion, even physically abusive. When she felt under the influence of her female, left side, "she spoke softly with seductive and gentle behavior."

At about this time, an event occurred which underscored the importance of Samantha's cats as externalizations of the split within her personality. Due to a bit of carelessness on the part of a maid, Marie-Jane fell from a second-story window. The cat's death failed to elicit grief in Samantha; instead she "assumed

Marie-Jane's purported stillness and composure," writes Volkan. This was followed by anxiety about the "wildness" she noticed in Maxie. Now, with the good and gentle cat gone, Samantha feared the domination of the wild and untamed aspects of her personality symbolized by Maxie. "She pondered whether he should not be destroyed and felt that she would be liberated from her own aggression if the animal, who reflected it in her perception, were done away with." After persuading her husband that Maxie must be destroyed, Samantha reported feelings of being "killed" inside and suffered a severe mental breakdown.

Samantha's complaints of having many "selves" corresponded to her appreciation of the split which existed within her personality. This expressed itself both in her attitudes toward Maxie and Marie-Jane and in her interests and everyday activities. In her dreams she saw twins and free-associated to Volkan that the twin figures represented her two "sides." She kept in her room a magazine with a cover illustration of a split brain: each hemisphere separated from the other as a result of a severance of the connecting link, the corpus callosum.

"She explained her interest in it," wrote Volkan, "by saying that her own brain was so divided and that at any given time she was sustained by only one half. Since she could not tolerate ambivalence, she adhered to the perception that her 'left' and 'right' sides were not coexistent, but had separate being."

Samantha's problems were caused, according to modern object relations theory, by failure of the developing personality to synthesize the positive and negative aspects of internal and external reality. In the normal course of development, as we've mentioned, the "good" and "bad" self and object images coalesce into an integrated concept which corresponds to the inherent ambivalence of reality: "nothing is perfect." Thus, overly idealized or unreasonably hated aspects of the self and others are neutralized and incorporated into an integrated whole. Psychoanalyst Joseph Lichtenberg, author of several papers on splitting, compares the result of successful integration to the difference between an A and a B movie.

"The child is able [after successful integration] to experience a wide range of feelings towards the object (himself and others). The difference between his former experience of objects and what he is now approaching, may be likened to the difference between a B movie and an A movie: In the former, the characters are all clearly good or evil, they are one dimensional; the characters in an A movie are more complicated, they have depth, they suffer from internal conflicts, and their characters have good and bad aspects."

It's the inability to deal with the "good and bad aspects" of human personality that is at the basis of splitting. The healthy and mature personality, the integrated self, is comfortable with the ambiguities and ambivalences which are characteristic of life experiences. Not only are people a mixture of good and evil but, in many instances, we're unable to discern their motives. This tolerance for uncertainty and ambiguity requires a degree of maturity which includes a healthy acceptance of self and others. But to the individual who uses splitting, such acceptance is impossible. To him, the whole world is divided into categories of good and bad. The self, too, is neatly divided into polarities, as with Samantha's "divided self," which was symbolically externalized via her attitudes toward the cats, Maxie and Marie-Jane. This division of the self, although it can be helpful and even provide a marginal adjustment, is brought about at a great personal price.

The self is never integrated; it remains impossible to relate to other people with love and hate simultaneously. (In this instance, "hate" involves not the attitude one holds toward an avowed enemy, but rather acceptance of the imperfections and deficiencies which are inevitable in any partner with whom we are engaged in an intimate relationship.) This incapacity to tolerate anger or aggressive feelings toward a loved one is the reason why splitting interferes with the establishment of rich and satisfying human relationships. The individual who uses splitting is literally unable to appreciate his own motives.

"The ability to appraise one's own motives is the core of a reflective self-awareness," wrote Dr. Lichtenberg. "It involves a functional differentiation in the ego, with one part observing the other. We may recontrast this to splitting which is characterized by shallowness in feeling, a lack of realistic self-appraisal and an impairment in empathy and intuition."

Splitting within the personality results in the rapid appearance and disappearance of mutually contradictory attitudes toward the self. At one moment an individual may be filled with confidence, striving and omnipotent feelings that all things are possible. Within days, this may be replaced by expressions of worthlessness, ineptitude and incapacitating inferiority. To an outside observer, such rapid alterations in self-appraisal appear inexplicable. How can a person shift so mercurially from grandiosity to self-abnegation?

By means of splitting, these polarities of thought and emotion are separated from each other. The memory is intact but the accompanying emotions which fueled the earlier attitudes and behavior can no longer be experienced. They are split off, separated from each other the way the islands in an archipelago are separated from each other.

Just Like a Piece of Cake

"Compare the process of splitting to the usual symptom formations seen in the neurotic," Vamik Volkan suggested to me during
a conversation one crisp fall afternoon in Charlottesville, Virginia, where Volkan is professor of psychiatry at the University of
Virginia Medical Center. "Let's imagine, for instance, that this
tape recorder here in front of us is a beautiful, tantalizing cake
that I would like to eat. Imagine further that the cake doesn't belong to me and I have no right to eat it; perhaps you have even refused to share it with me. If I were a neurotic in such a circum-
stance, I would respond with the development of a symptom.
Maybe I'd wait until you leave the room and then I'd take a bit of
the cake. At such a moment, I might develop an anxiety attack.
Or this might mark the beginning of a hand-washing ritual. In
any case, a kind of standoff is created: since I'm a neurotic, I
would simultaneously indulge myself and yet, at the same time,
punish myself. This is the meaning of the neurotic symptom.
Wanting the cake and not having a right to it causes a conflict.
This is solved by the development of a symptom. This is a form
of compromise in which the symptom both allows the expression
of an urge and punishes it at the same time. There is no split
here. The same self is involved in eating the cake and yet simultaneously experiencing the guilt that accompanies this act of petty
larceny. In order to solve the dilemma, a symptom results.

"Now let's compare that to the way I might respond to the
same situation if I were a borderline* suffering from a disorder

---

* We'll define the borderline personality in detail at a later point. For now,
it's sufficient to conceptualize the borderline personality as suffering from a
serious split within the integrity of the self.

within myself. On one occasion when you observed me, I would act as if I were above it all, as if the cake doesn't even exist. I would act like I did not want the cake or could care less about it. But if you saw me at a later point, you'd find me acting like an animal, literally devouring the cake. In this instance, there is no repression, no symptom formation. Conflict has disappeared by means of splitting. In this hypothetical example, I've solved my problem by fractionating myself into many components, each cut off from the other. Thus, if I were a borderline individual, I would see no contradiction while you would see an incredible contradiction: one minute I'm acting as if the cake is of no importance, while, at a later point, I'm devouring it without hesitation or remorse."

This process of splitting divides the psychic landscape into isolated fragments which are connected with each other only in general categories, broad brushstrokes of "black and white," "good and bad." The degree of fragmentation, the number of isolated, nonconnecting "islands," determines the seriousness of the disturbance. Freud speaks of the process via the metaphor of a shattered crystal. (It's uncanny how frequently the search through the labyrinthine literature on the mind leads on back to Freud. It's as if this typical Victorian Viennese possessed some kind of time capsule capable of projecting him into the fray of psychiatric controversies one hundred years in the future!)

"If we throw a crystal to the floor it breaks; but not into haphazard pieces. It comes apart along its lines of cleavage into fragments whose boundaries, though they were invisible, were predetermined by the crystal's structure," wrote Freud.

In a similar way, according to object relations theory, the infant-child who hasn't reached the point of integrating his perceptions remains like a faulty crystal with cleavage lines along which the personality may shatter when "thrown down" by the conflicts and stresses of life. In this case, however, not to push the metaphor too far, imagine the shattering to be a reversible process: stress causes temporary splitting along predetermined fracture lines. Later, a reconstitution takes place and the original situation is restored: lines of cleavage remain which are predetermined by the crystal's faulty structure.

The faulty structure of the crystal corresponds, in Freud's analogy, to the structural abnormalities of the psyche. Since early experiences have left the developing mind unable to synthesize contradictory or ambivalent aspects of reality, the adult individual is left in perpetual risk of "fragmenting" under stress, particularly the stress of close interpersonal relationships. To the individual with a self discoverer, the process of separation and individuation—establishing and maintaining a separate identity and sense of self—is fraught with complications. As we will examine more in detail later, the conflict often is solved either by merging with the other person, allowing oneself to be swallowed up, as it were, into the other's personality, or, at the opposite extreme, retreating into a "splendid isolation" of narcissism and grandiosity, where other people are unnecessary and dispensable. Once again, we return to the important insight that a firm grasp on the self must preclude any attempts at successfully interacting with others toward the establishment of intimacy. To the borderline, intimacy is threatening. As with Sonya, whom we met earlier, individuals with a disturbance in the sense of self are thrown into a panic whenever they feel themselves attracted to someone else. They become totally engrossed, captivated by their own emotions. Eventually the process is so painful that they feel they must break off the relationship or languish in exquisitely painful memories.

Marcel Proust captured the emotions of such a person in The Sweet Cheat Gone, the sixth volume of Remembrance of Things Past. "We suppose that we know exactly what things are and what people think, for the simple reason that we do not care about them. But as soon as we feel the desire to know, which the jealous man feels, then it becomes a dizzy kaleidoscope in which we can no longer make out anything."

The relationship of these feelings toward earlier experiences is rarely spontaneously voiced except by psychotics or artists of rare sensibility and insight. Here is Proust again on the connection between his grief at the departure of Albertine (the "sweet cheat" referred to in the title of the book) and his childhood experiences with his mother.

"Who would have told me at Combray, when I lay waiting for my mother's good-night with so heavy a heart, that those anxieties would be healed, and would then break out again one day, not for my mother, but for a girl who would at first be no more, against the horizon of the sea, than a flower upon which my eyes would daily be invited to gaze, but a flower that could think, and in whose mind I should be so childishly anxious to occupy a prominent place."

In response to the conflicts and anguish which intimacy brings in its wake, the borderline splits his perception of the other persons along with his own inner perceptions of himself. After Albertine's departure, the narrator—Proust himself, camouflaging autobiography by a first-person fictional account—writes:

"The memory of Albertine had become so fragmentary in me that it no longer caused me any sorrow and was no more now than a transition to fresh desires, like a chord which announces a change of key." Proust's response to Albertine's departure involves "fragmenting," not only of the memory of Albertine, but of himself as well: ". . . at every moment there was one more of those innumerable and humble 'selves' that compose our personality which was still unaware of Albertine's departure and must be informed of it; I was obliged—and this was more cruel than if they had been strangers and had not borrowed my sensibility to pain— to describe to all these 'selves' who did not yet know of it, the calamity that had just occurred."

Often, the process of splitting can be inferred from the responses certain people invoke in others. We're all familiar with the tendency for certain individuals to enjoy approval among one circle of acquaintances while, within another group, they're despised and spurned. Consider, as a typical example, an invalid whose disability understandably arouses sympathy from those familiar with the limitations imposed by the illness. But others, equally familiar with the invalid, often react with anger and frustration at what they, with equal validity, encounter as attempts to manipulate them into positions of subservience. Among the latter group, the invalid is a tyrant who employs his crutches to tyrannize the people around him. Typically, the invalid provokes such splitting of friends and associates into "warring camps" via the development of contradictory "selves." This is not a conscious process of "now I'll switch from Dr. Jekyll to Mr. Hyde." Rather the invalid is experiencing the divergent aspects of himself as isolated and cut off from each other. There is no sense of inner contradiction between, on the one hand, the impaired individual's legitimate expectations of care and consideration from others and, on the other, the whiningly complaining or cynically hostile verbal attacks he launches at some of the people around him. Lacking a firmly integrated sense of identity, the invalid experiences himself and others in absolute terms. There is his "crippled, helpless, dependent self" which he experiences and projects to those "good" people in the environment: those whom he experiences as caring and compassionate. At another point, the angry, hostile, devalued self enters awareness and reacts with rage and frustration at the "bad" persons who couldn't care less about his illness. The central point is not that the invalid's reactions are sometimes hostile (he may be quite correct that many people around him are uncaring) but rather that, as a result of his erratic behavior, large numbers of ordinarily reasonable people can't seem to come to any agreement about the invalid's essential character: those who encounter his "good" self respond compassionately; those who get caught up in the brambles of his "bad" self can only experience resentment.

At the basis of these fluctuations in behavior lies a shifting and varying sense of identity. A strongly enhanced sense of self may be replaced momentarily by a sense of annihilation, a kind of drifting away of one's sense of self like a mist passing over an early-morning landscape. In response to this diminishment of the self, the individual may react with panic, fear or, in the instance of the invalid, a carping irascibility. But in these instances, the experiences are typically described as extremely frightening and disturbing, responses which suggest that the process is deeply rooted in early infantile experiences when the self is first distinguished from the other people and things in the environment.

Object relations theory supports such an interpretation and suggests that a fragile sense of self may be the result of the coexistence of multiple, mutually contradictory self and object "representations" or "images." As each "image" replaces the other, varied and often contradictory behavior and attitudes may result. For instance, an individual may see no discrepancy in behaving, within a short time period, as if he were a powerful, grand or important person and as helpless and inadequate. Further, such individuals, perhaps on the basis of traumatic parental experiences, seem to possess an abundance of "bad" images over "good" ones. Other people are seen as primarily threatening and hostile and the world as a dangerous place which must be resisted and guarded against at all costs. Since the majority of images, or introjections, as they are termed by psychiatrists, are negative and menacing, such individuals lack internalized standards by which their own behavior can be evaluated. Other people must tell them what is good and bad. Thus, they become overly dependent, even addicted to the approval of others.

Along with "good" internal images—mostly derived from positive experiences with parents—the individual destined for a disturbance of the self possesses an abundance of threatening, hostile images which are never successfully united with the pleasurable ones. The personality is overwhelmed with negative images to which it reacts with anger and hostility. Since these contradicting "good" and "bad" images of others have never been successfully joined, they exist in their "split" state. Thus Kernberg's patient, described earlier, could alternate without feeling any sense of contradiction between obsequious requests for help and rageful attacks. Further, such an individual alternates between his conflicting states without awareness of the sense of contradiction and confusion his words and actions instill in other people.

Of greatest interest for our understanding of disorders of the self, however, is the peculiarly intense self-interest exhibited by such individuals. They are totally involved with themselves and thus are commonly referred to as narcissists, after the Greek youth Narcissus.

IV

The Narcissist

KING: I see myself. Behind everything, I exist.
Nothing but me everywhere. Am I in every
mirror or am I the mirror of everything?

JULIETTE: He loves himself too much.

DOCTOR: A well-known disease of the psyche:
Narcissism.

Eugene Ionesco, *Exit the King*

Dr. Freud and the Narcissistic Cat

Originally, the term narcissism referred to a form of sexual perversion described by Freud as "the attitude of a person who treats his own body in the same way in which the body of a sexual object is ordinarily treated—who looks at it, that is to say, strokes it and fondles it till he obtains complete satisfaction through these activities."

Several years later, the term was expanded to include behavior not specifically sexual. For instance, self-admiration, vanity and self-preoccupation could also be considered a transformation of narcissism. The psychoanalyst Otto Rank referred to a female patient who "felt that men are so bad and so incapable of love, so lacking in ability to comprehend the beauty and worth of a woman, that she might better return to her former narcissistic state and, independent of man, love her own person." Rank considered narcissism to be present to some degree in everyone and his references to it as a "state" set the stage for the next major redefinition published by Freud in 1914.

"On Narcissism" describes the types of narcissistic love. A person may love according to the narcissistic type: "What he is, was, or would like to be." In each instance, the narcissist's choice is determined not by the unique qualities of the beloved, but rather on the basis of an identification with some aspect of the narcissist's own self. Thus narcissism can refer to a type of interpersonal relationship, an "object relationship," to use the formal terminology of early psychoanalysts.

Freud's thinking on the matter of narcissism resulted in a division of the term into primary and secondary forms. Primary narcissism referred to the earliest days of the infant's life, particularly to the infant's isolation and self-involvement, which is broken only by the first awareness of the mother's presence. Later—following attachment to the mother and, at a later point, to other people and things in the environment—the child can again withdraw his energies, his "libido," into an earlier state of self-absorption: *secondary narcissism*.

At the basis of this division of narcissism into its primary and secondary forms was the belief that a person's emotional life could best be understood in terms familiar to nineteenth-century physics. Thus, there was only a finite amount of "psychic" energy which could either be directed toward the establishment of relationships with others (object relations) or reinvested in the self as narcissism. Since this emerging emphasis on "object relations" is a preoccupation of psychological theorists which continues up to the present day, it might be advisable, at this point, to take a short detour in order to explain it further.

A person's relationship with others may depend on accurate perceptions of the differences existing among people of different backgrounds and persuasions. The ability to perceive and react to others on the basis of the unique features of their personalities is required in order to achieve what psychoanalysts refer to as "true object relationships." In contrast, a narcissistic relationship largely ignores the other person's needs, desires or reactions and concentrates, instead, on self-centered concerns. In each instance, a kind of psychic balance can be imagined in which, on one end of the scale, is placed the investment of psychic energy in others, while, opposing it on the opposite side of the scale, are the psychic investments in the self. In the narcissistic relationship, the scale is overbalanced in the direction of egoism. Freud's conversational description of a "narcissistic cat" recalled by the novelist and poetess, Lou Andreas-Salomé, captures the essence of the narcissistic relationship: one person existing merely for another's gratification:

"Most personal of all perhaps was his charming account of the 'narcissistic cat.' While Freud maintained his office on the ground floor, the cat had climbed in through the open window. He did not care much for cats or dogs or animals generally, and in the beginning the cat aroused mixed feelings in him, especially when it climbed down from the sofa on which it had made itself comfortable and began to inspect in passing the antique objects which Freud had placed for the time being on the floor. He was afraid that by chasing it away he might cause it to move recklessly in the midst of these precious treasures of his. But when the cat proceeded to make known its archaeological satisfaction by purring and with its lithe grace did not cause the slightest damage, Freud's heart melted and he ordered milk for it. From then on the cat claimed its rights daily to take a place on the sofa, inspect the antiques and get its bowl of milk. However, despite Freud's increasing affection and admiration, the cat paid him not a bit of attention and coldly turned its green eyes with their slanting pupils toward him as toward any other object. When for an instant he wanted more of the cat than its egoistic-narcissistic purring, he had to put his foot down from his comfortable chaise and court its attention with the ingenious enticement of his shoe toe. Finally, after this unequal relationship had lasted a long time without change, one day he found the cat feverish and gasping on the sofa. And although it was most painstakingly treated with hot fomentations and other remedies, it succumbed to pneumonia, leaving naught of itself behind but a symbolic picture of all the peaceful and playful charm of true egoism."

Classically, narcissism is considered the opposite of what psychoanalysts call "object love." Only in this instance, "object" doesn't mean what we usually mean when we refer to an object (a book, a table and so on); in this sense, it is anything other than the self. Thus, the object can be another person, even our memory of another person who has died or otherwise passed out of our life, at least in the "here-and-now" sense. Deep and abiding relationships; ideals; commitments to persons and institutions—all are "objects" in the sense that they exist outside the self but can be united with the self via relationships. To classical thinkers, narcissism (self-love) existed in an inverse relationship to object love (love for other persons and things). One psychoanalyst, describing the classical position, compares narcissism and object love with the image of fluid levels in a U-shaped tube: as the level rises in one side it sinks in the other. Thus, to the classicist, narcissism is a liability which detracts from the quality and intensity of relationships with others.

Traditional religious and ethical beliefs also inveigh against our concern and involvement with the self. A detachment from personal interests; an emphasis on spiritual rather than materialistic values; the stress on a communality of interests based on participation in an organized religion—all implicitly decry narcissism as an inferior, even detestable human propensity which must be suppressed or otherwise overcome. Nor is such an attitude a distinctly modern development. The myth of Narcissus, for instance, illustrates the destructive effect of self-absorption: Narcissus pines away while gazing at his own image reflected back to him from a pool deep in the forest. But despite the popularity of this version of the Narcissus myth, there exist other, less well known versions which also convey important attitudes toward narcissism.

Three Retellings of an Ancient Greek Myth

The early Greek geographer and historian Pausanias considered it "utter stupidity to imagine that a man old enough to fall in love was incapable of distinguishing a man from his own reflection." Pausanias reported in his first century A.D. *Description of Greece* that Narcissus had a twin sister who dressed exactly like him. The two of them lived in the forest and hunted together, eventually falling in love. When the sister died, according to the Pausanias version of the legend, Narcissus returned to the pool, fully aware that the face gazing up at him was his own but, in spite of the knowledge, "finding some relief for his love imagining that he saw not his own reflection, but the likeness of his sister."

The difference between the two legends is, of course, whether or not Narcissus recognized the reflection in the pool as his own or gazed upon it to evoke memories of his dead sister. Thus, even in mythology, which precedes by hundreds of years the first mention of narcissism, there is the suggestion that narcissistic attachments can be formed with another person: the narcissist can "love" others on the basis of what he "is, was, or would like to be."

Also basic to the myth is the theme of destruction. Narcissus is basically self-destructive, pining away because of neglect. In the classical version, he is absorbed with a reflection that he does not recognize as his own, thus falling in love with an unobtainable and unresponsive person whose beauty is completely engrossing and mesmerizing. If we accept Pausanias' version, Narcissus dies because of his total identification with his sister, a form of mourning: Narcissus, in order to escape from the intense mourning caused by the death of his sister, continues to gaze at his own image in the water. The intensity of his absorption is so overpowering that he eventually dies.

Other classical writers have emphasized even more clearly the destructive aspects of the Narcissus myth. Narcissus is said to have attracted many suitors, both male and female. But he rejected them all. After one such rejection, according to one version of the story, "one of these scorned youths, lifting up his hands to heaven prayed: 'so may he himself love and not gain the thing he loves.' "

In an earlier version of the myth, Narcissus reacted with more than simple rejection. He encouraged his spurned lover, Amenias, to commit suicide. When Amenias hurls himself on a sword in front of Narcissus' doorstep, after pleading with the gods to avenge him, Narcissus commits suicide himself after being tormented by "love of himself and by repentance." In yet another variation of the myth, Narcissus is murdered by a rejected suitor.

From the study of these alternative versions, it's possible to consider the Narcissus myth as involving an increasing internalization. Starting with the simplest version of the story (Narcissus is murdered by a rejected suitor) we progress to Narcissus killing himself because of a mixture of grief and "self-love." Still further along the continuum of internalization, Narcissus inwardly identifies with his sister and dies because of his inability to surrender his love for her in order to seek new love relationships. Finally, in the most subtle version of all, the classic rendering by Ovid, Narcissus dies because he becomes so absorbed with the reflected image in the pool that he cannot recognize it as himself. Narcissus' death provides a curious fulfillment of the prophecy made at his birth by the seer Tiresias. When asked by Narcissus' mother, Liriope, whether Narcissus would live to an old age, Tiresias replied, "If he ne'er know himself."

Throughout all the versions of the Narcissus myth, there's an emphasis on the destructive effects of self-love. While Narcissus' life can be looked at from the vantage point of a mythologized version of love gone awry, it can also be considered as a warning of the potential destructiveness of narcissism. The failure to establish a love relationship (Narcissus' rejection of Amenias); the establishment of a relationship which is based on loving oneself as seen in another (Narcissus' love for his sister); or finally, the purest form of narcissism in which a person directly and undisguisedly loves only his own self—each of these variations of narcissism are not only ultimately destructive but incompatible with a mature love relationship. This theme of the inadequacy of narcissism, after almost two thousand years of general acceptance, has recently come under reexamination. Is narcissism necessarily all bad?

Enter Dr. Kohut

In the late 1960s, several psychoanalysts, principally Heinz Kohut, a professorial lecturer in psychiatry at the University of Chicago, began speculating in print that narcissism may not be the liability everyone was considering it, but, rather, a completely independent line of psychological development. Furthermore, Kohut suggested that the condemnation of narcissism in the twentieth century had a deceptively disquieting resemblance to the Victorian attitude toward sexuality. At a lecture given at the New York Psychoanalytic Society on November 30, 1971, Kohut stated: "During quiescent historical periods, the attitudes in certain layers of society towards narcissism resembles Victorian hypocrisy towards sex. . . . I think that the overcoming of hypocritical attitudes towards narcissism is as much required today as was the overcoming of sexual hypocrisy a hundred years ago."

Kohut went on to detail the ways that narcissism provides the underpinning of so much of our everyday behavior. "We would not deny our ambitions, our wish to dominate, our wish to shine, and our yearning to merge into omnipotent figures, but should, instead, learn to acknowledge the legitimacy of these narcissistic forces."

Over the past decade, Kohut developed our understanding of narcissism through his study of what he referred to as "disorders of the self."

From clinical work with narcissistic character disorders, Kohut formulated a theory which is refreshingly at variance with the traditional analytic emphasis on primal drives, repression, the unconscious and so on—the "drive and defense" psychology so firmly entrenched in scientific circles as well as in the popular imagination.

Kohut takes as his starting point what he calls the *self object*. A child from its earliest moments experiences certain people in the environment as part of himself. The self and parent, for instance, are so intimately intertwined in the child's mind that self and object are one, merged into a *self object*. Further, the child's experiences at this early stage determine to a large extent whether the child's self will emerge, in Kohut's words, "as a firm and healthy structure or as a more or less seriously damaged one."

According to Kohut's theory, there are two kinds of self objects. The first, which he calls the *mirroring self object*, corresponds roughly to our everyday picture of the proud parent who, through encouragement and praise, builds up his child's sense of control, vigor and accomplishment. The second, the *idealized parent imago*, is a fancy term for a stable, calm and reassuring presence provided by the parent to the child. From this parental "imago" develops the child's sense of the world as a reasonably secure and predictable place. In addition, it is theorized that the child's future ideals and goals are at least partially shaped to the extent that the parents provide an image of "calmness, infallibility, and omnipotence." The emotional tone and attitude toward the child are more important at this point than any philosophy of child rearing. "It's not so much what the parents do that will influence the character of the child's self, but what the parents are," Kohut wrote.

Kohut emphasized the emotional state of the parents while downplaying the traditional analytic preoccupation with traumatic experiences or "primal scenes." For this reason, some critics consider Kohut's approach "unanalytic." But such criticisms overlook the vigorous emphasis Kohut placed on early parent-child *experiences* as a determinant of the quality of the child's emerging self. If anything, Kohut is even more "Freudian" than many of his critics with his insistence on the importance of early parent-child interaction in the formation of the child's future sense of self. But, rather than emphasizing events (who slept where? who saw what?), Kohut's emphasis is on the emotional tone conveyed by the parents.

"Their self confidence as they carried us when we were babies, their security when they allowed us to merge our anxious selves with their tranquility via their calm voices or via our closeness with their relaxed bodies as they held us, will be retained by us as the nucleus of the strength of our leading ideals and of the calmness we experience as we live our lives under the guidance of our inner goals."

Kohut compared the child's identification with the parent to the ingestion of protein in the child's diet. The ingested protein is split up into its constituent amino acids, which are then rearranged and incorporated into the tissues of the developing organism. No one would claim that the protein within the child is an exact replica of the protein in the infant formula. Rather, the constituents of the protein are rearranged into new patterns which are only vaguely similar to the original. In a similar way, the self-object relationships provide the model for the child's later emotional development. But, as every parent knows, a child is not just a miniature copy of its mother or father.

Normally—or perhaps one should say optimally—the interaction between the parent and child proceeds in directions which foster the child's independent psychological growth, in essence, the emergence of the self which Kohut defined as "an independent center of initiative, an independent recipient of impressions."

If all proceeds according to schedule, the child at about age two is beginning to achieve a firm sense of his own psychological continuity in both space and time. He is the same person today as yesterday; he can project himself into the future, at least the immediate future of wants and needs. And just as the infant is preadapted for certain specific requirements—the need for food, warmth, oxygen and so on—so too, psychological development requires a specific psychological environment: the presence of responsive self objects, principally the parents.

The parents' response to the child's emerging self exerts a critical influence on its subsequent development. If parents are securely established as independent selves, then they can engage with the child in what Kohut referred to as "mirroring." The growing self of the child requires a mature, cohesive, parental self that is in tune with the changing needs of the child. In essence, if the parents have a firmly grounded sense of self, then they can assist the child in its progress from early consciousness to the achievement of a secure self.

"If the parents are at peace with their own needs to shine and to succeed in so far as these needs can be realistically gratified, if, in other words, the parents' self confidence is secure, then the proud exhibitionism of the budding self of their child will be responded to acceptingly."

In those instances where the parents possess a fragile or insecurely established self, the self-object experience of the child is distorted. The parent who ignores the child, habitually refuses praise or encouragement of the child's early accomplishments, deflects attention from the child as a means of bolstering the parent's own flagging self-esteem—such a parent frustrates the child's achievement of a healthy self. "Faulty interaction between the child and his self object result in a damaged self—either a diffusely damaged self or a self that is seriously damaged in one or the other of its constituents," wrote Kohut.

The emphasis on the influence of childhood experience on adult behavior and emotional health is, of course, traditionally of psychoanalytic interest. At an optimal time—somewhere between six months and two years, the exact period varying according to which authority you consult—the child's emerging sense of self will be established. It can be coherent, vigorous and experienced as a unity or, in the case of a pathogenic self-object experience, "the adult self may exist in states of varying degrees of coherence from cohesion to fragmentation; in states of varying degrees of vitality, from vigor to enfeeblement; in states of varying degrees of functional harmony from order to chaos." Difficulties in any of these areas form the basis for Kohut's conception of "self psychology."

"Significant failure to achieve cohesion, vigor or harmony or a significant loss of these qualities after they had been tentatively established may be said to constitute a state of *self disorder*."

In adults, the lack of a sense of self often emerges as a chronic, aching insecurity which typically lies hidden behind a façade of invulnerability. Today, such women and men constitute a significant portion of a psychiatrist's practice. Although they often initially present with neurotic complaints, phobias, anxiety attacks and so on, the difficulties eventually turn out to involve a self disorder. They exhibit specific vulnerabilities with unusual sensitivity to failures, disappointments and rejections (even being passed over at a department store counter can trigger paroxysms of self-doubt and irresolution). Rather than simple inferiority feelings, however, those suffering from a self disorder exhibit several recognizable and frequently encountered types.

Based on Kohut's theory of early infant and childhood development, several problem areas emerge, each capable of compromising and distorting the child's developing self. In those instances where the parents, either through absence or, more commonly, through emotional unavailability, fail to provide a "mirror" in which the child's emerging self can be sympathetically responded to, the self develops, in adult years, into an *understimulated self*: the personality lacks vitality and vigor, experiences itself as boring and inadequate.

Burdened with crushing feelings of inertia and deadness, the understimulated self frantically reaches out to the world in order to grasp the excitement and vitality which it inwardly lacks. Forms of self-stimulation replace natural and spontaneous excitements. Frantic efforts are employed to critically stir up a sense of aliveness and vitality. Addictions, sexual promiscuity and perversions, alcohol and drug-induced "highs," dangerous sports and recreational activities (hang gliding, motorcycle racing, etc.)—all are, in the last analysis, attempts to artificially repair the chronic state of understimulation, to make up for the failure of the earlier self-object relationship to provide a source of sympathetic responsiveness. In the social sphere this lack may be expressed by a flight into hypersociability: superficial contacts with large numbers of people, friends compulsively collected as sources of social or sexual stimulation. But despite large numbers of "contacts" the understimulated self remains alone and misunderstood. In the midst of various activities, the understimulated self experiences what Kohut termed "empty depression."

"Individuals whose nascent selves have been insufficiently responded to will use any available stimulus to create a pseudo excitement in order to ward off the painful feelings of deadness that tends to overtake them."

At the opposite pole are those suffering from self disorders brought on by overstimulation. Here, the early self-object experiences included excessive and heightened encouragement for the child's emerging capacities, but without those realistic limitations which parents normally impose on their child's tendency toward grandiosity and self-display. Intense and unrealistic ambitions—totally unrealizable in most instances—restrict the development in the child of a healthy self. Instead, healthy confidence is replaced by feelings of anxiety and fright in the face of challenges involving self-expression.

Along with restraints on these early tendencies toward grandiosity, the child must be provided with an opportunity to identify with what Kohut refers to as "an image of calmness, infallibility and omnipotence." In most cases, this image is the parents', the usual self object from which the child's *self* emerges. When the parents' soothing presence is absent, the self winds up overburdened, lacking the capacity for managing on its own the inevitable anxieties of everyday life. Since the earliest emotional experiences were unshared, the self is later equally unable to share emotional discomforts with other people. Painful emotions are thus experienced in isolation and the world is perceived as a dangerous and threatening place in which other people can be of little assistance in terms of emotional coping. In essence, the self is overwhelmed and overburdened.

As a result of distorted experiences in the early self-object relations, the developing self may end up extremely susceptible to fragmentation in the face of self-esteem threatening situations. While this can happen, to a minor degree, to just about everyone, the fragmented self is particularly susceptible to becoming "unglued." This may take the form of undue preoccupation with the body, or some aspect of health. An ensuing hypochondria may result with the conviction of an incurable illness or, perhaps, that something is terribly wrong with some body part. In these instances, the normally integrated feelings of the body as a totality are fragmented. The self is experienced as a series of body parts, each of which is somehow defective. In other instances, the fragmentation is more psychological, leaving the person with a feeling of mental vertigo: a loss of the sense of continuity in space and time, an absence of the personal cohesiveness that forms the underpinnings of identity. In most instances, these feelings of fragmentation are triggered by real or imagined rebuffs—often trivial in degree by most people's standard—but nonetheless experienced by the person given to fragmentation as a potent threat to self-esteem.

Common to each of these disturbances of the self is a narcissistic wound, a weakness in the area of self-esteem. For this reason, Kohut's theories of the self are based on a theory of narcissism. But narcissistic disorders are only one of the many disorders of the self. Nevertheless, the study of narcissistic disorders has provided the foundation for self psychology. More importantly, the application of new knowledge, drawn from object relations theory on the one hand, and Heinz Kohut's concept of early mirroring and the importance of the parental imago on the other, allows for the recognition and prediction of certain behavioral patterns.

All of us are familiar with persons who exhibit an insatiable need for other people's approval and praise. In fact, everything they do is motivated by the intense desire to attract attention. Often given to dramatic gesture, they must be the main topic of all discussion or they lapse into a petulant despondency. Above all, they seek approval and acceptance. Kohut labels such individuals *mirror-hungry personalities*, a reference to the failures such people experienced early in life when the parental self objects failed to respond and reinforce ("mirror") the earliest expression of their emerging self. Naturally, relationships in which one member of a pair requires constant emotional stroking are eventually doomed to dissolution. But the mirror-hungry personality suffers only a momentary setback before quickly striking up yet another relationship in which he or she can, at least for a while, occupy the center of attention.

An even more common disorder of the self is exhibited by what

Kohut terms the *ideal-hungry personality*. Frustrated in their early attempts to identify with an idealized parent, such people are forever in search of perfection in those around them. They seek to associate themselves with persons of wealth, beauty or power. When in the presence of these charismatic individuals, the ideal-hungry personality feels complete and whole, thriving in the reflected glory of the hero or heroine. The ideal-hungry personality requires association with an admired and glorified individual in order to feel "real" and experiences an inner void when left to his own devices, cut off from some association, however trivial, with persons he can idealize. Every entertainer and sports figure and most politicians are plagued by sycophantic hangers-on who derive their sense of reality from their association with the "famous." Not all are ideal-hungry personalities, of course, but the tendency for many to drift from one celebrity to another (rock groupies are a conspicuous example) suggests that the relationship to a celebrity, any celebrity, is more important than a sustained relationship with any specific one.

If the process of identification progresses far enough, ideal-hungry personalities merge into the much sicker *merger-hungry personalities*. Here, the self structure is so weak that other people are required to provide what little sense of self the mirror-hungry personality possesses. So intimate is the relationship here that the merger-hungry personality cannot separate his own desires, impulses and thoughts from those of the individuals he so strongly identifies with. In these relationships, the admired individual must be constantly present or the weakened self is threatened with complete dissolution.

In instances where the sense of self is better developed but still fragile, an *alter-ego-hungry personality* may result. Here, the weakened self seeks association with a person who shares common opinions and values and, in some instances, even physical appearances. The emphasis here is on a near-perfect correspondence, a kind of twinship. But these relationships, too, are usually doomed to failure. No two personalities can ever exactly correspond: differences arise; personalities which seemed at first exactly parallel turn out, later, to differ in many important areas. "The alter-ego-hungry discovers that the other is not himself and, as a consequence of this discovery, begins to feel estranged from him," says Kohut.

The final disturbances of the self described by Kohut comprise the *contact-shunning personalities*. Driven by an intense need for other people's approval, these individuals are the hermits, the loners who seem totally free of any dependence on others. But their assumed independence is only a sham. In reality, their need for approval and acceptance is so intense that it can never be satisfied. And, in response to this failure, they totally withdraw. Dostoyevsky's underground man is a literary example of the contact-shunning personality who conceals beneath the façade of self-sufficiency and arrogance a gaping wound of inadequacy. Unable to extract the praise and goodwill of those around him, Dostoyevsky's hero dwells in an underground cellar in St. Petersburg. At the basis of his reclusiveness is an unsatisfied grandiosity which can never be realistically achieved in the "real world."

Since he cannot be appreciated as he wishes, he withdraws and fantasizes himself "riding a white horse and crowned with laurel. I couldn't even conceive of playing a secondary part, and that is why in actuality I quite contentedly filled the last of all. Either a hero, or dirt, there was nothing in between."

By thinking of himself as a "hero," the underground man is able to justify his isolated and miserable existence. Things are not as they seem, he tells us. "In the mire I comforted myself with the idea that the rest of the time I was a hero, it was the hero who was wallowing in the dirt: for an ordinary man, I felt, it is shameful to roll in filth, but a hero is above really becoming filthy, and so I can let myself experience the dirt."

Kohut's therapy is aimed at providing his patients with the empathic mirroring which, he has found, was missing in their childhood and resulted in one or more of the above-described distortions of the self. To this extent, Kohut's approach to his patients is a supportive and gentle one, perfectly attuned to his own appearance and demeanor.

A small trim man with white hair and a soft Viennese accent, Kohut spoke with great feeling during our interview. Despite a chronic illness which would kill him within a year of our talk, he displayed a vigorous determination that I understand his point that many of his patients were "deprived" of the normally expected mirroring responses. He envisioned the analyst's task as helping the patient gain a sense of self-worth through the re-creation in the treatment situation of an empathic, approving relationship in which the patient is effectively mirrored in the analyst's response. To this extent, Kohut's approach is at variance with the traditional psychoanalytic emphasis on the twin forces of sex and aggression.

In Kohut's formulation, one hears little about aggression. Instead, the concentration is on failures of nurturing or caring in the early child-parent relationship. To Kohut, the Oedipal conflict—the central dynamic around which classical psychoanalysts have constructed their theories—is only a breakdown product: if the self is fragmented then it cannot handle the pressures of sex or aggression, and the resulting symptoms (the classical work and sex problems resulting from these Oedipal failures) are considered an inadequate response brought about by a failure in the unity and coherence of the self. To this extent—and this is a primary criticism of Kohut's contributions—all emotional disorders can be reformulated as self disorders.

Pathologic Narcissism

Among the critics of Kohut's approach to narcissistic personalities is Dr. Otto Kernberg. An associate of the New York Psychoanalytic Institute and fifteen years Kohut's junior, Kernberg is the author of *Borderline Conditions and Pathological Narcissism* and until Kohut's death shared a reputation as the most knowledgeable people in the world on the subject of narcissism.

While Kohut's approach emphasized the empathic failures that have resulted in the narcissistic patient's lack of self-esteem and integration, Kernberg takes a more traditional analytic approach which retains the importance of aggression as a key element of human personality. Kernberg's experience with narcissistic personalities has resulted in a formulation in which the negative emotions (anger, envy, rage and depreciation) play a prominent part in the patient's problems. Rather than just providing the mirroring which the patient lacked earlier in life, the analyst's activities, according to Kernberg, must involve working with the patient's sense of deprivation along with the resulting anger and frustration such deprivation has created within him. Thus the treatment situation can often be a stormy one, creating extraordinary tensions and pressures within the analyst. "I wouldn't advise anyone treating more than one or two narcissistic patients at one time," Kernberg says. "The pressures and tensions are just too great."

Kernberg has divided narcissism into the more common, everyday narcissism we all express to one degree or another and a more disturbed version he calls *pathological narcissism*.

On the subject of pathological narcissism Kernberg has written: "These patients present excessive self-absorption hand in hand with a superficially smooth and effective social adaption, but with serious distortions in their internal relations with other people. They present various combinations of intense ambitiousness, grandiose fantasies, feelings of inferiority, and overdependence on external admiration and acclaim; they suffer from chronic feelings of boredom and emptiness, are constantly searching for gratification of strivings for brilliance, wealth, power, and beauty, and have serious deficiencies in their capacity to love and to be concerned about others. Other predominant characteristics include a lack of capacity for empathetic understanding of others, chronic uncertainty and dissatisfaction with their life, conscious or unconscious exploitiveness and ruthlessness towards others and, particularly, the presence of chronic, intense envy and defenses against such envy."

In the spring of 1980 I met with Dr. Kernberg in his office at the Westchester Division of the New York Hospital–Cornell Medical Center. A small, precise man who speaks with a Viennese accent, Kernberg displays an erudition combined with a formal charm that reminded me of my fantasy of Hercule Poirot minus the glistening mustache.

"When we talk about narcissism we are talking about disorders of the self," Kernberg commented early in our discussion. "But we are also talking about the world of object relations; you can't separate the self from its relationships."

To make this a bit clearer, Kernberg compared the "infantile" kinds of relationships to their more adult counterparts. The infant, for instance, relates in a dependent, demanding and power-oriented manner, forcing the mother to carry out the infant's grandiose demands. At the other end of the spectrum is the normal "adult self-centeredness which combines a mature, enlightened self-love condensed with a mature investment of the object in depth." Although both infant and adult narcissism are "self-centered," the self-investment of the normal adult is fashioned principally for mature goals, ideals and expectations. When the adult regresses from this state of normal narcissism into clinging, demanding relatedness, we have first the condition of infantile narcissism and finally pathological narcissism. Kernberg has found that patients with narcissistic personalities function along a broad range of social effectiveness. They may appear perfectly "normal" to the casual observer and may require an in-depth exploration in order to reveal their underlying self-centeredness, excessive need to be loved and admired, and what Kernberg describes as "curious contradictions between a very inflated concept of himself and occasional feelings of extreme inferiority." Accompanying this is an excessive need for other people's admiration, a shallow, directionless emotional life, and an incapacity to appreciate other people as separate, distinct individuals in their own rights. The outward signs of narcissism may thus extend from relatively mild to completely disabling forms of the disorder. In its worst—the condition of pathological narcissism—the personality is marked by impulsiveness and a tendency toward explosive or chronic rage.

Is narcissism more prevalent today than in times past, or are we more conscious of it now than we were before?

"This is a very difficult question to answer," Kernberg replied. "For one thing, there are no epidemiologic data that could help us. Psychiatrists have only developed the techniques for treating narcissistic personalities within the last fifteen years or so." (Kernberg's modesty evidently precluded his adding that one of the two most successful techniques for the management of the narcissistic personality was developed by himself.) "My hunch is that such patients existed before, but simply weren't recognized. It's all a matter of how a person presents his problems and that's terribly dependent on cultural expectations. The person in the past who complained of lacking a zest for life, or who expressed a general lack of interest, would today come in and say something like 'I can't find myself.' "

As Kernberg spoke, I reflected on the ubiquity of narcissism. We all engage in narcissistic behavior in our everyday relationships. In fact, if we were to completely eliminate narcissistic concerns from our lives, we would probably go crazy. Most of our everyday interactions are, in the final analysis, basically narcissistic.

For instance, consider the typical behavior we all engage in when out on a shopping trip. For the purpose of illustration, let's imagine the situation of a shopper, say a woman, who is intent on selecting an autumn wardrobe. In one store, the woman may sit viewing models who display, for her pleasure, various styles of the latest Paris fashions. In half an hour, perhaps ten or twelve models may parade by, each model attired in clothes which exert varying appeal to our shopper. Overall, the models are comparatively anonymous: each could be replaced by another with minimal disruption to our shopper's routine.

Fifteen minutes later the shopper is at another store, sorting through clothes displayed on a rack. She remembers very little, at this point, about the models in the first store. In fact, they never really existed in their own right, that is as people the shopper might wish to know. Rather, the models are objects, little more than animated mannequins who serve their purpose at one moment and then can be conveniently forgotten. The relationship was narcissistic—a means of fulfilling the shopper's needs. While these needs may remain stable (purchasing clothes which are self-enhancing), the individuals capable of fulfilling these needs (the models) may succeed each other in dizzying rapidity. If the shopper were fickle enough, hundreds of models could be pressed into service to display a whole storeful of outfits.

In yet a third store, the shopper may find herself unable to decide between two dresses. Each has its own appeal but she can afford only one. To help solve her dilemma, the shopper is likely to question the salesperson, inquiring about materials, design, fashionableness and so on. She may try on the dresses and listen attentively to the suggestions of the salesperson, retaining, of course, her own firmly entrenched opinion about what does and does not enhance her appearance. Although an animated conversation may ensue between the shopper and the salesperson, their relationship is as narcissistic as the one that existed with the models. The salesperson doesn't exist in her own right either, but only as a means of satisfying the wants of our shopper. In fact, each participant in the dialogue is very restricted to self-centered aims: the customer wants to choose the outfit that is the most enhancing to her; the salesperson wants the customer to select *something* from the available merchandise that will earn for her a commission. The relationship, although certainly cordial, is inherently self-centered: narcissistic.

In both instances, these narcissistic relationships are the most logical and sensible approaches under the circumstances. Imagine, for instance, what would happen if the shopper were required as a condition for purchasing her clothes that she somehow respond to all sorts of intimate details about the salesperson's private life. Although such a recounting might be temporarily distracting or amusing in its own right, say, by satisfying one's sense of curiosity about a total stranger, it would ultimately be tiresome to have to engage, in every human interaction, with an equal degree of intimacy and concern. To put it at its plainest, some people we care about as people while others exist in our minds as, well, only animated things.

Now at a certain point our shopper will finish her junket and return home, where her husband and children may be required to act as an audience assembled to comment on the wisdom of her selections. On the way through the door, the shopper may be besieged with details about her children's day at school, their exhilarations and despairs. The husband, too, may enthusiastically break into a recounting of the things which affected him during his day at the office. In these instances, the barrier of anonymity and self-centeredness breaks down; the relationship has become less narcissistic and self-centered. The shopper shows an entirely different "self" to her family than she did to the models or the salesperson. This alternation doesn't involve hypocrisy or splitting. Rather, certain kinds of relationships are impersonal and inherently narcissistic while others, typically a family situation, demand a shared communality.

Now, to complete our analogy, let's imagine a very different kind of shopper who arrives home to relationships which are essentially narcissistic. In this instance, the husband and children share the inner changeability of the models and salespeople. Perhaps this is a second or third husband; maybe the children are his; her own children are off somewhere living with their father. To a listener, the exchange between the woman and her family may sound impersonal, distant, overly formal—in fact, reminiscent of a shopper conferring with a salesperson. To this woman, her home is only a kind of living theater wherein the family exist as actors chosen to play a series of roles intended to enhance her own self-esteem. To the casual observer, the inherent narcissism in the relationships may be difficult to detect. It may, in fact, only be detected by inference: the woman's lack of meaningful, prolonged relationships over time, her exhibitionism, her total self-preoccupation. To her, the husband and children are on the deepest level little different from the models and salespeople she encountered earlier in the day.

The basic issue is not whether narcissism is present or absent in our relations—in some cases it's absolutely essential for our psychological survival—but rather, whether we are able to transcend our narcissistic concerns and enter into more intimate and emotionally demanding relationships with others.

"There are three considerations that I think bear on the question of the incidence of narcissistic disorders. First of all, narcissistic pathology comes into prominence at times of rapid social change: narcissistic personalities have a capacity for leadership under conditions when most people would despair at the chaos and meaninglessness," commented Kernberg.

"Secondly, narcissists are power-driven, they gravitate toward positions where they are the center of attention. Thus, we are more aware of them.

"Finally, narcissists correspond uncannily to our present cultural ideals. The drive towards mass consumption; towards external adjustment contrasted to internal life; the breakdown of traditional authority with the consequent development of chaotic group situations. All these developments tend to bring the self-sufficient, self-aggrandizing, childish, exhibitionistic, and consumer-oriented personality to the forefront. This is, in essence, your narcissistic personality."

Kernberg's study of history has convinced him that there is a relationship between cultural norms and certain types of psychopathology. Victorian Europe, for instance, with its "official morality" and sexual repression, was a natural setting for hysteria with its division, within the hysteric, between instinctual urges and the barriers which prohibited gratification of these urges.

In times of social breakdown or rapid change, more severe types of pathology arise which, according to Kernberg, are ordinarily held in check by social institutions. The social structure, under ordinary conditions, "controls" the more severe forms of psychopathology. In the event of social breakdown the sicker kinds of pathology are, in Kernberg's words, "smoked out." For this reason, we are seeing not only an apparent increase in pathological narcissism—or at least an increase in the visibility of these types of character disorders—but, in addition, new "malignant" versions of narcissism.

"One of the most distressing developments over the past several years has been the appearance of a subgroup of narcissistic personalities in which there is an infiltration of the pathologic, grandiose self with aggression. This aggression typically takes the form of a pride at being cool or callous, pride at not caring about others or not needing anybody. Within this malignant, distorted version of narcissism, you get heavily sadistic elements. The Marquis de Sade had an astonishing insight into this kind of character disorder, which he described so well in *The Hundred and Twenty Days of Sodom.*

At this point in our conversation, I began speculating about what directions narcissism and self disorders might take over the next decade. If we agree with Kernberg that personality, particularly psychopathology, must change with changing social conditions, then who, at this point, might be the forerunner of how things may be in a few years? Narcissism infiltrated by aggression and sadism . . . of course! None other than the architect of the horrors of Guyana!

"I agree with you," Kernberg replied, with a quiet smile in response to my query. "Jim Jones had this quality of grandiosity infused with ruthlessness, manipulation, psychopathy and sadism which eventually led to mass murder."

A Psychic Spider Web

Kernberg's experience with narcissistic patients began during his training analysis, a period of supervised psychoanalytic practice with a series of patients. He recalls one patient in particular:

"There was one man I treated many years ago who was a distant, ironic man whom I could never seem to reach. Most striking of all was his unavailability. Even though we met daily for over three years, it was often as if he were the only one in the room. The sessions were unbearably frustrating and boring. I had to fight against a chronic sense of being somehow unskilled. Even though he was attentive and seemed to consider my interpretations carefully, I was unable to reach him. I was treated by him as a captive audience for his self-aggrandizing fantasies. Finally, because I was moving to another city, I transferred this patient to the care of a colleague. The colleague was mildly critical of how little had been accomplished in three years of work. He felt that the case had not been touched and seemed to have definite plans on how he would proceed. Well, three years later I went back there and met my colleague, who informed me that the patient had stopped his treatments after several months. 'I couldn't reach him either,' he said.

"I thought about that case for several years, wondering as to the reason why an obsessive-compulsive personality—the diagnosis that, at the time, seemed to best fit the man's picture—responded so poorly. After that I discovered similar patients. From the study of their relationships, fantasies, as well as their reaction to me in the transference, I eventually detected a repetitive pattern. Their feelings alternated between expression that I was the greatest analyst, while they were only a shadow or appendage to me, to a complete reversal of this type of position: *they* were the important person and I was just an appendix to them, a captive audience who must sit and listen to their grandiose exhibitionistic monologue. Once I was alerted to this oscillation, I began analyzing what these patterns could be protecting the patient from. It turned out that it protected these patients against underlying feelings of rage at earlier experiences with a frustrating, manipulating, nongiving mother . . . against conflicts that were usually pre-Oedipal and were intensely infiltrated with aggression. I have inevitably found this pattern in the narcissistic patients I have treated."

Seventeen years later, Kernberg, at a party, met the man who had inspired him to develop his concept of narcissism, culminating in 1975 with the publication of *Borderline Conditions and Pathological Narcissism.*

"The change in this man was shocking; he was disheveled and deteriorated. I hardly recognized him. He spoke to me briefly about how lonely and empty his life had become. In middle age his narcissistic defenses had failed him and he was left utterly alone in both the physical and the emotional sense. I've never forgotten the sad spectacle of this man who previously, superficially, seemed to be functioning so well. Such middle-age deterioration is quite characteristic of the narcissistic personality."

In recent years, Kernberg has turned his attention to the long-term implications of pathological narcissism. Do narcissistic personalities always lead to breakdowns as dramatic and far-reaching as this patient? Or is the narcissist able to regroup his psychic forces later in life? In general, the picture which emerges is not a happy one.

The narcissist exists, according to Kernberg, "in a strangely atemporal world," where are found cycles of wants, temporary idealizations, greedy incorporation and, eventually, spoiling disappointment or devaluation. "The narcissistic person learns from experience that the 'exciting new' is one more edition of the 'disappointing old'; and he misses what is really new in any relationship because of his serious limitations in grasping the depth and uniqueness of human beings," Kernberg has written.

Gradually, as these processes continue, the narcissist discovers himself painfully alone in the face of mid- and later-life assaults on the things he most values (youth, good looks, prestige and so on). The aging narcissist's own internal world is bleak and depopulated. "Since he has never related to people as unique and independent beings, they don't really exist for him. . . . There is a gradual deterioration of the narcissistic patient's internal past. It is as if he lived in an eternal present; the passage of time and aging represent an external situation that overcomes him in a bewildering way, without the normal sensitive awareness and preparation for the changes that occur with time."

Kernberg's description of the aging narcissist reflects an unhappy, isolated individual filled with vague regrets of opportunities missed, particularly in the area of interpersonal relationships. Most distressing of all is the absence of an inner life filled with fond and happy memories of shared experiences and affections. This bleakness of the internal landscape is accompanied by the inevitable external physical and mental failings which accompany increasing age. But for the narcissist, aging brings no consolation or compensation. Neither wisdom nor respect are the narcissist's lot since he has never laid the necessary groundwork from which can come rich and rewarding experiences with children, grandchildren and long-term friends. The narcissist's reliance on manipulation makes him unable to relinquish responsibility to others. He projects his own brutal uncaring attitude onto relatives and friends, assuming that they harbor similar feelings toward him in his advancing years as he would hold toward them in a similar situation. Under normal circumstances, aging, and the ensuing dependence on others which it occasions, serves as a source of enhanced self-esteem: "They care for me, I must be important to them, therefore, I feel better about myself." With the aging narcissist, however, just the opposite situation prevails.

"Realistically needed support or dependence induces shame, a sense of failure and humiliation," according to Kernberg. Usually, we don't think of the acceptance of dependency as a stress to our sense of worth. But to the aging narcissist, dependency is equated with vulnerability: "The future prospect of having to depend is to be shamefully inferior, to be exploited and deprecated. The narcissist believes that neither gratitude nor care, but only pity or depreciation can be expected from grandchildren or the young in general."

In defense against these increasing feelings of vulnerability, the aging narcissist flees into hypochrondriacal concerns. Who isn't familiar with the aged parent or grandparent whose every word is part of a litany of physical complaints? In this way the young can be kept at bay and manipulated into the role of caretakers. Control under these circumstances remains with the aged narcissist who, by means of his hypochondria, is able to exploit those around him.

Overall, the aging narcissist's final end can be a sad one. Isolation, bitterness, loneliness and petulant rage form the nucleus of the attitude with which the narcissist greets his final years. In defense against the failings of later years, the aging narcissist, according to Kernberg, can adopt one of several "compromise formations."

First, as we've mentioned, hypochondriacal concerns and "health fads" can provide some feeling of control over failing physical performance. Thus, as the narcissist becomes less and less able to deny the inroads of aging, he may throw himself into sports or athletic rituals. Compulsive jogging, for instance, may serve as a denial mechanism of the aging process.

Secondly, again according to Kernberg's clinical experience, the aging narcissist may align himself with a religious cult as a means of making up for the perceived failures and loss of youth. This may coexist with claims of love and unity "for all humanity" along with an accompanying inability to get along with individuals in the narcissist's immediate social environment.

Third, the aging narcissist may attempt to maintain his exalted version of himself by restricting his social interchange to people he perceives as his inferior, thus maintaining, in Kernberg's words, "the function (or the reality) of the great man unknown wandering among the ordinary people."

Fourth, a deviant life-style (homosexuality, chronic alcoholism, drug addiction and so on) may be selected as "self-erasing" mechanisms that make possible marginal adjustment to an ever narrowing and frightening social horizon.

Finally, the aging narcissist may seek a bleak and unstimulating environment in which he may live out a routine and unrewarding social life. It is as if the narcissist has solved his internal disquiet via "self-effacing and anesthetizing abandonment of previous aspirations and grandiosity."

Contemporary cultural patterns and expectations tend to confirm several of these compromise formations. Advertising minimizes the effect of aging on the personality. In many ads, older people, if they are depicted at all, appear different from their younger counterparts by only a few gray hairs. The elderly are encouraged, under the guise of "keeping fit," to engage in arduous athletic endurance contests. Marathons for senior citizens are one example of this phenomenon. Everywhere, the aging narcissist is confronted with cultural rationalizations for his inability to accept the inevitable decline of physical performance which accompanies advancing age. The message that comes across on TV is that aging, *as aging*, is unwanted and unacceptable. Therefore, what is more logical than a "flight into youth," a last-ditch effort by means of dress and cosmetology to recapture one's lost past? But eventually the battle is lost. Youth cannot be recaptured. The inroads of aging can be hidden only partially and for limited periods of time. At some point, the aging narcissist is faced with the reality of his own mortality and death. Thanks to his deeply pathological narcissism, he is uniquely and tragically unprepared for this internal confrontation. Life is empty, unfulfilling, hopeless. There is no sense of having performed well in the past nor little comfort in the memories of earlier personal relationships. A lifetime spent in manipulating others has precluded the narcissist from appreciating the depth and complexity of other human beings. To him other people have always existed as stick figures. It is only the narcissist's interests which are of any importance. For this reason, the past—the repository of happier memories that ordinarily provide some measure of comfort in advancing years—is as empty and barren as the present.

Although this book is not about treatment, it would be unnecessarily grim to leave matters at this point: the aging narcissist trapped in a psychic spider web waiting only for his inevitable consumption by the forces of despair. In many cases, often through psychoanalytic help, the aging narcissist is able to come to terms with his lifelong tendency to devalue and manipulate the people closest to him in life. Thus his depression may trigger an inner awareness of how much other people really do care. He may be comforted by renewed interests in things outside himself: the beauty and continuity of the seasons; the intellectual rigor of science; the grandeur of art; the unity of the cosmos—in such instances the aging narcissist has the opportunity for allying himself with processes which are transcendent. He is able, thus, to "get out from under" the burden of his own heightened, painful self-consciousness. How this is accomplished and with what results is a matter that extends beyond our present concern. As with the ghost of Christmas Future, I wish, at this point, only to sketch a vision of what Kernberg has found may lie ahead for the narcissist who cannot or will not change.

The Natural History of the Narcissist:
Clever Me and Stupid You

Narcissists are primarily interested in themselves. They suffer, in fact, from a heightened self-interest which relegates friends, co-workers, even husbands and wives, to the status of second-class citizens. But behind this self-absorption lies a deeply hidden, usually unconscious inability of the narcissist to experience himself as an independent being.

I hope it's clear by now that this *sense of self* is entirely different from the more commonly described *sense of identity*. "Who am I?" is the question that we ask during a crisis of identity. It can be answered by pointing to any one of a dozen attributes. I am the doctor writing this book, a thirty-nine-year-old neurologist living in Washington, D.C., the husband of Carolyn, the brother of Louise and Christopher, etc.

The *sense of self*, in contrast, points to a more fundamental reality: "Am I?" is the question appropriate here. Am I the same person today as yesterday? What about the person who, ten years ago or so, attended college or graduate school? Is he the same person writing these words? These are the questions that trouble the narcissist and they also provide the best explanation for his behavior.

The narcissist's feeling of continuity is constantly threatened by fragmentation. He defends against this process via efforts aimed at bolstering his sense of self. To do this, the narcissist envisions himself in constant competition with everyone else. If they are important, he is a nonentity. If other people can reap rewards of wealth, influence or power, then he is somehow made smaller and his self dissolves into the mists of anonymity. But if the narcissist can somehow devalue the other person, then his own self-perception and self-esteem is bolstered, at least momentarily.

For the narcissist, life consists of an unending round of maneuvers aimed at bolstering self-esteem—hence the sense of self—via devaluating and manipulating other people. Persons and events who serve to bolster the narcissist's self-esteem are valued. Any person or thing which challenges the narcissist's superiority must be destroyed or, at the very least, devalued and held in contempt.

Superficially, the narcissist's requirement for continual boosts of self-esteem seem similar to the self-centeredness of a child. But while the child is genuinely capable, at least momentarily, of interest and absorption in the people and events around him, the narcissist never loses his preoccupation with his fragile sense of self.

A threatened gas shortage? The narcissist ignores the worldwide political implications and ruminates about how he can be first in line to obtain his own private fuel supply.

A recent death of a friend? The narcissist carefully weighs when he should make his inquiry about purchasing his friend's house, which he has always admired.

In every conceivable situation, the narcissist is bogged down in the simple perspective of how people and events can be manipulated to his own advantage. But in all instances, he lacks the child's ability to imaginatively suspend belief and personal identity in order to enjoy play. To the narcissist there can be no play. Every tennis match is a me-against-him-or-her, a conflict in which there can be only one winner and the loser must suffer indignity and humiliation.

Typically, the narcissist, although superficially charming and attractive is cold, distant and aloof. This is inevitable since other people are important to the narcissist only as a means of bolstering his sense of self. Personal morality thus becomes dependent on shame and pride rather than guilt. While in an interpersonal situation the nonnarcissist is concerned with questions of responsibility (did I do the right thing?), the narcissist's morality depends on how others seem to be evaluating him. And since most interpersonal evaluations are indirect, the narcissist, like everyone else, must rely on his ability to correctly interpret other people's nonverbal and indirect communication. In this area the narcissist is at a distinct disadvantage: lacking a coherent sense of self; impeded at every junction by nascent feelings of fragmentation; threatened by the efforts of other people to achieve many of the same goals that the narcissist wants so desperately for himself—a more unfavorable setting for the mature evaluation of other people's intentions and motives could hardly be imagined.

At all times other people exist only to provide periodic "fixes" for the narcissist's failing sense of self. Those who contribute to the process of self-affirmation are lauded by the narcissist, while those who will confront or merely ignore the narcissist soon become the object of his intense—and to the uninitiated observer—puzzling animosity. Eventually, the world of the narcissist becomes peopled with the "all-good," who cooperate with the narcissist's increasing efforts at self-repair and the "all-bad," who, through efforts aimed at achieving their own sense of affirmation, seem intent on destroying the narcissist at his most vulnerable point: his sense of self.

If any human emotion could be considered most typical of the narcissist, it's envy. In a world where there are only winners and losers and, further, losing is associated with a loss of the sense of self—a veritable annihilation in which being itself is destroyed—in such a world the success of others is unendurable. Oscar Wilde summed up the narcissist's attitude in this area perfectly in his aphorism, "Anybody can sympathise with the sufferings of a friend, but it requires a very fine nature—it requires, in fact, the nature of a true individualist—to sympathise with a friend's success."

In a competitive world where another person's success is equated with one's own personal failure, a compromise solution is worked out in which people are gradually split into two warring groups: those who bolster the narcissist's sense of self-esteem, and those who oppose it or, at the very least, simply ignore it.

The narcissist is intent on using other people toward the development of what Otto Kernberg has termed the "grandiose self": the all-good, immensely wealthy, intelligent and powerful person the narcissist aspires to be. The reality of limitations and deficiencies which most people recognize as the "real world" is denied or raged against by the narcissist.

At times of lowered self-esteem, the narcissist experiences an intensely painful feeling of deprivation: other people have the treasures that he longs for so intensely. Later, as the seesaw of self-esteem rises, the narcissist attempts to grasp the treasures for himself, but always in the role of an actor in a psychic drama where the "goods" will never be sufficient for everyone. In such a world, those who possess the advantages the narcissist desires soon become hated and intensely envied.

Above all else, the narcissist suffers from a hypertrophied sense of entitlement: the wealth, power and influence enjoyed by others should be the narcissist's private possession. In a word, he is "entitled" to them and, hence, must work at ways of wresting them from their unlawful possessors. But how to do it?

If the narcissist is grandiose, rageful and self-centered, he's also intelligent, often charming and always keenly aware of the limitations in modern society of outwardly expressed hostility. Obviously, others are not going to willingly give up their treasures in response to the narcissist's blustering and, hence, ways must be developed to extract them. Physical force won't work. Persuasion is rarely helpful. Imploring is unlikely to lead to much in the way of power or influence. In addition, it must be remembered, the narcissist is interested in gaining his ends in ways that will not only bolster his self-esteem but result in the devaluation of others.

At first glance, the narcissist's task seems an overly formidable one. But narcissists, over the years, have developed a marvelous scheme that enables them to accomplish the twofold task of gaining their ends while humiliating their competitors.

What better way to proceed than through one-upmanship? If the other person can be fooled into relinquishing his possessions through trickery, the narcissist performs a kind of double whammy. He extracts the power, wealth, whatever, that the other person reasonably doesn't want to give up, while establishing his own psychic superiority. I am smarter, more clever, more important—in essence, *I am*. Thus the narcissist becomes keenly skilled at methods aimed at *manipulating* other people.

Manipulation is nothing more or less than employing deception to trick someone into giving up something he wouldn't otherwise voluntarily relinquish. It can involve lying, misrepresentation, stirring up another person's greed or merely promising things that one couldn't possibly deliver. But in all instances, the manipulative attempt is based on the narcissist's underlying dynamics: self-affirmation through the denial of the individuality and worth of the other person.

Psychoanalyst Ben Bursten refers to the narcissist's *modus operandi* as the technique of "putting something over," a term which captures perfectly the narcissist's combined need for a sense of exhilaration and contempt. To the extent that the other person is "fooled" or "tricked" into accepting the manipulation, the narcissist's sense of self-esteem increases. "Clever me and stupid you," the narcissist implies.

Con artists, as we will see later, develop this technique into an art form in which the "mark" provides not only money but an occasion for entertainment and sardonic amusement. At times, the need to "put something over" can be more powerful than the money or the material possessions involved in the con game. This in part explains why con artists, who are a particular variety of narcissists, often seem to behave so foolishly and self-destructively. At times they seem to engage in manipulation merely for the fun of it. This behavior, viewed from the usual vantage point, seems inexplicable. But the behavior makes a great deal of sense when it is considered as an attempt to bolster a failing sense of self-esteem via the demonstration of one's own cleverness contrasted with other people's stupidity.

The narcissist's difficulties involve the absence of a consistent, satisfactory relationship with others. Lacking a firm sense of self-worth, caused, most psychoanalysts believe, because of early life failure by the child to internalize feelings of love and affection from his parents, the narcissist is unable to give love to others. Instead, he must spend his life seeking a sense of self through other people's admiring responses. It's as if the narcissist uses other people the way another person uses a mirror. If the mirror is absent, then a person is left unsure how he looks, the cut of his suit, whether his hair is parted just right and so on. But to the narcissist his insecurities pertain to more than simply physical appearance. Filled with a generalized feeling of discontent, he seeks in others the confirming approval that he invariably lacks in himself. Neither the accomplishments of the past nor the prospects of the future can satisfy for very long since the narcissist, above all, doubts his own worth and remains endlessly caught up in a series of speculations about who he is and what he stands for. As a result, the narcissist has great difficulty in forming lasting and deep relationships with others, in fact may deny the desirability or even the possibility of such relationships. Since the other person is essentially a mirror used to reflect back to the narcissist the sense of worth which he inwardly lacks, people are never appreciated for their own sake but only as objects to be manipulated. Those who confirm the narcissist as a loving, worthwhile self are courted; those who are hostile or even indifferent to the narcissist become the object of his rageful attacks.

A narcissist can often be recognized on the basis of his need to put everybody down. Typically, the narcissist's conversation is peppered with references to other people's stupidity, inadequacy and incompetence. Implicit in such references is the narcissist's grandiose self-image. The narcissist would have us believe that only he is good, intelligent, clever and so on. Other people's failure to recognize and come to terms with these facts leads them to launch into activities which, the narcissist assures us, they're poorly equipped to carry out. A mood of sardonic humor usually accompanies such pronouncements, which superficially sound like well-reasoned criticisms rather than envious, rageful tantrums against anyone who dares to try to usurp the power and influence which the narcissist feels are rightfully his. For this presumption, other people will be made to pay a heavy price: the narcissist's attempt at manipulation in those cases where he can get close enough; and, in those instances where he can't, spiteful criticisms motivated by attempts at narcissistic repair and the maintenance of the grandiose self.

Manipulation serves several different but nonetheless complementary purposes. First, as we have mentioned, it provides a method for effecting narcissistic repair. If the narcissist is feeling low, he can rev up his narcissism by putting something over on another person, thus bolstering his self-esteem.

Second, the narcissist is able to separate himself from other people. In common with his "sicker" counterpart, the borderline personality, whom we will take up in the next section, the narcissist experiences intermittent but nonetheless serious difficulties in distinguishing himself from the people and events around him. What better way to establish one's identity than by manipulation? "I am the one who pulled off the trick, he's the one who fell for it."

Third, manipulation is often a highly adaptive and successful method to gain one's end. As we will discuss later, contemporary culture encourages manipulation in response to the inevitable fractionalization which occurs in every industrialized society. If one loses one's sense of continuity and other people are viewed only as potential competitors, then manipulation becomes a natural and not unreasonable approach to human relations. While homicide has not been tolerated since the age of the caveman, psychic murder via manipulation is now encouraged. People are only so many objects to be maneuvered, like pieces on a chessboard, into desired positions.

Finally, and closely allied to the last point, manipulation can be a form of successful adaptation. Prisoners soon learn to successfully manipulate their terrorist captors. Forms of pathologic adaptation can be successfully maintained by manipulation. For instance, the elderly narcissist who cannot bear the success of his own children may choose to interpret their attempts at autonomy as instances of rebellion and ingratitude which deserve his displeasure and ultimate disownment.

In all instances, it is important to distinguish pathological narcissism from the normal narcissism that we all exhibit to various degrees. There isn't anyone, except perhaps a confirmed masochist, who doesn't feel a need to bolster his self-esteem. We are all manipulators on occasion and, if we are honest about it, get a "kick" out of fooling certain people when it comes to professional accomplishments or even interpersonal triumphs. Who wouldn't engage in a little manipulation in order to meet certain people of influence or be able to enter socially prominent circles?

The process of manipulation isn't pathologic; rather the pathology stems from the narcissist's powerful need to devalue others and to express his contempt for them by reducing everyone else to the level of a thing, an extension of his own fragile sense of self; in essence, people are nothing but "fixes" for his failing narcissism.

The narcissist differs from the nonnarcissist both in the depth of his narcissism (self-absorption) and in the fact that his very identity is dependent on bolstering his self-esteem toward a pathologic and ultimately unattainable grandiose self. The narcissist is seeking perfection on earth, but within the confines of his own psyche. While the saints in medieval times attributed perfection to God alone, the modern narcissist seeks perfection within himself. "There is no God but me," wrote a particularly disturbed narcissist on a San Francisco billboard.

Panic and Self-Loathing Among the Singles Set

A common misconception equates increased sociability with the absence of narcissism. The person involved with other people, according to this point of view, couldn't possibly be narcissistic: invested in the self. Nothing could be further from the truth.

Many narcissists are, if anything, hypersocial. They claim innumerable friends and remain always caught up in an endless whirl of social activities. But behind this frenzy lies a self-preoccupation, a malignant form of narcissism in which other people exist as only bit players in a dramatic creation of the narcissist's omnipotence, grandiosity, power, beauty, intelligence, and so on. Accordingly, many so-called friends are abruptly dropped when they attempt to define the friendship in terms other than providing limitless narcissistic feedings.

It's the *quality* of human interactions rather than sheer numbers of people involved which determines whether or not a relationship is narcissistic. A person with a small number of deep friendships may be distinctly unnarcissistic. Behind the apparent isolation and loneliness may dwell profound emotional investments in other people, abstract ideas or altruistic principles. A monk, for instance, may interact with only a small number of people, but his life-style (prayer, monastic work, writing) may be directed to the edification and improvement of people everywhere in the world. Isolation and self-sufficiency aren't necessarily correlated with malignant forms of narcissism.

It's this discrepancy between appearance and reality, between narcissism and the number of social contacts, that makes an "objective" social science approach insufficient to the task of understanding narcissism. Most of the pivotal insights into narcissism, therefore, have come from those who take the time and trouble to explore individual attitudes and behavior. In our age, this is the province of the psychoanalyst. Despite theoretical formulations which are anything but obvious or inevitable to "outsiders," the psychoanalytic relationship has allowed for the gradual unfolding of individual human dramas, a development which was essential for an understanding of narcissism. Many of the psychoanalysts specializing in narcissism and disorders of the self have recently made their cases available. Their insights provide support for the basically narcissistic nature of many "love" relationships.

Jonathan, a twenty-five-year-old industrial engineer, sought psychoanalytic help because of unhappiness, inability to perform adequately on his job and a general preoccupation with the meaninglessness of his life. A tall, good-looking man who dressed with care and taste, he spoke of his need to date continuously. According to his analyst's notes, Jonathan could not bear to be alone, "just with myself." Even solitary activity such as reading required the presence of a girlfriend. As a result of this fear of being alone, he dated compulsively but experienced little pleasure in the relationships which he required in order to quiet his fears and anxieties. Not surprisingly, this "addiction" for other people soon extended to his psychoanalyst and the treatment process itself. For instance, he compared the disappointment and anger he felt at the ending of his sessions to his feelings at the end of a night spent with one of his girlfriends. "When she says, 'You better go now,' I can't. I have to say that! I can't tolerate *her* saying it. I have to break them into the pattern."

But behind his repetitive and histrionic sexuality lurked an ennui that had become unbearable. He found intercourse "dull as hell" but carried around with him at all times a book of phone numbers and addresses of the women he was involved with. "They serve as an outlet. . . . It's also a great athletic endeavor, adventuresome, it's also like having a cocktail, but I don't like to drink, so I have an orgasm instead."

On a typical evening, Jonathan would show up at a woman's apartment unannounced, make love to her and then leave in the middle of the night only to repeat the performance in another apartment somewhere across town. He spoke of "performance anxiety" and related his behavior to boredom or the fear of being alone. Once he was established with a woman, however, his "performance anxiety" would arise anew and he would embark on further compulsive sexual foraging at another apartment. The sadistic and exploitive elements of Jonathan's behavior didn't escape his analyst.

"If you treat them badly they'll do everything you want them to do," he exclaimed on one occasion after recounting how he had urinated on his "lover" of the moment. Coupled with these aggressively sadistic elements, there lurked a fear of the basic split within his personality. "We are getting down to the *real* me now, and I don't like it too intense. I can't handle it . . . I'm absolutely exasperated being *me*." He was both frightened and fascinated at the prospect of moving emotionally close to either the analyst or one of his deprecated lovers.

At the basis of Jonathan's anxiety was an extreme need for admiration and approval. "My whole life needs an acknowledgment to know I exist; I always need a stamp of approval." There was never a middle ground between the ecstatic heights of self-sufficiency and the depths of self-loathing that almost approached annihilation. "He always felt that he was either fantastic—the best—or nothing," his analyst noted. Affectionate feelings were something to be hoarded like food or gold lest they be dissipated and lost forever. "When I feel I have gotten enough from you," he said to his analyst, "then I have a lot to give to others . . . otherwise it's like I have to save all I've got for myself."

Most interesting and revealing about the nature of the narcissistic self-image was Jonathan's description of himself as a "splat on the wall—when you throw hot rubber against the wall it hardens and it's like an octopus with suckers on it, clinging to the wall. Then nothing matters, only the clinging like a splat. It can't tolerate the crumbling of the wall. Any disconnection is a threat to the survival of the splat. That's how I am with T. [a lover]."

When alone, Jonathan had "a burning feeling to call somebody, grab a girl; nothing else counted, no pride, no dignity. It was more than loneliness, worse than hunger, deeper than hunger."

Behind this mixture of panic and self-loathing was a fear of being emotionally shut out in ways similar to his own shutting out of other people. "One of my problems is separation—if I lose somebody, the anxiety I get is that I might as well be dead." At other times the anxiety took the form of fears that he would not be "appropriately responded to." His analyst noted that not being taken seriously, not being understood, was the most painful response anyone could accord him. At such times, Jonathan would stir up his narcissism via "some exciting sensations, some kicks to get me out of it."

Characteristically, these efforts at self-stimulation took the form of further sexual exploits marked by compulsivity, shallowness and fear of the loss of his identity. He approached others addictively. In place of heroin or alcohol he was addicted to people since they served, principally, as periodic boosts for his flagging sense of self. To the casual observer, Jonathan has a plethora of social relationships. But basically he is narcissistic, manipulative and deeply enmeshed in sadistically exploitive "love" relationships.

Painters Who Never Paint

A common variation of a narcissistic identity disturbance is a relentless but seemingly endless effort toward the achievement of some type of professional goal. Rather than a matter of economic or social position, however, the effort to "become" a lawyer or a doctor or artist, whatever, represents a search for a sense of identity which the person can finally cling to as the "real me." The striving for this goal, rather than its accomplishment, becomes the focus for the individual's sense of self. To achieve the goal and thus form a stable identity as a doctor, for instance, throws the person into a panic. The important issue seems to be an inward dedication to "becoming" something which will confer status, a sense of purpose and, most of all, an identity.

Fearful of failure and at the same time unable to bring to bear sufficient inner resources to achieve a particular goal, this variety of narcissist displays a life-style which is remarkable for its lack of productivity. Painters who do not paint; writers who never seem to develop the necessary inspiration; graduate students whose dissertations drag on for years; actresses who never seem to be in the right place at the right time to land a part—these are some of the most commonly observable life-styles in which identity seems more tied up with the process of "becoming" than actual achievement. If one dabbles around with paint and a brush, for instance, it's not too difficult to convince one's friends that one is an artist. Or the publication of poetry via a "vanity press" bestows upon the poet an identity as an author. But to actually paint or write creatively implies an effort which may result in failure, an agonizing and unbearable blow to the narcissist, whose already fragmentary

sense of self responds to such experiences with the feeling of annihilation described by Sonya and Jonathan.

This reference to annihilation recurs with intriguing frequency
throughout the writings and discussions of psychiatrists who specialize in treating patients with identity disorders. Their patients
express fears of a sudden loss of themselves, engulfment into a
void, a kind of psychic black hole from which they will never return. Since such fears are often expressed by individuals of impressive professional accomplishment, the statements have a ring of
unreality about them. How could a person be so successful and
yet possess such a fragile concept of himself? And what is the
basis for this fear of acute annihilation?

Dr. Peter Giovacchini, psychiatrist at the University of Illinois,
has studied disorders of identity for more than a quarter of a century. Beneath his patients' veneer of self-sufficiency and compla-
cence, Giovacchini had found a deep-seated sense of inadequacy
and worthlessness. "Underneath a strong and arrogant exterior,
the analyst is frequently confronted with a frightened and confused, helpless, infantile orientation," Giovacchini has written.

Such self-attitudes lead, according to Giovacchini, to efforts of
overcompensation which are often rewarded in our culture where
a great emphasis is placed on material success and less emphasis
on human qualities such as affection and self-esteem. Success, in
turn, stimulates the formation of a narcissistic identity heavily dependent on continued material rewards, praise and attention. If
this feverish search for self-affirmation is successful, "one sees a
picture of narcissistic fulfillment, a well integrated organism with
a minimum of human qualities and failings."

Typically, such a person is hardworking and immensely ambitious yet, in Giovacchini's words, "plastic and perhaps unscru-
pulous." When in a position of power, the person may actually
affect the world for the better as a side effect of his accomplishments, all of which are directed at further increasing the
sense of self-esteem. But whatever benefits may result for other
people from the narcissist's efforts, his orientation remains purely
selfish. His efforts are directed toward creating and maintaining a
sense of self-esteem which protects the narcissist from underlying

feelings of helplessness and inadequacy. To relinquish contact to another person or share responsibility or pause, even momentarily, from the compulsive drive for additional money and recognition is, to the narcissist, equivalent to psychic collapse.

"Collapse would mean a state of helpless vulnerability; he would find himself at the mercy of external forces and assault, in other words, at the mercy of an external world that would use him for its own needs and, thereby, stamp out all vestiges of individuality and autonomy," Giovacchini has written.

The search for total control and invulnerability provides the basis for the narcissist's success. In our society, positions of great importance frequently seem to be occupied by people who arrogate total control and absolute power to themselves while demanding unquestioning "loyalty" from those around them. This is the narcissist's formula for success. Monetary rewards and acclaim provide the narcissist with "infusions" of confidence and self-esteem, while any attempts on anyone else's part to share in the rewards are bitterly opposed as an attack on the narcissist's psychological as well as material integrity—the annihilation the narcissist refers to so frequently.

Annihilation, within such a mind-set, is equivalent to anything that threatens the narcissist's identity as a "successful," "wealthy," "popular," etc. individual. Wealth or popularity thus becomes an integral part of the narcissist's sense of identity, a crucial component of his self. The narcissist maintains the precarious sense of self by satisfying his continual need for acclaim and material possessions. In a sense, the narcissist is "hooked" on self-enhancement and power. Lacking a firmly grounded sense of self which can exist independently of material possessions or other people's esteem, the narcissist is trapped into a compulsive and driven search for continued affirmations of his "success."

The boredom and ennui experienced by many workaholics over the weekend or on vacations is an attenuated form of narcissistic distress: if one's sense of self is rooted entirely in a professional role, then the results of stepping out of that role, even briefly, can range all the way from boredom to a paralyzing and panicky loss of identity. To the outside observer the narcissist is a paradox:

superficially he appears successful and confident, yet his attitude and behavior implies a deeply experienced sense of insecurity. Grandiose evaluations of his own abilities and talents alternate with fearful, almost paranoid expectations that others are out to "get him," another variation on the theme of annihilation.

What we now know about narcissism was learned partly from observations of the attitudes about the self expressed by many successful narcissists. The greatest contribution to our knowledge, however, comes from the studies of narcissistic "failures": people whose achievements were insufficient to provide them with a sense of identity.

Lacking wealth, fame or even personal acclaim within a small circle of acquaintances, the narcissist begins to display a series of characteristic symptoms based on dissolution of his sense of self. Who am I? What is life all about? are typical questions raised by the narcissist. Rather than being questions of a philosophical or epistemologic nature, however, they originate in a fragmentation of the personality and an imperiled sense of identity.

Analysts who specialize in the treatment of narcissistic disorders emphasize above all else the narcissist's extreme vulnerability in the area of identity. Threatened by a sense of impending annihilation, the narcissist fights back by developing an inflated, grandiose sense of his own importance. Vain, egocentric, pompous, arrogant, snobbish, the narcissist treats others with contempt, holds them at a distance and devaluates them as a means of bolstering his own self-esteem. But these deprecatory maneuvers are successful for only a short time. Eventually, the pendulum swings to the opposite pole: the narcissist's ebullient self-centeredness shifts into an equally intense feeling of worthlessness, rejection and hypochondriacal anxiety.

"Narcissists of this type thus suffer regularly from repetitive violent oscillations of their self-esteem," according to psychoanalyst Annie Reich. "It is as though the warded-off feeling of catastrophic annihilation which had started off the whole process originally were breaking through the elegant façade each time."

The narcissist's cycling between periods of intense self-inflation and hopelessness is based, as we discussed earlier, on disturbances in integrating the "good" and "bad" images, a failure of "fusion" which, ordinarily, results in the appreciation of other people's basic ambivalence summed up in the everyday phrase "Nobody's perfect."

But to the narcissist, some people are perfect and to be lionized, while others are all bad and must be reacted to with hate and resentment. "The infantile value system knows only absolute perfection and complete destruction," according to Dr. Reich. "It belongs to the early time in life when only black and white existed, good and bad, pleasure and pain, but nothing in between. There are no shades or degrees, there are only extremes."

Coupled with this inability to realistically evaluate others, the narcissist is equally incapable of self-evaluation. "Like tolerance for others, tolerance for oneself is a late achievement," writes Reich.

Both "love" and "hate" are experienced by the narcissist in extremes. Aggression is evident in his sometimes flamboyant efforts to put down other people. Money, fame, property—all provide visible tokens of the narcissist's superiority which he often forces on other people in almost physically intrusive ways. "See what I own —my beautiful wife, my lovely home . . . etc." The narcissist's public proclamations of self-admiration involve at its source a deep contempt for everyone else.

Later, as the façade of grandiosity and self-display begins to wear thin, the narcissist experiences an equally intense period of self-hatred and his aggression is turned inward. Typically, the stimulus for this turnabout is a rather trivial occurrence.

Perhaps the value of a stock falls one or two points; a contract has to be renegotiated at slightly less favorable terms. In another instance perhaps something as trivial as contracting a slight cold or flu may set the narcissist at odds with himself. But to the narcissist nothing is trivial but, instead, may represent a potential threat to his very existence.

The cold may, in fact, be lung cancer, necessitating a trip to the doctor, whose reassurances about the narcissist's good health are ignored.

The renegotiated contract may be the start of a business failure, a total financial wipe-out. In the space of a few days or even, in some cases, a few hours, the narcissist's grandiosity and self-assurance can be transformed into feelings of inner dejection, worthlessness and hypochondriacal self-preoccupation. He may claim to be "dying" or "coming apart at the seams" or other destructive phrases. At such a point the outward aggression formerly employed to bolster the narcissist's grandiose self has been turned inward, creating anxiety and a panic state.

The portrait of the narcissistic personality presented in the last several chapters provides the framework for understanding the various types of manipulators we will encounter in the remainder of this book. Narcissism is the process which enables us to understand the confused, distorted and often deeply disturbed personalities of the borderline, the psychopath and the impostor. The underlying dynamic of all these character disorders is a disturbance within the narcissistic realm. They all, in part, suffer from a self disorder of different intensity and seriousness. No matter how complicated and bizarre their stories, they can all be understood by reference to the principles set out in this section of the book. They all suffer, to a greater or lesser extent, from narcissistic pathology. Whichever form this disturbance ultimately takes depends on a host of environmental factors. To this extent, they all exist along a continuum. But, in telling you this now, I'm anticipating myself somewhat.

Let's move on now into deeper and more troubled waters, where we will encounter increasingly serious, extreme but nonetheless subtle distortions of personal integration.

V

Crossing the Border

"Impairment in the integration of the self is central to most, if not all, metapsychological constructions of the borderline state."

The Borderline Syndrome,
Michael H. Stone, M.D.

A Hard and Tough Lover

At age thirty-six, Anita was a successful interior designer, the wife of a wealthy attorney, the mother of two children and an insatiable nymphomaniac. Her sexual activity over the previous two years had increased to the point that she was in constant danger that her liaisons—brief, impulsive flings—would be discovered by her husband. Finally out of boredom and an acute sense of the utter ennui of her marriage she told her husband of the affairs and, almost immediately, filed for divorce.

After her divorce, the sexual encounters increased in frequency, always involving men who, for one reason or another, were unmarriageable. In addition, her frigidity and failure to reach orgasm—a state of affairs she blamed on her husband and the loveless marriage he had provided—continued unabated. (The only exception was an intense orgastic experience with her divorce lawyer which took place on the floor of his law office. She reached orgasm by fantasizing that she was a prostitute he had picked up on the street and brought back to his office.) Finally, in desperation, she sought psychiatric help in order to "settle down" and remarry.

Anita's analysis, carried out over a two-year period, provides an insight into the dynamics of a woman suffering from a serious disorder of the self. Her analyst's notes concerning his impressions of Anita have been suitably altered to conceal her identity. The facts are true, however.

To the casual observer, Anita's disturbances would be hard to pinpoint. In fact, unless the observer were aware of Anita's sexual liaisons nothing would appear to be amiss. Her outward appearance and behavior were, to quote her psychoanalyst's words, those of a "beautiful, seductive woman, dressed in high mod fashion—a lively, spontaneous and articulate woman, likeable and quite popular, who gives an impression of warmth." Beneath the veneer of social adjustment, however, lurked a personality that was disjointed, fragmented and at odds with itself.

Most striking of all were certain contradictions in Anita's behavior which she failed to acknowledge even after they were repeatedly pointed out to her. Her sexual relationships, for instance, were based on two opposing expectations. While she took a "hard and tough" approach to her lovers, reveling in the sensuous delights of anonymous, unrestrained and often perverse sexuality, she expected quite another set of attitudes from her partners. Repeatedly, the affairs broke off after bitter and acrimonious confrontations concerning her lovers' unwillingness to grant exclusivity to their arrangement. She expressed, on several occasions—to the amused dismay of her lover of the moment—that she considered their affair a possible preamble to marriage. Realistically, this was unlikely for several reasons, not the least of which were the kinds of men she was involving herself with: not at all sufficiently "rich" or "refined" for her social requirements. Rather, she wished that her companions be bound to her while she remained free to move on to the next relationship.

And move on she did with a ruthlessness and vigor. Often, over a space of only a few hours, the lover, formerly the object of her exclusive attentions, would simply "disappear" from her mind. Rather than anger or revenge, Anita's motivation—or, perhaps it would be more correct to say, lack of motivation—to "forget" sprang from an inner discontinuity. In her mind people replaced each other rapidly and without warning, drawn, as it were, into a kind of psychic black hole. If a lover disappointed her or frustrated her, he simply disappeared, no longer existed.

In the event of frustration, one lover was exchanged for another, who could then be interchanged with yet a third and so on. Throughout it all, her contradictory expectations about her relationships continued: the carnal, cynical woman speaking earnestly of forming a "lasting" union with a devoted man. All attempts at resolving these inconsistencies were unsuccessful; the compulsive sexuality continued unabated. "Interpretations had no effect on the course of her next affair," her analyst wrote.

Anita's inconsistency, it turned out, was the most striking aspect of her personality, the inner dynamic which helps us to understand her. As another example of this inconsistency, she lacked the ability to appreciate any similarities between other people's behavior and her own. For example, on one occasion before the breakup of her marriage, she fought with her husband because he had "become hysterical" and shouted at their daughter. She rebuked him bitterly and demanded that he control his temper lest his outburst cause psychological harm to their child. Yet moments later, when confronted with a report card detailing the daughter's failing grades, Anita lashed out at the child, even proceeded to the point of calling up the teacher and angrily abusing her over the phone. Despite questions, probings, and outright confrontation, Anita saw no similarity between her husband's earlier behavior and her own.

Once alerted to Anita's inconsistencies and lack of integration, her analyst was able for the first time to make sense out of the chaos of her life. It was as though the continuity of her experience was perpetually susceptible to fragmentation, particularly whenever she encountered resistance, indifference or simply a strong impulse. Her awareness of time, scheduling, the ordering of her life, other people's expectations of her—all dissolved along with her sense of self. She literally "lived for the minute," unable to maintain her own structural organization over time.

"The patient's distorted sense of time was intimately connected with her urgent impulses. When a strong new need appeared, impulsive or less discernibly so, the world connected with the abandoned aim and object would disappear," writes her analyst.

Although Anita exists in her own right, and her uniqueness cannot be captured by a label, her behavior and experiences correspond to what psychiatrists now describe as a *borderline personality*. The history of this concept provides a crucial insight into the development of our modern concepts of the self.

In 1925 Wilhelm Reich, the originator of the orgone box, wrote a monograph entitled "The Impulsive Character." Here he described his attempts to apply psychoanalytic treatment to patients in the Vienna clinic where he worked. Most noteworthy in his writings is the description of a severe mental disorder marked by "the grotesque quality of their symptoms." As Reich put it, "the compulsive thought of killing one's child, as conceived by the simple neurotic, appears trite and innocuous in comparison to the compulsive urge of an impulsive individual to roast his child slowly over a fire."

But as Reich makes clear elsewhere in the monograph, he's not describing a psychotic, an individual who might, under certain circumstances, actually carry out such a grisly deed. Nor was he illustrating the dilemma of a neurotic who may be tortured with obsessional thoughts: "Am I likely to kill my child? Could I ever do such a horrible thing?" Rather, Reich was impressed with the ability of these patients, the compulsive characters, to simultaneously maintain sharply contradictory emotional states without any conscious discomfort. To accomplish this, Reich speculated that these patients somehow "split off" parts of their personality, thus explaining their ability to entertain their morbid fantasies without evident discomfort.

Over the years, other psychiatrists began observing additional features by which these impulsive characters could be recognized. These included a constitutional feeling of inferiority accompanied by consistent failures in the maintenance of self-esteem; a strong tendency to blame all personal problems on other people, often relatives or friends; narcissism; oversensitivity to mild criticism or rejection; frequent engulfment in "emergency emotions" of anger, fear, hostility; and, most intriguing of all, a deficiency in the individuals' power of empathy with other people.

But this was not the end of the matter by any means. Nor did this list cover all the suggestions by which the disorder could be recognized. Individual psychiatrists emphasized additional features: chaotic sexuality; the frequent occurrence of phobic fears; the inability to experience pleasurable sensations and so on. Reading the literature published in the twenty-five years after Reich's monograph, one is impressed with the diversity of opinions expressed. There seem to be as many views on what constituted this disorder as there were psychiatrists seriously thinking and writing about it. Along the way, the term *impulsive character* was replaced by the term *borderline,* implying that the patients didn't fit clearly into psychosis (outright madness) nor was the seriousness of their conflicts adequately relayed by the benign term "neurosis."

In 1954 a psychiatrist and psychoanalyst at the Menninger Foundation, Robert Knight, wrote a now-classic paper which describes the disorder as a weakening of what, at that time, was referred to as "ego functions." Adapting the analogy of a retreating army, Knight suggested that many of the previously described disturbances of adjustment (phobias, obsessions and so on) constituted a kind of "holding operation" in the front lines of the battlefield while the main personality forces were positioned or rather regressed far behind these lines. The value of Knight's contribution stems from the emphasis he placed on what psychoanalysts now refer to as a person's "synthetic functions." These include such things as anticipation of the future; the maintenance of a firmly grounded sense of self; logical thinking; realistic planning; the ability to postpone momentary pleasures in the interests of future benefits. In addition, Knight drew on his considerable powers of observation to pinpoint certain peculiarities in the patients' use of language. Most noticeable was the borderline patient's tendency to remain oblivious to the obvious implications of many of his statements. Since this is a subtle but nonetheless crucial point, let me digress here for a moment and illustrate what Knight was talking about.

The Victim

Esther, a forty-one-year-old mother, was referred to me several years ago for the evaluation of her persistent, repeated, and increasingly frequent beating of her young child. An attractive, charming and even, on occasion, amusing woman, she vividly recounted to me how she "absolutely flew off the handle." "On occasion I wanted to literally kill Susan." She described with animation and dramatic gesture how she would suddenly be overcome with an impulse to "murder that kid," whom she consistently referred to as "the victim." Throughout all this, she sought reassurances from me that her problem might be due to epilepsy. "Couldn't all this be explained by some kind of a seizure?" she asked.

A few minutes of questioning revealed that Susan was an adopted child and a victim of cerebral palsy which had left her seriously crippled. Esther described an afternoon walk: "When we go out together I walk ahead so that Susan can see which way I'm turning. (With her crutches it's hard for her to turn suddenly and she has to watch which way I'm going.) People often stop her on the street and say kind things to her. They don't know that Susan and I are together. 'It's so sad and so pathetic,' they'll turn and say to me, unaware of the fact that Susan is with me. At such times I get so angry because I know Susan is hearing and enjoying this. She absolutely *revels* in self-pity. Her greatest pleasure involves getting people to feel sorry for her, and here I am standing in the street having to listen to some stranger's pity about *my* child. If Susan is crippled and ugly, what does that say about me? Now, Doctor, getting back to the more important question of epilepsy, couldn't these rage episodes which come out of nowhere be secondary to an epileptic attack?"

"Possibly, but do you think there could be any other explanation?"

"Like what? I absolutely adore Susan." She laughs and makes a hugging gesture with her arms. "I want *so much* to help her. Do you know that it's through Susan that many people in the neighborhood know who I am? 'That's Susan's mother,' they all say. She means so much to me. What other possible explanation than epilepsy can account for these *insane* rages against that pathetic child?"

Esther's tortured explanation for her aggression fails to grasp the "splitting" which exists within her with regard to Susan. Her maternal feelings are shocked by the physical abuse she heaps on the child. Simultaneously, she resents having to accompany a cripple, be taken for the mother of a defective child, in fact have her very identity defined as "that's Susan's mother." But most important and absolutely critical for our appreciation of splitting, these contradictory attitudes coexist within Esther's mind as separate "islands" cut off from any communication with each other. In her mind, the "true" explanation for her aggression has nothing to do with her feelings but must involve something mysterious and unaccountable: an epileptic seizure.

Both Esther's and Anita's problems stem from failures in integrating internal processes which, in most people, create a unified sense of self. Overall, both women demonstrate a bland tolerance for contradictions in thought and behavior, with no need to unify or reconcile their drastically opposing attitudes and actions. To Esther, her deeply conflicting attitudes toward her daughter—expressed so patently that the listener feels surely she *must* realize the implications of what she's saying—coexist with repeated reiterations of her conviction that her aggression toward the child must be due to "some kind of seizure." Esther's emotional responses are split off from the ideas and insights which she expresses, often correctly, about the threat Susan poses for her identity. She doesn't want to be thought of as the mother of a "cripple" but, at the same time, "loves the child dearly"; she wishes to help Susan, yet walks so far ahead of her on the street that it appears to bystanders that the child isn't with her.

Turning now to Anita, her sexual life is marked by rapid turn-over and superficial attachment. Her own contemptuous attitudes toward her lovers exist side by side with the unrealistic idea that a relationship which to her is only a fling would somehow be invested by her partner with feelings of commitment, dedication and the wish for permanency. When things turn out differently she shuts off her emotions and promptly forgets her lover's existence. Her analyst has written: "If the object disappoints her, it disappears. It's not a case of sour grapes or revenge. The person indeed no longer exists for her. This is not amnesia due to repression, but rather a case of out of sight out of mind." Once again the self is fractionated into separate islands, each existing in isolation from the other.

The French psychoanalyst André Green compares the mental topography of such a person to an archipelago: isolated islands of the self surrounded by the void of a vast and empty psychic ocean. Thanks to the process of splitting, the self becomes transformed, using Green's analogy, from something like a continent—where differing aspects of the personality like neighboring countries, gradually and imperceptibly merge—into, instead, a string of disconnected islands existing in lonely isolation. Within such an inner landscape, communication between the islands becomes impossible, hence the presence of widely varying and often contradictory thoughts, fantasies and emotions corresponding to the different selves.

To the borderline personality, the subjective experience of such a disconnection process consists of a vague and periodic sense of discontent, emptiness and uneasiness. To observers, in turn, such people appear aloof, disjointed and unpredictable as though one were dealing with several people at a time rather than a single individual whose identity changed very little from one occasion to another. On this subject of the borderline's effect on others, Green has written: "The discourse of the borderline is not a chain of words, representations or affects, but rather, like a pearl necklace without a string, words, representations, affects contiguous in space and time but not in meaning."

Within such a world, distinctions begin to blur in regard to one's own thoughts, emotions and inner representations. The self is constantly threatened by its disappearance and transformation into a new self. Further, feelings of unreality, nonexistence and threat—in a word, annihilation—are encountered in the form of anxiety and panic attacks. At such times, puzzlement about identity and purpose can begin to intrude into everyday matters, sometimes resulting in what Erik Erikson has described as "identity diffusion."

Lacking an integrated view of the self, the borderline personality is thus incapable of forming stable impressions of other people. A borderline's description of his experiences frequently sounds like a series of contradictory impressions of a person or event as seen through the eyes of a group instead of a single person. Frequently, the described inner experiences are contradictory as if involving two people with opposite and irreconcilable points of view.

One of Dr. Otto Kernberg's patients, for instance, expounded on the disgust she felt for men who viewed women as sex objects. She elaborated further on her narrow escapes from sexual involvements, the end result of which had eventually led to a self-imposed limitation on her social life. A few seconds later and almost as if the previous recitation had never taken place, the patient commented casually about her job as a "bunny" in a Playboy Club.

Such contradictions can also include past events reinterpreted in the present by a "new self" in such a way that their occurrence is either denied altogether or, when this is impossible, are experienced as involving another individual. "I wouldn't want to be Linda Lovelace," said the former porn queen during an interview. "I wouldn't want to have anything to do with her, that's not the way I am at all. That wasn't me."

One of the best indications of splitting comes from the reactions frequently reported by other people in response to their perceptions of discontinuity shown by the individual affected by splitting. Observers often describe the borderline personality as a "puzzle" or a "mass of contradictions." Their inconsistency may even arouse anger and remorse about "hypocrisy," as if somehow one attitude is being put on for show while inwardly, it's suspected, just the opposite feelings are retained. "Insincere," "selfish," "self-centered"—the emphasis in all these pejoratives is on the perception that the affected individual is somehow incapable of caring about anything other than his own personal concerns at the moment. But as with Esther and Anita, what appears as a lack of concern is actually an inability to appreciate the discontinuity and lack of synthesis which characterize their lives. As Anita's analyst writes at one point in his notes: "It took me a long time to realize that the need for consistency was only in *my* mind, not hers. She felt no need for it."

A Companionship of Shadows

In Lawrence Durrell's novel *Justine*, the main character, described at one point as a sufferer from hysteria, actually exemplified the splitting process characteristic of a borderline.

"I remember her sitting before the multiple mirrors at the dressmaker's, being fitted for a shark-skin costume, and saying: 'Look! five different pictures of the same subject. Now if I wrote I would try for a multi-dimension effect in character, a sort of prism-sightedness. Why should not people show more than one profile at a time?'"

The narrator, hopelessly in love with the enigmatic and exotic Justine, captures at many points in the novel the fascination and despair that Justine's multidimensionality arouses in him. "The speed with which she moved from one milieu to another, from one man, place, date to another, was staggering. But her instability had a magnificence that was truly arresting. The more I knew her, the less predictable she seemed."

Arnauti first meets Justine on the evening of a carnival in Alexandria, Egypt, where, outside the open door of a tall ballroom, they encounter each other's reflections in a long mirror, Durrell's symbolism for the narcissistic realms in which their love is destined to tortuously unfold. Impressed with the "hungry, natural candor" of Justine, Arnauti turns from the reflected image to the "real" Justine. And thus begins a love affair which Arnauti compares to a "syllogism in which the true premises are missing."

From the first moment, Arnauti is fascinated, tortured and mesmerized by this mysterious woman whose personality is as difficult to grasp as her mirrored reflection. Recalling his feelings years later, he writes: "It is idle to go over all this in a medium as unstable as words. I remember the edges and corners of so many meetings, and I see a sort of composite Justine, concealing a ravenous hunger for information, for power through self-knowledge, under a pretence of feeling."

At once passionate and aloof, childlike yet all the while tantalizingly carnal, Justine leads Arnauti into sensual experiences where contradictions abound and logic and consistency have no place. Arnauti can never get a fix on Justine's personality, can never understand the forces which impel her into actions which appear alternately impulsive, dissolute, innocent, refreshing but, at all times, maddeningly unpredictable. Even in moments of greatest intimacy with Arnauti, she remains a creature of the mirror:

". . . at times when I had felt myself to be closest to her, I felt nothing very sharp in outline: rather a sinking numbness such as one might feel on leaving a friend in a hospital, to enter a lift and fall six floors in silence, standing beside a uniformed automaton whose breathing one could hear."

Throughout the diary, Arnauti captures the fractionated aspects of Justine: "With her one felt all around the companionship of shadows." At moments when he feels closest to her, Justine reveals herself as a creature of a thousand different aspects, a brilliant and beautiful gem whose appearance alters according to the vagaries of perspective and illumination.

"Of course I knew as much as could be known of the psychopathology of hysteria at that time. But there was some other quality which I thought I could detect behind all this. In a way she was not looking for life but for some integrating revelation which would give it point."

Justine's lack of integration is what both attracts and repels Arnauti. As he encounters the various psychic "islands" of her personality, each separated from the other by the process of splitting, he is alternately fascinated and horrified at this woman of Alexandria who, in love, gives out nothing of herself, "having no self to give." While she seems to love Arnauti, he is painfully aware something is lacking in her feelings. At first he speculates that his perceptions of Justine may be distorted by jealousy. But, as their love affair unfolds, it becomes clear that Justine is not one person but many separate selves. "You know I never tell a story the same way twice. Does that mean that I'm lying?" she asks.

At one point in the narrative Justine creates in Arnauti a state of mind corresponding to her own highly charged ambivalence. It is a marvelous literary exposition of the contradictory feelings that coexist as a result of splitting: "And later again, thinking about her as I did and have done these past few years I was surprised to find that though I loved her wholly and knew that I should never love anyone else—yet I shrank from the thought that she might return. The two ideas co-existed in my mind without displacing one another. I thought to myself with relief, 'Good. I *have* really loved at last. That is something achieved'; and to this my alter ego added: 'Spare me the pangs of love *requited* with Justine'. This enigmatic polarity of feeling was something I found completely unexpected."

As the work progresses, Arnauti begins to suspect that his feelings of deep ambivalence toward Justine are a response to the "enigmatic polarity of feeling" which she both experiences in herself and excites in others. Essentially there is not one Justine but rather an infinity of mirror images which, though each can be enjoyed for its own exquisite beauty, must remain forever unfulfilling.

"There is no pain compared to that of loving a woman who makes her body accessible to one and yet who is incapable of delivering her true self—because she does not know where to find it," he writes.

And to love such a woman is to risk one's mental and physical well-being since she consumes other people's emotions without experiencing emotions herself. "To such women how fatal an error it is to give oneself; there is simply a small chewing noise, as when the cat reaches the backbone of the mouse."

Arnauti's passionate infatuation with Justine cannot achieve the status of love because Justine and others like her are incapable of loving. "The word [love] implies a totality which was missing in my mistress, who resembled one of those ancient Goddesses in that her attributes proliferated through her life and were not condensed about a single quality of heart which one could love or unlove."

Throughout it all, Justine is vaguely aware of her own inner lack of integration. Her multiplicity of selves engages in frantic attempts to achieve some kind of synthesis leading to "a perpetual flow of ideas, speculations on past and present actions which pressed upon her mind with the weight of a massive current pressing upon the walls of a dam. And for all the wretched expenditure of energy in this direction, for all the passionate contrivance in her self-examination, one could not help distrusting her conclusions, since they were always changing, were never at rest. She shed theories about herself like so many petals."

Justine's myriad tangle of relationships which enfold in the course of the novel represent her attempt to achieve a sense of order and integration. But the effort is a failure, the personality a composite of hopelessly contradictory selves which, though often brilliant and sensual, are always incapable of becoming unified into a single self. "Justine and her city are alike in that they both have a strong flavor without having a real character," notes one of the participants in Justine's chaotic life.

Justine, of course, is a work of fiction and one must exert care lest one reads more into the work than the author intended. Nevertheless, striking similarities exist between Justine and real-life personalities afflicted by splitting. For instance, Anita's analyst has written a short summary of his impressions of her. It reads like a description of Justine, almost as if the two personalities, one fictional, the other taken from real life, were interchangeable: ". . . if you met her you would find her a warm, attractive, lively, passionate woman, vigorous, life seeking, who attracts men and women, not in the way of some cold, narcissistic beauty, but rather like a charming child. As a matter of fact she seduces people by an active show of interest in them, which proves at the bottom to be narcissistic. A one day acquaintance sounds like a lifelong friendship. She seeks desperately to find a firm identity for herself. With half blind, impulsive lunges she tries to establish some design in her life scheme. Here is the tragi-comedy of an actress who only half understands her part."

Just Disappearing into Thin Air

Narcissists and borderline personalities differ in the degree of discontinuity in their inner experience. The borderline individual's self experience has larger gaps and holes. Or, as one psychiatrist put it, "the borderline patient has integrative deficits in self constancy which are manifested by persistent fragmentation and splits in his self structure, occurring in times both cross sectionally and longitudinally. As a result, his present self experience is not securely placed within a context of past and future selves. Instead, his ongoing experience of himself contains continual potential newness, unfamiliarity and dissonance—more than the usual discontinuity in the self over time."

The borderline's discontinuity is responsible for the great difficulty he experiences in maintaining a firm sense of self. The narcissist's self, in contrast, is freer and less at risk. Deficiencies and periodic crises in self-esteem, rather than self cohesion problems, are typically the lot of the narcissist. The borderline employs extreme measures in order to regain the sense of continuity and meaning within his life.

"At times this may be accomplished by fanatical dedication or infatuation with causes, religious movements, or other sources of dedication which allow the borderline to gain some sense of definition of self and a corresponding sense of identity," according to psychiatrist and Jesuit priest William Meissner, a specialist in borderline and narcissistic character disorders. "However, these commitments tend to remain inconstant and often are subject to sudden shifts of conviction in quite different directions. Such involvements in extrinsic causes tend not to be characteristic of narcissistic personalities."

But the most essential difference between these two personality types involves the ways an individual sense of self is constructed. With the narcissistic personality this involves specific self-esteem vulnerabilities. As long as the narcissist can maintain some element of his "grandiose self" he is satisfied and often functions rather well. The borderline, in contrast, not only requires the maintenance of his sense of importance but must also deal with a heightened aggressiveness. He envisions himself as a victim and responds accordingly. Anger and frustration along with a sense of victimization—this is the personality constellation of a borderline.

"Whereas the pathology of the narcissistic personality is more or less confined to the narcissistic sector of the personality as it affects the integration and functioning of the patient's self, the more prominent intrusion of issues having to do with the vicissitudes of aggression makes the picture considerably more complex for the borderline personality," says Meissner. "The disruptive influence of unresolved aggressive elements . . . contributes an additional burden and an additional set of vulnerabilities."

If the narcissist suffers from periodic disappointments in other people's failure to enhance his self-esteem, the borderline goes one important step further: he reacts with rage and disintegration to what he interprets as a deliberate frustration of his needs. He storms, rages and may engage in verbal, even physical abuse. At times the uproar may be so extreme that the borderline appears to have stepped *over* the border into outright psychosis. Given time, however, the borderline reconstitutes, reintegrating his fragile sense of self. But he remains clinging and demanding, marked by what Meissner has termed a "sense of peremptory and uncompromising entitlement." Since the other person is never capable of satisfying the borderline's demands, all intimate relationships eventually become hostile, yet dependent.

The borderline both needs and resents other people. He needs love but can't accept it. He wants to be taken care of but can't tolerate the feeling of dependence on others. Borderlines are like a magnet which both propels and attracts, never quite achieving intimacy yet forever in search of it. As a result, the borderline is constantly disappointed in others, frustrated in his attempts to establish a relationship. "In such states they can become sullen and pouting, whining and complaining in their attempt to wheedle the necessary response from the important other," says Meissner.

Most fascinating of all is the borderline's superior functioning under conditions that other people might consider stressful. Meissner cites a girl in her thirties with a severe borderline character disturbance who successfully manages a busy office.

"This is a conflict-free area," Meissner told me during a break in the meetings of the American Psychoanalytic Association. "She places great emphasis on her practical abilities, her capacity to function under the stresses of a busy office. This is the basis, in fact, for her self-esteem. She does very well indeed. But in intimate relationships, say a budding love affair, she regresses into conflicts regarding aggression and hostility. Intimacy is her area of weakness and powerlessness. As long as her relationships call forth the practical, intellectualized part of her personality, she does well. But anything involving intimacy evokes quite another response. It's as if the borderline has chosen an internalized leit motif around which he or she chooses various externalized versions. The self is the final product of these internalizations. Thus, the victim introject or the aggressor introject may come to dominate the person's sense of himself, and in a less stable and labile form of regressive expression, he may alternate between them, often quite rapidly and dramatically."

The lack of consistency and stability in the borderline's self-concept can be traced, many experts believe, to the early infant-parent relationship. There are differences of opinion about the exact timing, but the infant's emerging self becomes firmly established somewhere within the first two years of life. Examination of this development has provided support for the approaches of many psychiatrists toward certain forms of psychosis which they view as deviations from this orderly process of early separation-individuation.

In the first phase of infant development, somewhere during the first month of life, it's postulated, the infant is completely merged psychologically with its mother. There is only the slightest hint of a self.* This is called the *autistic* stage. Later, somewhere between two and five months of life, the infant enters a symbiotic phase in which the mother is experienced as part of the infant's earliest gropings toward a sense of self. Since at this stage the infant fails to completely differentiate between himself and mother, the parent is experienced as part of the infant, hence the term *self object*, which is often used to describe the fused image of the infant and mother. Gradually the infant goes through several phases of separation from the mother, a process that occurs between one and three years of age and leaves the infant with a firm sense of a self as separate from others. He's able, by this time, to retain a firmly established *internalized* version of himself and others.

But in borderline individuals, the sense of self is incompletely individualized. They suffer from a chronic lack of a consistent sense of identity, a term aptly described by the psychoanalyst Erik Erikson as identity diffusion: the absence of an integrated self concept and an integrated and stable concept of others in relationships with the self. Further, disturbances in differentiating the self from others in the adult borderline leave the borderline individual with a self that can only be realized in relation to others, a merged self object.

"Within this self concept there is no individual subject (as 'I') and no separate object (as 'thou') connected by a relationship. Instead, subject and object are fused into a 'we' and the self is expressed *as the relationship*," according to Dr. Thomas H. McGlashan, director of adult studies at Chestnut Lodge, a residential treatment center in Rockville, Maryland, known throughout the world for its psychoanalytically oriented explorations into the causes and treatment of serious mental disorders. Dr. McGlashan bases his theory about the borderline personality on a thorough understanding of the literature—dating back approximately twenty-five years, as we have said previously—and the ongoing treatment of borderline patients at Chestnut Lodge. Out of Dr. McGlashan's experience has emerged a series of observations that

* Recent research suggests that this assertion may require revision. See my article "Newborne Knowledge" in *Science* '82 Jan.–Feb. '82.

provide a framework for our understanding and identifying the borderline personality.

First of all, for the borderline there is never a sense of an "I" which can be defined without the presence of another. This requirement for another person can take physical form such as the desire to be touched or caressed in order to feel "alive." The compulsive sexual encounters which Anita displayed can occur as one expression of this need. In the absence of a physically confirming gesture, the borderline may complain, as one of McGlashan's female patients did to him, that she feels alone in the room despite the physical presence of others. Even the other person's silence or lack of comment is experienced as an "absence," a sense of emptiness. At the basis of these feelings is a disturbance in the borderline's capacity to define himself at a particular time and place. Somehow this matter of presence, whether or not one actually feels *present* in the here-and-now situation—depends principally on the responsiveness or unresponsiveness of others. One borderline young man described the situation:

"It's so hard to explain—yesterday I was sitting in the Student Union watching someone who was smoking a cigar—I was feeling lonely, you know, depressed—suddenly as I watched the smoke going up and out, I felt that was me, just disappearing into thin air."

Accompanying these feelings there is often a terrifying sense of unreality, as with a twenty-six-year-old woman who complained: "I have depression spells and feel I'm insane . . . the world is unreal and so am I and all my friends . . . there's a need to hit myself in the head and knock myself out or to have pain, for that feeling would be more real." This requirement for pain as a confirmation of "realness" can, in the absence of support from another person, lead to bizarre and seemingly inexplicable self-mutilations.

Will the Real Catherine Deneuve Please Stand Up?

I can recall my first meeting with Rhonda. She entered the emergency room at St. Vincent's Hospital in New York City and registered with the simple statement: "I'd like to talk to a psychiatrist." Thirty minutes later she and I were sitting in a cramped interviewing room down the hall from the minor surgery suite.

She was a beautiful woman of about twenty-seven with blond hair, pale, perfectly textured skin and a pair of remote, coolly appraising eyes which rarely blinked. Aside from the obvious distress that she was feeling, she reminded me of a cool and distant Catherine Deneuve. The problem, as she put it, was her inability to "feel" anything. She spoke of food that had become tasteless, skiing and tennis activities that were no longer enjoyable, and when she spoke of sex it too sounded dull and mechanical, as if, in her words, "it was all happening to somebody else."

As she continued to speak, I was struck by two things. Her voice was flat and unemotional, absent the normal variations in rhythms and cadence that make human speech interesting. Secondly, although it was summer and the tight cubicle we were in must have been 90 degrees, she was wearing a heavy woolen turtleneck sweater. I said nothing, however, and let her continue.

She lived with a girlfriend in the Village and from the way she said "friend," I knew that she had tried *that* too and had found it as unsatisfying and wooden as the love affairs with men she had described moments before. Her manner was matter-of-fact, almost as if she were reciting a list. In a word, her affect was flat, one of the four primary symptoms of schizophrenia. But she had none of the other three signs: her speech was sequential and made sense; there were no loose associations; she didn't express any evidence of ambivalence, a term implying the simultaneous experience of contradictory attitudes or emotions toward the same person or situation.

The monotonousness of her tone coupled with the muted affect caused me next to consider depression. Yet she wasn't exactly depressed either. She never cried, continued to eat regularly and slept fairly well—three key areas in which the depressed patient usually experiences difficulties. If she wasn't schizophrenic and she wasn't depressed, then what *was* she? As I reflected on this I was, of course, momentarily distracted from what she was saying, in essence wasn't really listening to her. And since my first and most important task was to *listen* to my patient, I put an end to my theoretical musings and sat back, this time really looking and listening. But try as I might to concentrate on what she was saying, I kept coming back to the question of why someone would be wearing a heavy woolen sweater in July. Finally, my curiosity got the best of me and I interrupted and asked, "Aren't you hot in that sweater? Why do you wear it?"

She looked intently at me and then quietly started to take the sweater off. It all happened in an instant, but nevertheless, I can still recall the mixture of feelings I experienced as each rapidly replaced the other: surprise, shock, embarrassment, lust, annoyance and finally horror!

Sitting before me was a girl with hundreds, perhaps thousands, of festering sores each about half an inch in length but deep enough in some cases to have penetrated into the muscle layers. Many were infected, oozing a whitish, milk-like pus. Her breasts were inflamed too, with the tiny incisions extending into the nipple areas. Suddenly the room was filled with an overpowering stench of infection and decay. As I sat there numb and totally unable to function, she reached into her handbag and drew out a razor blade and gently placed it against her forearm. Before I could stop her the blade was pushed, hard, into the skin and then withdrawn, leaving another freshly bleeding incision.

But what was most startling was the appearance on her face as she dug the razor into her skin: she looked at me and smiled with an expression which—there is no other word for it—was positively orgastic. Her mood then altered, within split seconds, and she began to cry softly. Then, as quickly as these expressions had appeared, they disappeared with equal abruptness, leaving a girl with a blank facial expression and hideous lacerations on her breasts and arms.

She spoke then of never feeling "alive" or "real" except when she briefly experienced the paroxysmal pain of her razor-inflicted injuries. Whenever she cut herself, she told me, she felt whole and alive. At other times she spoke of being inside of a shell, of not being certain if she were alive or dead. Only through pain was she able to confirm her sense of wholeness and integrity.

At that period in my life I was unacquainted with the forms that severe disturbances in the sense of self can take. I have since learned that the individual who feels empty and incomplete may attempt to experience, however briefly, an identity based on pain. In the case of Rhonda, this pain was self-inflicted, a form of masochism. In other instances, the pain may be inflicted on others. The victim's suffering when witnessed by a sadist may provide him with his own sense of identity. Thus, sadism and masochism may contribute a sense of cohesion to the person suffering from a sense of personal fragmentation.

"In an individual with a diffuse or dissolving self-representation, the masochistic search for acute experiences of pain can be understood as a means of acquiring a spurious feeling of being real and alive, and thereby re-establishing a sense of existing as a bounded entity, a cohesive self," wrote Dr. Robert Stolorow in 1975 in the *International Journal of Psychoanalysis*.

On the subject of sadism, Stolorow wrote in the same paper: "Sadism may function to restore a fragmenting self-representation along pathways analogous to those followed by masochistic activity. The sadist may vicariously acquire a feeling of being alive and real through a process of identification with the acute pain he induces in his victim. Dramatically shocking and forcing attention from a real or imaginary audience through his cruelty, may provide the sadist with the vitally needed experience of self-authentication."

Stolorow, among others, has pointed to the ubiquity and

seriousness of sadism and masochism and how they relate to self disturbances, particularly narcissistic issues. This concept provides a new way of looking at the phenomenon of violence combined with sexual perversion.

If you doubt the pervasiveness of sadomasochism as a component of sexuality for a significant proportion of the population, a visit to a pornographic movie will convince you. In each of three movies chosen completely at random, I discovered one or more overtly sadistic or masochistic acts, i.e., beating with chains or whips, sexual intercourse involving pain or humiliation. This lends some credence to the belief, often expressed by those who would ban pornography, that there is an inevitable association between the introduction of pornography into a community and heightened levels of violence.

The infliction of pain on oneself (masochism) or on others (sadism) is often combined with sexuality in sadomasochistic perversions. Here, too, the underlying dynamic is the attempt to achieve a sense of cohesion.

Most individuals experience during orgasm a feeling of both intense self-realization and surrender. Orgasm is intensely self-confirmatory and, at the same time, an occasion for merger with a loved one. In the mature personality, this momentary loss of the self through orgastic merger is pleasurable. But in the individual with a deficient sense of self, the experience is disorienting, shattering in its effect on the sense of continuity. In an effort to preserve some sense of self, the sexual experience is tinged with masochistic or sadistic features. In the case of the masochist, as with Rhonda, the self is integrated by means of experienced pain. With the sadist, the integration comes from inflicting the pain on others. In each case, sexual satisfaction can only result if the threatened self-dissolution accompanying orgasm is offset by the pathologically integrating rituals of sadomasochism.

"The Janus-faced quality of the orgasm in both offering the promise of self-articulation and posing the threat of self-dissolution may account for the elaborate ritualization with which the structurally deficient individual must surround his perverse acts," writes Stolorow.

Sexual perversions typically illustrate sexuality used to combat a threatened dissolution of identity. The psychiatrist M. Masud R. Khan, after a lifetime spent in the study of sexual perversions, summarized his findings in 1979 in the already classic *Alienation in Perversions*. "All perversions entail a fundamental alienation from self in the person concerned and the attempt is to find personalization through the elaborate machinery of sexual experiences."

The personality of the pervert often turns out, according to Khan, "more like a collage than an integrated, coherent entity." The pervert often experiences himself as separate from his body; he often requires confirmation of his own existence through the mechanism of shared body experiences. What was sought in many of the cases studied by Khan was a shared body fusion. Through polymorphous perverse sexual activities, the individual achieves a state of euphoria, followed later by feelings of confusion, excitement, trauma and, in one patient's words, the sensation of having been "gorged."

"Contact by touch, penetration, sight and incorporation (the taking of the other's sexual organs in the mouth) was often imperative to bring about the euphoria and the establishment of body fusion which is experienced as both intensely pleasurable and anxiety provoking." As one of Khan's patients described his oral sexual encounters, "I feel it is more than an indulgence. I am trying to find out something. I know my body from outside only. I have no sense of being in it. I know other people exist, like my wife exists, but I have to *feel* it before I can be sure of her existence. I am sorting myself out into a separate person and getting to know and feeling my own body reality."

As with sadism, masochism and sexual perversion, polymorphous perverse bodily experiences lead to the temporary augmentation of the sense of identity. This is only temporary, however. "It's very important about these body experiences, that in spite of their excited and ecstatic quality and value for the patient, they are, at the same time, felt to be traumatic, bewildering and shaming," according to Khan. After many years of studying various forms of sexual perversion and polymorphous sexual activity,

Khan has drawn a composite picture of the individual driven to the achievement of these experiences.

Typically, such people appear normal in every respect and their outward behavior is, in Khan's words, "characterized by amicable cleverness, tidy appearance, compliance and apathetic docility." They have little capacity for real initiative and tend to be "intrigued, provoked or seduced into doing things." They quickly form acquaintanceships but derive little pleasure from these hastily constructed relationships. Their enthusiasms disappear as quickly as they are formed. People rapidly replace each other in their affections. Most characteristic of all is what Khan refers to as their "latent emotionality": "a confused, formless, obsessive state of tension which they nurture diligently, although it is both painful and exhausting." This state of tension leads to fervent, short-lived attachments pursued with passionate intensity and then, just as suddenly, abruptly dropped in the manner of Anita. They seek comfort and contact through clinging, dependent behavior and, as with all dependencies, ambivalence and even hatred develop toward the person they feel themselves becoming dependent upon. To solve this dilemma created by their requirement for closeness, despite an inability to tolerate the accompanying dependence, they respond by creating moods of tension, in fact, a craving for tension.

"It is a trait of this type of ego distortion that it builds up a craving for tension. It feeds on tension just as avidly as it is compulsively trying to discharge it," writes Khan. According to Khan's formulations, which are admittedly speculative, such persons are unable to experience their own aggression. This failure leads to indirect and subtle ways of handling aggression. For example, aggression is typically transformed into sadism, the need to control and manipulate others. The sense of control is gratified by involving other people in their activities which entail merger and intimacy by means of perverse physical contact. But ultimately, this intimacy turns out to be bewildering and traumatic. In the words of one of Khan's patients: "I feel I get involved in a game to which I have lost most of the clues."

The need for other people, when combined with fear of the loss of the self through merger, leads to experiences in which the other person serves as the measure of the borderline person's reality. This may even extend to the way the borderline individual experiences his own body. Most curious of all is the borderline's relationship to his own thought processes. There often exists the feeling that the other person can tell him what to think, how to respond, and can even engage in thought reading. "If you're so sure that I have something on my mind, then you should tell me what it is," beseeched one of McGlashan's patients in response to his query, "What's on your mind?"

Such a response may be followed up with a request that the other person provide the thoughts and feelings which are experienced as missing. Thus the momentary contents of consciousness are determined by the contributions of the other person, who may, after a while, even be experienced as the initiator of the borderline individual's own mental activity. McGlashan describes this as a *projective identification process* "wherein not only the content of mind gets projected into the other but also the mind-capable-of-initiating-mental-activity gets projected into the other. The other becomes the responsible agent of one's subjective experience." If continued long enough, this attribution of one's inner processes to another can lead to a form of madness in which one's own thoughts are somehow controlled by outside malevolent forces.

At the turn of the century, a brilliant young psychoanalyst, Victor Tausk, himself later a victim of suicide, described the process in a classic paper, "On the Origin of the 'Influencing Machine' in Schizophrenia." Tausk showed that machines or electronic gadgetry may be delusionally identified as the source for a disturbed individual's "insane" thoughts. But, as we've mentioned repeatedly, the borderline individual is not insane, at least not according to the standard meaning of the term, nor do his projections usually extend to outright declarations that he is under alien control. In its attenuated form, however, it can appear as a suspicion that the other person is out to do harm.

"Eloise often, for example, expressed a breakthrough of suicidal thoughts in our sessions which were usually split off and successfully denied," McGlashan has written. "Since such thoughts occurred with greater frequency and intensity while she was with me, she felt I was responsible for their presence and concluded (with terror) that my hidden agenda was her suicide!"

In milder forms, the other person becomes the source of one's own subjective experience: Am I really thinking these thoughts because they're *my* thoughts or are *you* somehow responsible for the thoughts that I'm now having?

At this point it's necessary to again remind you, the reader, that not all borderline individuals display all of these characteristics. They may, in fact, display only some of them and then only in attenuated forms. Again, the absence of an inner sense of self may remain confined to the subtle forms discussed earlier, such as a pervasive feeling of emptiness, meaninglessness and personal deadness. The experience may be described as "loneliness," "depression" or a prevailing sense of inner unfulfillment. Typical of this is Lynn.

Among the Barracuda

Lynn is an attractive thirty-five-year-old freelance writer with a secret: over the years she has built up a dependence on Valium and barbiturates which, if discovered, could threaten her professional career. Since she's now unable any longer to obtain her drugs through legitimate channels, she depends for her supply on "street" suppliers. The self-destructive, even physically dangerous aspects of her behavior aren't lost on her, however. "The pills make me feel, I guess you might say, kind of depressed. But at least when I'm depressed I feel real, it's the real me. I always feel alone even when my husband and four daughters are around. Funny"—she laughs without mirth—"I feel abandoned living in an eight-hundred-thousand-dollar house with five other people." When I inquired why she took the medication she responded with a question of her own. "What do you take to feel good?"

Lynn speaks of an abiding need to be cuddled, held, caressed and fondled. Such body experiences serve, in her words, "the purpose of confirming my identity and self." A chronic feeling of "depletion" drives her toward "suckling behavior," which, more often than she wishes, results in episodic affairs, "sport fucks," as she refers to them. She feels that parts of her body are "ugly," particularly her breasts.

"Love serves as a means of filling a gaping hole inside me," she explains when expressing her sexual preference for fellatio. "It's as if somehow this emptiness inside me is filled by taking it into my mouth and gulping it down. Briefly, but only briefly, I feel warm and feel filled. The emptiness isn't so painful."

Last year, Lynn's drug use and feelings of emptiness became so alarming to her that she went to a psychiatrist. She recalls the need to touch and be touched by her psychiatrist, a procedure he severely limited and ultimately forbade altogether. "To me, I only feel real when I'm able to touch another person . . . just talking seems somehow so unreal. Often I would just take his hand. He permitted that for a while and then said he'd come to the conclusion that such behavior was, in his words, 'ultimately destructive.' I still go to him twice a week, but it's not the same thing since he forbade the touching. This doesn't help my feelings of being abandoned and alone."

Lynn's activities include frequent and extravagant shopping forays, during which she adds to her collection of rare paintings. Over the years her collection has grown in size and value. She is proud of her business acumen and speaks frequently of the advantage her "superior I.Q." gives her when negotiating with other people. To her, life is a battlefield in which one's guard can never be let down, even for a moment. Other women are "barracudas who'll chew right into everything you've got if you let them." Even her own mother isn't to be trusted, can't be depended upon to play any other role than that of a "spoiler." "No matter what I have, I can count on my mother driving over from across town to spoil it for me. That's why I call her the Spoiler."

Lynn speaks scornfully of others as if they don't quite measure up as human beings. One day she said to me, "Take somebody like you, I bet your wife is a very ordinary person. That's the way it always is: a man with a lot on the ball is married to a cipher while, if things were fair, somebody like you would be married to somebody like me." Since she knows nothing of my wife, Lynn's speculations are based on fantasy. In this case a recurrent one: she is a superior being forced by fate into taking "second place to a bunch of ciphers."

What makes Lynn of particular importance in regard to the matters discussed in this book is the consequences which follow from her precarious sense of self. Insecure and vulnerable despite wealth, professional attainments and social position, she is driven into promiscuous sex and destructive drug use in an attempt to restore a sense of ease. "Sometimes I think this hole inside me will never be closed up." But she's unable to derive comfort and satisfaction from revealing herself to others.

"The world is filled with a lot of failed people who can't cope and therefore try to screw you," she comments. Coping to Lynn means the acquisition of wealth and professional attainment. But when it comes to the establishment of satisfying and enduring interpersonal relationships, she would have to admit, if she thought about it at all, that she, too, is, in a sense, a "failed person." For her, relationships must always take on a primitive quality involving touching, caressing, smelling, tasting and so on.

In order to restore her sense of wholeness and aliveness, Lynn abuses herself with drugs, which, while providing a momentary sense of cohesion, are ruining her health and threatening her career. The continuity of her own boundaries shifts from the momentary, drug-induced sense of wholeness to later frantic, desperate efforts to "feel alive" once again through sex, particularly primitive, chaotic sexuality heavily tinged with masochism and degradation. To be sexually "used" by another person provides the requisite shame, anger and disillusionment which she then quells by means of her drugs. Behind all this desperation and frenzy is an inner restlessness that reaches out repetitively to other people for satisfaction. But since other people in their individuality are "ciphers," they have nothing to offer Lynn but the impersonality of their bodies. But this, too, is threatening. Since Lynn discovers the "real me" in sexual intimacy, she's dependent on the other person. As they leave they, in a sense, take the most important part of Lynn with them.

Masud Khan wrote of the experience of such a patient: "These bodily intimacies created a mild state of euphoria while they lasted. Touching, licking, devouring with eager eyes, played a large part in the foreplay. What was quite often frightening for the patients was the sudden realization during such an episode that they had lost sense of their own body image. This fusion of body images is significant. They felt confused, excited, traumatized and gorged . . . some of the oral and tongue play was aimed at establishing this primary body fusion with the partner."

In Lynn's case, the body intimacies are frustrating, leaving her more vulnerable and needful of pills. "This gaping hole inside me can't be filled by anything or anybody . . . so when I want to get some real relief . . . want to sometime get into contact with myself I take some pills and turn off all things that usually fill up my days: the clothes, the shopping trips, the inane people whom I can't communicate with because they're so stupid . . . I just turn it all off and descend into myself where it's very quiet . . . the pills make me kind of, well, depressed is the only word I can think of to describe it. With the pills I can get into myself, at least when I'm depressed I'm really feeling something . . . the depression is real. I'm real. It's really me."

The instability in the sense of self, as exemplified by Lynn, Anita, Esther and Rhonda, results, according to modern object relations theory, from the person's previous failures many years earlier to internalize soothing, dependable anxiety reducing relationships with a mother or mother substitute. As a result of this failure, the person destined for a self disorder is peculiarly vulnerable over his or her lifetime to disruptions in the sense of who he is. When under stress, for example, particularly the stress of establishing or maintaining a close, intimate relationship, such persons "come apart" emotionally. Since they have never established stable internal sources of self-esteem, they experience themselves as abandoned and terribly alone. Their identity has, in a way, been stolen from them, purloined by the abandoning person, whom they now hate with the deepest of passions. "Scratch a lover and find a foe" is an experience that the borderline relives over and over.

At some point the borderline individual's feelings and behavior further regress to earlier infantile stages which the "normal" person has outgrown years ago. Envy and rage intensify, thus contributing even more to the sense of loneliness and utter abandonment. On the one hand lacking all internal sources of support and self-affirmation, and on the other unable to trust others to provide what is missing in himself, the borderline personality experiences an annihilating sense of fragmentation.

But why are borderline personalities so susceptible to abandonment? What is it in the loss of a love relationship, for instance, that the borderline tolerates so poorly? Most psychiatrists who specialize in the treatment of borderline disorders consider the borderlines' specific vulnerability to rejection as stemming from their failure to establish and maintain comforting and sustaining memories of important people whenever these people are physically absent. Once again, the analogy is to earlier stages of development.

Normally, at about eighteen months of age the child forms an *evocative memory capacity* that enables him or her to retain a concept of the permanence of other people through the incorporation of internalized images and memories of these people as part of the self. Mother and child are, in a sense, one within the developing mind of the eighteen-month-old.

In the case of borderline personalities, the evocative memory capacity is postulated to be missing or poorly formed. When stressed by the threatened loss of an important and sustaining relationship, the borderline regresses to what psychiatrists call *recognition memory capacity:* others must be physically present in order for them to be experienced as real. A child at this stage of *recognition memory*—prior to the formation of *evocative memory* —requires his mother's physical presence in order to experience comfort. Only later, after the child achieves evocative memory, is it possible to gain comfort merely from the expectation of encountering mother a few hours later. In the meantime, the child can rely on his internalized images of mother to sustain him. In fact, the image becomes part of himself.

To the borderline such identifications are impossible: the self is experienced as fragmentary and extremely dependent on the *actual presence* of the loved one. In response to absence—like the child limited by his recognition memory, to whom mother no longer exists as she closes the front door—the borderline experiences an acute sense of abandonment. Lacking any sustaining or supporting fantasies of those who are important to him, the borderline rages against the feelings of helplessness which swell up and threaten to strangle his internal life altogether.

Naturally concepts derived from childhood cannot provide a totally satisfactory explanation of adulthood problems in self experience. Nevertheless, the cautious formulation and employment of object relations theory provides a workable model or framework to understand the borderline personality's fragile sense of self.

"The end result in the adult borderline is an inability to depend on internal sources for soothing and self-esteem and a concomitant inability to trust the external environment to provide what is missing within the person," according to Dr. Gerald Adler, a psychoanalyst at the Boston Psychoanalytic Institute.

An environment that cannot be trusted is an environment that must be combated and fought against at every moment with all the strength and vigor that can be commandeered. This is the motto of the psychopath. As we move along the continuum from the borderline personality to the psychopath we enter the realm of the psychic outlaw, the desperado. The dynamics, however, are the same: the psychopath, as with the narcissist and the borderline, is an individual with a fragile sense of integration who bolsters his failures not just by exploitation but, if the occasion demands it, by violence. What makes this particular manipulator so interesting are the implications that his behavior has for both the legal system and our broader social environment. But in order to appreciate the full impact of the psychopath, it's necessary to delve into some history.

VI

The Psychopath

"We are now confronted by a band of psychopaths in motley, in their various ways evil and sometimes beneficent, headlong and magical, louts and schemers, children unrestrained and charged with energy . . . drunkards and forgers, addicts, flower children, Mafia loan shark battering his victim who can't pay up, charming actor who makes crippled little boys and girls laugh, charming orator, murderer, the prophet who makes us love life again, gentle, nomadic guitarist, hustling politician, hustling judge, writers and preachers coming back with a vengeance to visit retribution on the middle classes that rejected them, whore and pimp, cop on the take, changers filling the multitudes with joy, prancing Adonis of rock concerts, the saint who lies down in front of tractors, a student rebel, icily dominating Nobel Prize winner stealing credit from laboratory assistants, the businessman who then steals the scientist's perception, turning it into millions . . . all, all doing their thing, which is the psychopathic commandment."

Psychopaths, Alan Harrington

Chains, Dungeons and Bloody Noses

In 1793 Philippe Pinel, a young physician from the south of France, was appointed director of Bicêtre, one of the largest mental hospitals in Paris. Pinel's principal claim to fame now stems from his audacious and, at the time, widely criticized release of the mental patients under his care from their chains and dungeons—the routine "treatment" provided the insane in prerevolutionary France. But perhaps equal in importance to Pinel's efforts to free the mental patients from inhumane treatment were his observations concerning a wealthy nobleman confined for life to a mental hospital after brutally murdering a peasant woman.

"An only son of a weak and indulgent mother, was encouraged in the gratification of every caprice and passion, of which a violent and untutored temper was susceptible," Pinel wrote. Apparently, the man's temper was both prodigious and unpredictable. "Every instance of opposition or resistance, raised him to acts of fury." When riled he "assaulted his adversary with the audacity of a savage." And, by the time of the murder, had established a pattern of putting to death dogs, horses or "any other animal that offended him."

This explosive man's contacts with his neighbors, although stopping short of homicide, frequently ended in raucous brawls. "If ever he went to a fete or any other public meeting, he was sure to excite such tumult and quarrels, as terminated in actual pugilistic encounters and generally left the scene with a bloody nose."

But the most interesting aspect of Pinel's patient was the contrast between these violent episodes and what appears to have been his "normal" personality. When unmoved by passion, he showed a sound judgment, managing an estate without assistance, and was described by Pinel as distinguishing himself by "acts of beneficence and compassion." Such intervals of quiescence alternated regularly, however, with "wounds, lawsuits, and an unhappy propensity to quarrel." Finally, a fit of rage directed against a peasant woman who had verbally attacked him led to his hurling her into a well, killing her. This was too much, even for the relatively permissive standards which prevailed at the time in the relations between the nobility and the peasants; the nobleman was captured and confined to Bicêtre.

After reviewing the nobleman's records and conducting an interview, Pinel was puzzled concerning the nature of his patient's insanity. There certainly didn't seem to be any doubt that a person must somehow be insane to have carried out such a brutal act, but of what did his insanity consist? At no time did he display the emotional outbursts which ultimately had led to murder and subsequent confinement. At all times he was capable of reason and persuasion; he was totally cooperative, and displayed none of the usual rantings and ravings that Pinel customarily encountered among the other inmates of Bicêtre. Certainly such a person was hard to reconcile with contemporary theories concerning mental illness.

In the eighteenth century, mental illnesses were considered disorders of the intellect, hence, partially corrected by "reason." Several of the early textbooks on mental illness, in fact, were written by philosophers rather than physicians, including two works contributed by Kant and Hegel. If mental illness stems from diseases of reason, it seemed reasonable, in turn, that treatment should be provided by those skilled in "right reason," i.e., philosophers.

But the nobleman suffered from no defect in his reasoning capacity; in fact, if anything, he displayed a kind of "insight" into his difficulty, correctly recognizing that his "emotions" or "feelings" were not under the control of his "reason." Although today we have no problem with such distinctions, it was in direct contradiction to contemporary thinking during Pinel's time.

Starting as far back as the Greeks and continuing up to Pinel and his nobleman patient, the defining characteristic of mental illness was a derangement of reason (delirium). Thus in the Age of

Reason, peculiarities and abnormalities of behavior (mental illness) were the result of deficiencies and distortions of reason. To lose one's reason was to be insane; conversely, insanity stems from a defect in normal reason.

But Pinel's experience with his violence-prone patient forced him to the revolutionary proposal that insanity can exist without defects in the reasoning capacity, a state of affairs described by Pinel as "manie sans délire." Once such a possibility was recognized, Pinel had no difficulty in discovering other patients in whom reasoning was preserved despite the presence of clear-cut mental illness.

"I was not a little surprised," Pinel wrote, "to find many maniacs who, at no period, gave evidence of any lesion of the understanding but who were under the dominion of instinctive and abstract fury."

Other students of mental disease confirmed Pinel's observations that emotional disorders could exist without affecting a person's rationality. An American physician, Benjamin Rush, a man with interests which ranged far beyond medicine or mental illness (he was one of the signers of the Declaration of Independence and an ardent opponent of slavery and capital punishment), took things a step further by suggesting that certain character traits formerly associated with "vice" might, in fact, be the products of "disease." To prove his point, Rush, like Pinel, cited a nobleman who, despite every social and economic advantage, behaved so bizarrely that Rush was convinced the person must be insane.

Drawing on the description of a sixteenth-century French statesman, Maximilien de Béthune, Duke of Sully, Rush analyzed at a distance of almost two hundred years a notorious character named Servin.

Like Pinel's nobleman, Servin appears to have enjoyed every advantage: he was a wealthy landowner; a master of philosophy, theology and mathematics; an accomplished and persuasive speaker; a dramatist, poet and musician; an excellent horseman, dancer and accomplished athlete. According to the duke's description, however, Servin was also grim, false, given to "every conceivable vice," a liar who could not be trusted or depended upon and a man whose drinking and carousing ended not unexpectedly in his death while in a brothel "blaspheming."

According to Rush, Servin's character illustrated what he called "moral derangement." In such a person, the "moral faculty" is affected in the same way as memory, judgment or imagination might be affected. Citing cases from the medical literature in which physical illness affected those latter abilities, Rush suggested that the "moral faculty" could also be altered unfavorably by physical conditions and, hence, constitute illness rather than vice.

Rush's interest in moral insanity stemmed, no doubt, at least partially from a strict Scottish Presbyterian background. To such a man a "moral faculty" seemed a natural expression for the human mind which also included "the principle of faith, conscience and the sense of deity." But Rush's conviction that certain acts formerly regarded as criminal or sinful might indeed spring from a diseased mind, provided a new and intriguing way of looking at many formerly inexplicable human behaviors. The will can be diseased, Rush claimed, "when it acts without a motive by a kind of involuntary power." The image he evoked to explain such a mechanism was, predictably, a medical one: "Exactly the same thing takes place in this disease of the will that occurs when the arm or foot is moved convulsively without an act of the will, or even in spite of it."

Despite the limitations of a concept which compared certain disordered behaviors to epileptic seizures, Rush's ideas on "moral derangement," along with Pinel's mania without delirium, did away with a firmly held but incorrect demarcation between mental health and illness. The discovery that mental illness could exist in the presence of a normal intelligence and understanding opened the way for confusion that persists today concerning the distinction between sanity and madness. It is from within this misty no-man's-land between the ill and the merely ill-intentioned, between the insane and viciously inclined, that the *psychopath* first appeared to haunt the conscience and to confound the judgment of psychiatrists and lawyers up to the present day.

Insanity Trials

If a person can be insane yet retain normal ability to reason, is he responsible for his actions? In the instance of Pinel's nobleman patient, the dilemma was conveniently solved by locking him away in an insane asylum. If the murder had occurred in England, however, the nobleman might very well have ended his days swinging from the end of a rope. While changes in attitude toward mental illness were well under way within the medical profession, a similar but much more restrained and groping reevaluation was occurring within English law in regard to guilt and innocence.

It's not always appreciated that medicine and the law exert mutual and often contradictory influences upon each other. While today we're accustomed to the testimony of psychiatrists and psychologists within the courtroom, their very presence in an eighteenth- or nineteenth-century court would have been unthinkable. At that time, the law, especially criminal law, was committed to the theory that a person was strictly and totally responsible for his actions. This flowed naturally from the theological idea that people possess free will and are free to choose. If they choose wrongly, so the theory goes, they must take the consequences, however harsh and unpleasant they may be.

In English law, a man thrusting a woman into a well was fully responsible for such "vice" and if, in addition, anyone bothered to demonstrate that the assailant was ordinarily capable of sensible and reasoned discourse, so much stronger was the argument that he should be done away with. But there were changes soon to come about that would turn the proposition of will and total responsibility on its head. The stimulus for this was a series of color-ful and controversial "insanity trials."

In 1724 Edward Arnold was put on trial on the charge of at-tempted murder. Arnold was accused of shooting and wounding a Lord Onslow. At the trial the prosecutors established, along with Arnold's guilt, that he could bargain, make purchases and calcu-late correctly and, most interestingly, that he had been under medical care for a series of strange and troubling personality quirks that came to light during the trial.

On occasion Arnold had complained to friends and relatives that Lord Onslow had cast a spell on him, hidden "bugs" in his body and had even taken physical possession of him in order to torment him. Such information was troubling to the judge, who, despite the legal precedent limited to the matter of strict account-ability, charged the jury to weigh in the balance whether or not Arnold's peculiarities interfered in any way with his capacity to "distinguish between good and evil." Certainly it seemed beyond doubt that Arnold had actually fired the shot that wounded On-slow, but in what state of mind and with what intention?

"If he was under the visitation of God, and could not distin-guish between good and evil, and did not know what he did, though he committed the greatest offense, yet he could not be guilty of any offense against any law whatsoever; for guilt arises from the mind and the wicked will and the intention of the man. If a man be deprived of his reason and, consequently, of his inten-tion he cannot be guilty; and if that be the case, though he had actually killed Lord Onslow, he is exempted from punishment."

At this point, perhaps carried away by the implications of what he had been saying, the judge introduced a key reservation in his charge that the jury should assess Arnold's reason and intent.

"When a man is guilty of a great offense, it must be very plain and clear before [he] is allowed such an exemption [from re-sponsibility] . . . it must be a man that is totally deprived of his understanding and memory, and doth not know what he is doing, no more than an infant, than a brute, or a wild beast."

The judge's qualification requiring the jury to consider whether Arnold was "a wild beast" served to undo the unprecedented and courageous remarks the judge had made earlier. Arnold—pitiable as he was with his delusions and fairly obvious derangement—was obviously not on the level of a "wild beast" and, hence, was sentenced to be hanged. Three quarters of a century later, a second "insanity trial" forced the issue of intent even further.

On May 15, 1800, in London's Theatre Royal in Drury Lane, James Hadfield, a twenty-nine-year-old former soldier, fired a pistol in the direction of the King. Apparently, Hadfield's alleged assassination attempt was carried out from so far away that few people believed that he actually intended to harm the King. More important for the defense than Hadfield's amateurism, however, were the circumstances leading up to the assassination attempt.

An exemplary soldier throughout his career, Hadfield had been severely wounded about the head and neck six years earlier in France at the battle of Roubaix. According to medical reports, his head had almost been severed from his body and a portion of his skull sheared completely off. Upon his recovery, Hadfield demonstrated dramatic changes in personality, including the belief that he was King George. In addition, Hadfield began complaining of the imminence of a fiery Armageddon in which God would destroy the world. One way of preventing this, Hadfield believed, was to sacrifice his own life. But since Hadfield held strong reservations about suicide, he dreamed up the scheme whereby the state could do the job for him as a punishment for an attempt against the life of the King.

With all of Hadfield's bad luck in the past, the time had come, it seems, for things to begin looking up. The change in his fortunes came principally in the form of his defender at his trial. His court-appointed attorney, rather than an inexperienced and, as is usually the case, unwilling defender, was one of the most brilliant and successful lawyers in London, Thomas Erskine, later to be appointed lord chancellor.

Erskine, from the very beginning, set out to demonstrate Hadfield's insanity. To do so, however, he first had to overcome the earlier precedent set in the Arnold case: Hadfield was no closer to a "wild beast" than Arnold before him and if that were to be the sole criterion of sanity, Hadfield clearly was doomed.

Focusing on the writings of several eminent legal commentators, Erskine set out to show that their insistence on a total deprivation of memory and understanding was not only foolish in conception but impossible in attainment.

"If a total deprivation of memory was intended by these great lawyers in the literal sense of the word:—if it was meant that to protect a man from punishment, he must be in such a state of prostrated intellect as not to know his name nor his condition, nor his relation to others—that if a husband, he should not know he was married; or if a father, he could not remember that he had children; nor know the road to his house . . . then no such madness ever existed in the world."

After making this telling point, Erskine went on to detail his impression of the insane. As he correctly pointed out, most emotional disorders do not affect all but only some aspects of the personality. In addition, different personality characteristics are affected by different emotional disorders. As Erskine rather flamboyantly put it: "Reason is not driven from her seat, but distraction sits down upon it along with her."

In essence, Erskine was arguing amid the hubbub of a crowded London courtroom what Pinel had grasped in the comparative seclusion of his consulting room within an insane asylum: reason and insanity are not mutually exclusive.

"Delusion . . . where there is no frenzy or raving madness, is the true character of insanity . . . I must convince you not only that the unhappy prisoner was a lunatic, within my own definition of lunacy, but that the act in question was the immediate offspring of disease."

Apparently Erskine succeeded fairly well in convincing the jury and Hadfield was acquitted, an affirmation of the presiding judge's final charge to the jury: "If a man is in a deranged state of mind at the time, he is not criminally answerable for his acts."

Following these trials, English and American psychiatrists began concentrating on what was known at the time as "moral insanity."

James Cowles Prichard, an anthropologist and early ethnologist as well as a psychiatrist, wrote in 1835 in his *Treatise on Insanity and Other Disorders Affecting the Mind,* "The morbid phenomena which this disease displays in the moral constitution or feelings are independent of any corresponding affection of the understanding . . . the sudden anger of a person laboring under moral insanity and subject to paroxysms of rage is not the result of fantasied provocation which the individual has sustained from him who is the victim or object of his malice. It is not the revenge of supposed injury, but an immediate impulse arising spontaneously in the mind which is diseased only in its moral constitution."

Prichard's new perspective is reflected in his classification of mental disorders. He speaks of "monomania" as a "partial insanity"; mania as "raving madness"; and dementia as "incoherence." These three classifications affect the "understanding or rational powers" and therefore, according to Prichard, are forms of "intellectual insanity." Thus far, his classification is very much in line with earlier conceptions in which insanity remained a matter of impaired reasoning. But Prichard didn't stop at this point. The originality of his contribution consisted in the distinction that he made between "intellectual insanity" and what he called "moral insanity": "a madness consisting of a morbid perversion of the natural feelings, affections, inclinations, temper, habits, moral dispositions and natural impulses without any remarkable disorder or defect of the intellect or knowing and reasoning faculties, and particularly without any insane illusion or hallucination."

Prichard's observations were to have far-reaching implications in both psychiatry and the law. In many respects, they were similar to Pinel's mania without delirium. Prichard had gone further, however, in suggesting that moral insanity often consists in disturbances or changes in the emotions that are so minor as to go unnoticed by the untrained or inattentive observer. Often, only those who know the affected individual are likely to notice that he has somehow changed.

Prichard, in effect, was emphasizing that moral insanity may amount to little more than an accentuation of certain personality traits which have characterized the affected individual since childhood, thus blurring the margins between behavior caused by disease and that which is secondary to eccentricity or disturbances in normal character. This, of course, opens the door for wide-ranging speculations concerning the presence of "moral insanity," as an explanation for certain heretofore inexplicable crimes.

"In fact, the varieties of moral insanity are perhaps as numerous as the modifications of feelings or passion in the human mind," Prichard wrote in *Treatise on Insanity*.

Seven years later, Prichard spelled out the implications as he saw them with the adoption of the concept of moral insanity. "The admission of such a state as really existing is very important in a legal point of view; it brings with it many inconvenient results and it seems, in some cases, to confound insanity with eccentricity, or natural singularity of character."

Prichard apparently was fully aware of the implications of what he was saying: that in certain cases, criminals might be excused from punishment from crimes that they had committed. "But it is vain to shut our eyes against truth whatever inconvenient results may follow from admitting it."

The Taint of Degeneration

Prichard's concept of moral insanity was imported into the United States in the early years of the nineteenth century. Its most ardent defender was a thirty-one-year-old general practitioner, Isaac Ray. Ray also divided mania (insanity) into "intellectual mania" and "affective" or "moral" mania, with both of these variants further distinguished by their general or particular nature. Thus, Ray supported Prichard's distinctions, which placed the emotional side of the mind on an equal level with the intellectual; both could lead to various forms of insanity.

At the basis of Ray's theory (it was truly a theory since Ray was a rural general practitioner who had little direct contact with psychiatric patients) was the modern-sounding concept that the brain was the substrate of the psyche. "It is an undoubted truth that the intellectual and affective powers are connected with abnormal conditions of the brain."

Despite the modernity of these views on the origins of mental disorders, Ray's theoretical ideas were based ultimately on his unbridled enthusiasm for phrenology—strict localizations of mental faculties within the brain. In some instances, these "centras" could be located by skillful palpation of the skull while, in other instances, the centras could only be inferred. What was important in Ray's conception of moral mania, however, was his insistence that subtle disturbances of the emotional sphere could exist without affecting the other aspects of mental life. This is a pivotal distinction that prevails in our present-day concept of the psychopath.

"In this form of insanity, the derangement is confined to one or a few of the affective faculties, the rest of the moral and intellectual constitution preserving its ordinary integrity." As examples of such limited disorders, Ray cites an irresistible inclination in an otherwise honest person to steal or the inability to tell the truth despite any discernible motive for lying.

Not unexpectedly, Ray's equation of "crime with illness" raised an uproar among American psychiatrists and legal theorists which continues today. "It is a mere question of words and saves the trouble of thought," wrote one commentator at the time. "All that comes out of it is to deprive the word 'insanity' of any real meaning."

These sometimes acrimonious cavils among nineteenth-century specialists involved infinitely more than mere hair-splitting distinctions. They brought about important changes in our medical and legal definitions of insanity. For one thing, the formerly distinct but false line separating sense from madness was done away with through the discovery that grave emotional disturbances could exist that were not due to disorders of understanding. Thus a person with moral insanity could be reasonable, free of delusions and, on most occasions—at least to the superficial observer—not behave out of the ordinary. The concept "moral mania" referred to asocial, ethically inferior behavior which stemmed not from "normal evil" but from illness.

If moral mania was due to a brain disorder, it was only a step to considering it hereditary. In the middle and late nineteenth century, particularly in Europe, specialists in the nervous system developed a theory that mental illness was the result of "degeneration." In some instances, degeneration ran in families as a hereditary disposition, while in others the disturbances were acquired secondary to life experiences. In either case, the "taint of degeneration" once acquired caused a mental imbalance. "Their mental situation can be explained with a single phrase: the equilibrium between all the cerebral function has been destroyed," wrote an authority at the time. "No degeneration without mental imbalance."

For several years, strenuous efforts ensued aimed at recognizing individuals afflicted with the "mental imbalance." Various physical traits were cited as characteristic of what one authority referred to as the "born criminal":

"Generally speaking, the ears of the born criminal are handle shaped, with thick growth of hair on the head, sparse beard, sunken eye cavities, enormous jaw bone, chin squared or jutting, broad cheek bones—in short, a mongolian or, perhaps, a negroid type."

In time, such pseudoscientific claims were revealed as nonsense. More important and less easily dismissed, however, were certain trenchant behavioral observations concerning one subclass of "degenerates" known as *psychopaths*.

At the basis of psychopathy is what an early writer on the subject described as an "irritable weakness." "The tainted are, with uncommon ease, strongly engaged by the most varying stimuli and impulses. That is to say that they are irritable but the function thereby released has no real force, nor is it properly lasting. The nervous force of the tainted is rapidly drained and, thus, their irritability is allied to weakness."

According to nineteenth-century authorities, the psychopath formed strong personal attachments but, after a time, the positive feelings cooled or even were replaced by enmity. Psychopaths are sometimes cruel and often paradoxical in their behavior. They enjoy drawing attention to themselves. They revel in fantasy and are often boastful and proud. But since their behaviors are not usually looked upon as symptoms of mental illness, "laymen consider these individuals to be sensitive, lazy, cruel, mischievious and incorrigible children."

At the heart of the diagnosis of psychopathy was the recognition that a person could appear normal and yet close observation would reveal the personality to be irrational or even violent. Over the next fifty years, psychiatrists in France, Germany and England argued over how the psychopath could be defined. A representative selection drawn from the literature of the time illustrates the difficulties authorities were having in agreeing upon a definition of the condition which defied existing conventional psychiatric wisdom:

"A permanent mental condition independent of any sort of psychotic attack which manifests itself in the inability of the individual to commit himself to and follow a harmonic lifestyle in accordance with his best interests, a lifestyle adapted to the conditions in society."

"Permanent inadequacies in the area of emotion and will which are manifested primarily in an inability or difficulties to adjust to communal life."

1. "a lack of feeling quality to other humans, described by some as affectionlessness and others as lovelessness. In extreme cases he may be quite without feeling sense";
2. "a liability to act on impulse and without forethought";
3. "a combination of the previous two leading to aggression";
4. "a lack of shame and remorse for what has been done";
5. "a inability to profit by or use experience";
6. "a lack of drive or motivation leading to a general inadequacy of conduct so that a person does not use his apparent abilities."

"Unusual emotional reactions are almost universal in members of this class. They are often egocentrical, selfish, irritable, very suggestible, and easily fatigued mentally."

"They are self centered, self loving, obeying instinctively the law of self preservation which takes no thought for the welfare or well being of others and acting as if the immediate present were the only thing to be taken into account. Their conscious activity seems to be ruled almost entirely by the 'feeling' aspect instead of by thought and reflection. While they appear intelligent, they have a peculiar twist in their makeup that amounts to a defect in their power of discriminating between values."

With the rise of psychoanalysis to a position of prominence in America in the 1920s, definitions of psychopathy took on a distinctly "analytic" turn. While this involved some shift in emphasis, very little was gained in the way of clarification of the concept of psychopathy. "There seems to be little doubt that the special features of psychopathic behavior derived from a profound hatred of the father analytically determined by way of the inadequate resolution of the Oedipus conflict and strengthened through fears of castration," wrote Lindner in *Rebel Without a Cause.*

Despite the jargon and generally unhelpful references to such things as "incest" and "parricidal fantasies," psychoanalysts did agree among themselves that the psychopathic personality structure was "narcissistic," an observation which provides a pivotal insight into our contemporary understanding of these disorders of the self. Thus, psychopaths, rather than forming a distinct category completely separated from other emotional and mental disorders, are best thought of as a variation along the continuum of narcissistic disorders.

"In order to understand the psychopathic personality, it is essential to understand the evolving conceptualization of the narcissistic personality, since it is our opinion that psychopathic personalities represent one form, a severe form, of a narcissistic personality structure," according to Dr. Louis A. Leaff, associate professor of psychiatry, Medical College of Pennsylvania.

Leaff's statement was made in 1978 and it's mentioned here only as a preview of the directions that subsequent theories about psychopathic personalities would take over the years up to the 1980s. But in telling you this, I'm getting slightly ahead of myself. To really understand the psychopath and place him along the continuum of manipulative behaviors, it's necessary to step back four decades and examine the contributions of Hervey Cleckley, the man who brought the psychopath to world attention.

The Mask of Sanity

In 1941, Hervey Cleckley, a psychiatrist living in Augusta, Georgia, published a book, *The Mask of Sanity*. Cleckley was later to become famous as the psychiatrist who diagnosed and treated a case of multiple personality which was dramatized in the book and movie *The Three Faces of Eve*.

From his own experience on the wards of a neuropsychiatric hospital, Cleckley had become convinced of the failure of the traditional divisions of mental illness into "neurosis" and "psychosis" —along with such controversial conditions as schizophrenia—to adequately account for a new type of patient many psychiatrists were beginning to encounter in increasing numbers in their consulting rooms or, as in Cleckley's case, on the wards of the nation's mental hospitals.

In *The Mask of Sanity*, Cleckley described this new patient, the psychopath, who seemed totally free of the traditional symptoms of mental illness. For instance, psychopaths rarely shouted or screamed at their psychiatrists; failed to express any ideas that seemed delusional or "crazy"; rarely appeared nervous or ill at ease.

On the contrary, Cleckley's initial impression of his psychopathic patients included such items as "an easy security," "a freshness, artlessness, and candor"; "well informed, alert and entirely at ease, exhibiting a confidence in himself that the observer is likely to consider amply justified."

Such descriptions, coming from a psychiatrist who was well acquainted with mental illness and, in addition, possessed in abundance the considerable skills required to unravel sometimes convoluted and hidden emotional disorders, seemed inconsistent with Cleckley's claim that psychopaths "present a sociologic and psychiatric problem second to none." If psychopaths were so charming, rarely did physical harm to themselves or others and, finally, weren't deluded or anxious, in what sense were they a problem?

As Cleckley expressed it, a true understanding of the psychopath could never emerge if psychiatrists apishly followed the standard procedures of the time. In a face-to-face encounter, for instance, the psychopath appeared totally candid and relaxed and seemed to have little to fear. When asked about his difficulties, the psychopath in turn almost always provided convincing arguments either that the problems didn't exist or, failing this, that other people were primarily to be blamed for them.

Although Cleckley recognized his patients' explanations as self-serving and diverting rationalizations for the behavior which had led to their difficulties, he was also the first to suspect a smidgen of truth in the things the psychopath was telling him: their difficulties always stemmed from their relationships with other people.

"The disorder can be demonstrated only when the patient's activity meshes with the problems of ordinary living. It cannot be even remotely apprehended if we do not pay particular attention to his responses in those interpersonal relations that, to a normal man, are the most profound."

Cleckley's emphasis on interpersonal relations led him to conduct extensive interviews with relatives, spouses, teachers, employers—almost anyone who was willing to talk.

"To know psychopathy adequately, one must try to see them not merely with the physician's calm and relatively detached eye, but also with the eye of the ordinary man on the street, whom they confound and amaze," Cleckley wrote.

Alive and still in active practice in Augusta, Georgia, Cleckley at seventy-eight years of age is recognized today as the world's authority on the subject of the psychopathic personality. Cleckley has drawn up a list, culled from his more than fifty years' experience, of sixteen personality characteristics by which the psychopath can be identified. The list remains unequaled today for its brevity and precision.

1. Superficial charm and good "intelligence"
2. Absence of delusions and other signs of irrational thinking
3. Absence of "nervousness" or psychoneurotic manifestations
4. Unreliability
5. Untruthfulness and insincerity
6. Lack of remorse and shame
7. Inadequately motivated antisocial behavior
8. Poor judgment and failure to learn by experience
9. Pathologic egocentricity and incapacity for love
10. General poverty in major affective reactions
11. Specific loss of insight
12. Unresponsiveness in general interpersonal relations
13. Fantastic and uninviting behavior with drink and sometimes without
14. Suicide rarely carried out
15. Sex life impersonal, trivial and poorly integrated
16. Failure to follow any life plan

One of Cleckley's most famous patients was described under the pseudonym Anna. She was first seen by Cleckley when she was forty years old, and, writing several years later of the experience, Cleckley described her: good-looking, composed, yet giving the distinct impression of energy, playful spontaneity and vivid youth. She was, Cleckley writes, well informed on current affairs and able to discuss the music of Brahms, Schopenhauer's views on women, even Hamlet's essential conflicts as she saw them. Cleckley was clearly impressed with Anna and wrote of a "rather remarkable woman . . . with evidence of high intelligence and considerable learning . . . her manner suggested wide interests, fresh and contagious enthusiasm, and a taste for living that reached out towards all healthy expression. Having a cup of coffee with her or weeding a garden would somehow take on a special quality of fun and delightfulness."

At the time of Cleckley's first meeting with Anna, he had collected voluminous details on her life. And despite the reliability of his sources (parents, friends, the family doctor, a previous psychiatrist), Cleckley was at first inclined to believe that "the well authenticated facts of that record should be ignored since they were so thoroughly contradicted by the obvious characteristics of this appealing woman."

The "facts" regarding Anna began at around sixteen when she was discovered to be the inspiration for a boys' club at her local high school. The club was organized around group sexual activities and orgies. Eventually, the size of the group reached the proportions of a small army who visited Anna in a shed, or behind her house. As Cleckley discreetly put it: "Its former hayloft afforded reasonable privacy."

Initially, the existence of the "animal crackers," as the club was dubbed, came to the attention of Anna's parents, with the inevitable result. The wisest approach at the time seemed to have involved the parents putting the best possible face on the matter and hustling Anna out of town to a boarding school. Her "sincere" expression of repentance and regret softened the parents' reserve somewhat, but after discussing things with Anna, everyone agreed that she could no longer continue to attend school in their small southern town.

After several months at boarding school, Anna was caught cheating on exams, was suspected of several thefts within the dormitory and, most characteristic of all, produced a series of "calm lies about matters that were accepted as points of honor." Anna was expelled from the school only to repeat her performance in half a dozen other schools around the country.

Even allowing for the conservative views on adolescent behavior that prevailed at the time—the mid-1940s—Anna apparently was too much to be endured by even the most liberal and tolerant of teachers. In Cleckley's words, "her behavior at each place fell into similar but not identical patterns. Like the persisting theme in a complicated work of music her actions took diverse courses but came always to an identical point which for her was failure."

On occasion, Anna was able to finish a year in one school and thus slowly but gradually reached the point where she was eligible to take the entrance examination for a small college for women.

Her excellent performance on the exam, despite her poor academic and conduct records, resulted in her acceptance by the school. But after a series of cynically humorous pranks (such as driving off in a teacher's car or stealing stockings and jewelry from classmates), she was expelled. On all occasions, unless absolutely caught in the act, she denied any wrongdoing.

Her "sincerity" was apparently so convincing that, on occasion, people disbelieved their own observations. Certainly in those instances where any reasonable doubt existed, Anna was able to convince her accusers of her innocence. Furthermore, she established her innocence so convincingly that many times the authorities were taken completely off the track and resorted to accusing other students who failed to provide equally "convincing" protestations of their innocence. As with all psychopaths, Anna's expressions of denial were made with absolute conviction and sincerity.

On one occasion, Anna's father received a report indicating her failure in four subjects. This came as a surprise and shock since over the previous few months Anna's academic performance had been quite good. Puzzled and annoyed at this development, Anna's father called her for an explanation. Her relaxed manner and lack of anxiety led him to believe Anna's explanation that a mistake had occurred in the dean's office and that Anna's grades had been mistakenly confused with those of another girl who was doing poorly. Temporarily convinced but still somewhat doubtful, Anna's father was put completely at ease several days later when the promised official announcement arrived from the dean's office regarding the "mistake." Typed on the official school stationery and signed with the dean's signature, the revised report card was even better than Anna's performance over the previous several months. Soon, however, the true explanation emerged in the form of a separate letter from the dean detailing Anna's poor academic performance along with misconduct that threatened her immediate dismissal. At this point, confused and alarmed, her father personally visited the school, where, after a conference with the dean, Anna's deception was unmasked.

During a lull in the school day, Anna had wandered into the administration office and stolen the stationery and report card forms, which—personally typed and submitted by her—spoke so glowingly of her performance. When faced with the facts, Anna reacted with equanimity, apologized in a convincing way for her mistakes and admitted that it had been foolish of her to think that her deception could go undetected for long. Most interesting of all, she was unable to offer any reason why she had acted as she did. Nor was she at all curious or concerned about the possibility of discovering a reason for her behavior.

Over the years, Anna entered into numerous marriages. Her first husband, a wealthy architect, discovered soon after their marriage that Anna had seduced his younger brother, infecting them both with gonorrhea which she had contracted from a homosexual interior decorator with whom she had had an affair.

After the divorce, Anna entered a period when, in Cleckley's words, "she had fallen into the habit of marrying on an impulse apparently as trivial as what might lead another woman to buy a new hat." Among her husbands were taxi drivers, bar companions and welfare recipients. Her feelings toward these men were superficial and fickle. They were forgotten soon after the divorces and never mentioned again. Her sexual exploits included numerous bisexual affairs as well as group sex encounters, often with people she met casually in bars. "On being detected in activities that would produce fear, shame or consternation in others, this patient often showed simple insouciance," Cleckley wrote.

During the period of Cleckley's observations of Anna, his attitude remained one of bemused puzzlement and consternation. To him she always appeared poised, polite and "a paragon of happy behavior." His interviews with Anna's friends and relatives confirmed the impression of her genial good humor and feckless enthusiasm. One of her early husbands was impressed with what he called her unbelievable but somehow authentic innocence. No matter how sordid and chaotic the events of her life, Anna retained an attitude of calm persuasiveness. She was rarely angry, almost never showed any anxiety and, at all times, impressed others with her "sincerity and candor." She was accomplished in devising falsehoods on any subject and in making them utterly convincing, recalled Cleckley.

Years later, Cleckley attempted to organize his impressions of Anna. She didn't fit into the standard definition of insanity, yet her behavior was in many ways as "crazy" as that of individuals encountered in any mental institution who suffered from delusions or hallucinations. The nature of her "insanity"—if that is what it must be called—consisted in her incapacity to follow any life plan, an impulsivity which recognized no personal or social obligations and, most characteristic of all, her "failure to develop any sort of relationship with another human being that seemed to have much meaning for her or, to put it another way, that could influence her in any consistent, obviously purposive behavior."

In the course of his long career, Cleckley was to meet many others who exhibited similar traits. Because they appeared normal, exhibited few signs of discomfort or obvious "emotional disturbance" and yet reacted in ways that were clearly pathological, Cleckley evoked the image of a mask to describe the psychopathic personality.

The Mask of Sanity, the title of his classic work, implies that the psychopath—behind his façade of normality—actually suffers from a form of insanity. Although Cleckley never settled precisely the nature of the insanity, he remains convinced that the psychopath's fate is ultimately a tragic one.

"Without restraints and without any effective treatment, the psychopath continues progressively accumulating in his social wake, woe, confusion, despair, farce and disaster beyond any measure of these things I can convey."

At the time of the publication of *The Mask of Sanity*, little had been done about integrating Cleckley's insights into psychopathic behavior with newer ideas on narcissism. In the interval, it's become clear that the psychopath exists on the outer fringes of the manipulative personality. To him, legal, ethical and social restraints are completely irrelevant. He is a moral "outlaw," a "bandit," a desperado, a plunderer and marauder who holds himself above the, to him, petty confidences which bind the members of society together into everyday allegiance, however uneasy. Lacking a commitment to anyone other than himself and yet, at the same time, experiencing a paradoxical deficiency in the sense of his own integration—the extent to which he *is* a self—the psychopath creates a pseudo identity which he then proceeds to impose upon others. What he cannot extract by trickery, he'll take by force. His desperate insecurity and low self-esteem provide the trigger for impulsive, "unreasonable" and, on occasion, desperate behaviors and flights into fantasy. The most fascinating of these attempts at creating a mythologized grandiose version of oneself is encountered in a particular type of psychopath, the impostor.

The Misadventures of Mr. Honoré M'Biye

In February 1980, a thin, well-dressed black man walked into the Washington office of the World Bank and identified himself as a United Nations consultant. On the strength of his calm, authoritative manner, elegant Italian suits and claimed first-name familiarity with several well-known figures in the world of international finance, Honoré M'Biye was given an office on the eleventh floor as well as the use of a private secretary. His workday, however, was unlike that of any of the other consultants at the World Bank. Typically, he would arrive late in the morning and sit with his feet propped on the desk while he read the paper or talked on the phone (usually for the purpose of setting up luncheon appointments). He was polite, formal and, on occasion, imperious in his dealings with the other consultants.

The background on M'Biye was sketchy. He claimed to be a national from Zaire, a graduate of the Sorbonne and an expert on international affairs, specifically African affairs. In the 1980 World Bank telephone directory his name and telephone exchange were listed along with the designation CONS, for consultant.

Over the next five months, M'Biye's consultantship came under increasing scrutiny. An intensely private man with a low tolerance for questions regarding his personal life, M'Biye kept largely to himself except for a string of girlfriends he regularly took to dinner. Along with the wining and dining, he also "borrowed" small sums of money from these women. These "loans" were usually requested just prior to bank closings and weekends, or on other occasions when a trip to the bank was either impossible or merely "inconvenient."

After three months, M'Biye had run up several thousand dollars in debts, including $1,500 he obtained from a desk clerk in the hotel where he was living. But none of these creditors seemed worried that their money wouldn't be returned. On all occasions, M'Biye conveyed a quiet assertiveness and confidence capable of allaying all suspicions. Finally, in late April, several events occurred which stimulated the World Bank officials to begin checking into the background of their self-proclaimed consultant.

Identifying himself as a lawyer who earned $45,000 a year, M'Biye wrote a check for $7,000 in partial payment for a luxury sedan which he promptly drove from the showroom floor of a local foreign car dealer. The check bounced. When contacted, M'Biye apologized regarding the "misunderstanding" and gave the dealer another check. It also bounced.

In the meantime, M'Biye managed to obtain several thousand dollars in loans from two Washington banks. Nothing in the way of collateral had been required to secure these loans. He had no possessions other than several expensive suits and the car (repossessed after his second check to the dealer was discovered to be a phony). The money from the banks was obtained solely on the basis of M'Biye's connection with the World Bank. At this point, it was obvious that M'Biye's whole modus operandi depended on his identification as an employee-consultant to the World Bank.

A check into M'Biye's credentials revealed that a year earlier he had created a similar turmoil at the United Nations, where, after forging a director's name on a building pass, he had identified himself as a staff member of the U.S. mission. The pattern there was similar to his activity in D.C.: an elegant bearing, name dropping all over the place, flashy clothes and, most striking of all, an ability to convince seasoned professionals of the validity of his diplomatic and legal credentials.

Eventually, M'Biye's arrogance and personal defensiveness aroused curiosity at the United Nations. A belated credentials check turned up similar imposturing in Vienna, Paris and, most recently, Haiti. Confronted with the likelihood of arrest and imprisonment, M'Biye fled to Washington, where, unbelievable as it seems, the officials of the World Bank put off checking his credentials until, three months after his arrival, proof of M'Biye's fraudulent activities was brought forcefully home to them via an endless series of phone calls to the World Bank officials regarding "your consultant's" string of worthless checks. Finally the police were called and M'Biye arrested on charges of fraud.

My first contact with M'Biye took place in the lock-up section in the basement of the U. S. Federal Courthouse, in Washington, D.C., where, one early autumn morning, for the purpose of my interview, he was transferred from the D.C. jail. A guard led me through two sets of locked doors into a small room where, sitting quietly before a desk, was a small nattily dressed black man. He was wearing a three-piece gray pinstriped suit, gold designer glasses and alligator shoes. On his lap was a French-English dictionary upon which his hands rested peacefully. Overall, he looked like an elegant preacher ready to address a distinguished congregation on a passage drawn from Holy Writ.

When I introduced myself, he stood and bowed stiffly, his speech at once accented and scrupulously polite. The overall impression he created was that of a dignified, supercilious polyglot temporarily caught up in the details of an awkward and capricious misunderstanding.

"Mr. M'Biye?"

"You're the doctor? Fine. Please be seated."

M'Biye's appearance made it difficult for me to believe that we were sitting in a prison holding cell. His manner was what you'd expect to encounter when interviewing an ambassador who had reluctantly agreed to be interviewed on some arcane subject requiring patient and detailed explication. Although his command of English was excellent, he employed his bilinguality like a boxer slipping a punch. Any substantive question which even implied any wrongdoing on his part was met by a blank look. "I don't understand." Finally, I got the message: this man had been questioned by professional interrogators and wasn't likely to admit any wrongdoing to me. So I concentrated instead on his explanation of how he had gone from an eleventh-floor office in the World Bank to a basement lockup in the federal courthouse.

What emerged over several interviews was a cryptic, much-traveled man born in Zaire and placed by his parents at age twelve into a home of middle-class Parisians. Although Honoré is a black and deeply pigmented, he was in his own words "raised in a white household." He recalled with pride that through his childhood and teenage years he had worn suits and been driven to school in a car while many of the other children walked or took public transportation. His interest in clothes started at this early age, along with the sense of entitlement dictating that he continue to dress in the latest fashion. One must always be "in good condition at all times," he said. His sense of entitlement extends to all the good things in life and one senses in discussing the matter with him that he's of the opinion that the world should continue to provide him with the fine livery from which the costumes for his disguises can be created.

At all times his manner with me remained that of a cool professional conferring with another professional on a matter of shared concern. At no time did he drop his guard or relax while I found myself drawn into a discussion of *other people's* failures. One girlfriend, an attorney, offered her help at the time of Honoré's arrest. Later, for reasons Honoré failed to understand, she "stopped coming." In discussing her, his tone contained a sadness, a lingering disappointment that someone he once considered a good friend had betrayed him.

To hear him talk, one almost shared his pique at this turn of events, almost forgetting that Honoré was accused of extorting several thousand dollars from a variety of persons and institutions. For every question regarding Honoré's conduct, there was an explanation which was convoluted but eminently reasonable. Misplaced funds, failures of bank transfers, the hostility of the Zairian government, other people's incompetence—the list was endless and he could vary the routine to fit his audience and the needs of the moment.

With me the approach involved someone imposturing him! He focused on tiny discrepancies in the court papers (a one-numeral transposition of his passport number; a witness's faulty recall of a date) to fashion a theory that, in order to frame him the Zairian government had dispatched a look-alike to follow Honoré around and create general turmoil for him. But these explanations were not the delusions of a paranoid. They were presented coolly and objectively and formed only one of several alternative explanations of why he was unjustly accused. The most fascinating thing about these outrageous and preposterous claims was the lingering possibility that there just might be something to what he was saying. Again and again I found myself wondering: Could there be something to this? Is it possible, as he claims, that as a result of his membership in an organization dedicated to the overthrow of the Zairian government that they had carried out a vendetta against him? Nor was I alone in entertaining such speculations.

"He skirts on the naked edge of the truth, weaves a pattern of marginal credibility," his lawyer told me. "He has a strong sense of what different people will believe. Although he is only an amateur psychologist, he's still a master when it comes to dealing with the outer limits of credibility. After all, *anything* is possible. When dealing with Honoré, you find yourself constantly checking one excuse after another. Each discrepancy is covered by a succeeding one. The process continues until you find your head swimming and, throughout it all, there's the utter sincerity of this man. Your mind keeps saying 'he's lying' but your heart wants to believe him."

A similar discrepancy was revealed in interviews I conducted with several of Honoré's victims. One woman, a secretary at the bank whom he fleeced of several thousand dollars, revealed "He's not really lying, he firmly believes at the moment in the truth of what he's saying. He's convincing in ways you couldn't imagine. Even when you *know* something isn't true, he can convince you in five minutes that you're mistaken and that it is true."

Several days after my meeting with M'Biye, he provided me with a personal demonstration of his talent for mental legerdemain.

At three o'clock in the afternoon I was interrupted by a phone call from a parole officer. She asked me if I was "Mr. Restak" and then proceeded to interrogate me over the phone regarding Mr. M'Biye. How long had I known him? Was I regularly employed? What type of work did I do? The purpose of the call, she mentioned, was a background check on me since "Mr. M'Biye has given your name as long-term friend who might be willing to take him into your apartment in the event that he is released on bail." My astonishment was exceeded only by my eagerness to confront M'Biye at the outrageousness of his statement to the parole officer. Surely here was something that he could not dismiss so easily!

The next morning at our meeting I asked M'Biye regarding the parole officer's call. He vehemently denied that he had ever mentioned me in any context other than as a writer who wished to interview him. Before I could even inject a word in counterresponse, he went off on a tangent regarding the shameful duplicity of his landlady, who, he had learned earlier in the day, had moved all of his possessions out of his apartment and into a nearby garage. In his mind, his nonpayment of rent, to say nothing of his arrest and impending trial, were completely irrelevant to the matter of his landlady's "deceptive conduct." She had "breached her contract with me," he angrily asserted. Finally in frustration, he had thought of people who might help him. My name had come to mind: perhaps I could examine the landlady and certify her insanity. For this reason he had mentioned my name to the parole officer, who then "misunderstood what I was telling her, you understand?" he queried, meeting my gaze with unflinching eye-to-eye contact.

Needless to say, my confrontation ended in a standoff. His explanation, although unlikely, was not impossible. But I found out later, when discussing the situation with the parole officer, that M'Biye had spoken to her on several occasions about people who could help him recover his belongings from the garage where they were stored. She was adamant, however, that my name was mentioned in the context of a "lifelong friend who would be willing to provide a home for him in the event of his release on bail."

From this experience, I began to get a feeling for why M'Biye and other impostors are so successful. With the possible exception of a courtroom situation, it's almost impossible to pin down the exact details of any social encounter. There are always misunderstandings, distortions and outright errors in anyone's perceptions. It's these human failings that the impostor exploits to the limit.

Was the parole officer absolutely certain that she understood M'Biye correctly when he referred to me as a lifetime friend? "Well, not *absolutely*," she responded when I put the question to her, even though I didn't doubt her account for a moment.

Unless people are alerted ahead of time that someone is intent on deceiving them, their attention to conversational exchanges is fairly casual. Can you recall with absolute certainty the contents and sequence of remarks you made several hours ago? Probably not. It's this comparative looseness of social exchange that the impostor takes advantage of. He counts on people prevaricating when confronted with the challenge of absolute and total recall.

Another trick involves throwing the questioner on the defensive. After giving up on the parole matter, I asked M'Biye to discuss with me a string of bad checks which had led to the investigation and his indictment. He calmly surveyed me with the haughty disdain of a teacher dealing with an obtuse student.

"What check are you referring to, Dr. Restak? I can't discuss 'checks,' but perhaps I could help you if you bring up a particular check." Since I had been prepared beforehand for just such a response, I mentioned one of the more outrageous overdrafts of several thousand dollars, which he had written from an account that had never contained more than a few dollars.

Within seconds, my head was swimming with a barrage of details that he recounted in perfect English concerning money in a Parisian bank which was supposed to have been transferred to his account but, unaccountably, had never been transferred. When I countered that the FBI had called Paris and no such account existed, M'Biye paused, but only momentarily, and spoke of a "misunderstanding," "a mistake in the internal operations of that bank."

"A mistake?"

"Yes, the Zairian government, as I've already told you, is doing everything in its power to create trouble for me. The money in that account simply disappeared. And let me suggest another possibility. . . ."

M'Biye's possibilities are presented with the verve of a story-teller who regales his audience with puzzles capable of an infinite number of solutions. The artistry of the impostor is the artistry of the skilled raconteur who plays on the naïveté of his listeners. "I think that the most likely explanation involves an impostor sent by the Zairian government to impersonate me. It is he who, no doubt, withdrew the money."

"But there is no record of that large a sum of money ever having been in your account."

"I don't understand . . ." He pointed to the dictionary, imploring me with his eyes to provide the French translation for the words which I was certain he understood only too well. When I refused, insisting that he understood what I had said, he responded: "The records have been altered," and stared out into the hall where, at that moment, two guards were returning a prisoner to his cell.

M'Biye's juggling of circumstances and events provided the backdrop for a colorful and memorable trial. By the end of the first day, it was obvious that the jury was completely confused. For every alleged offense there was a perfectly reasonable-sounding alibi. In addition, there was always the cryptic possibility that this elegantly dressed man who sat with a pained and solemn look on his face just might be the victim of a political vendetta. Such a possibility worked more and more in M'Biye's favor. Halfway through the trial it appeared that he could be acquitted. But at that point he made a fatal error.

"Just when everything was proceeding as well as could be expected, M'Biye insisted to me that he wanted to take the stand in his own defense," his attorney told me. "I told him that I thought this would be the worst possible course of action for him."

The attorney went on to explain how, under common law, the defendant is judged on the basis of the act in question. References to other alleged misconducts cannot be introduced. When a defendant takes the stand in his own defense, however, "impeachment witnesses" can be called to testify as to the defendant's character as well as to other offenses that he has been accused of in the past. This is aimed at undermining the defendant's general credibility.

"It proved a fatal mistake, as I told him it would. The prosecutor brought in an army of people who had been stung by bad checks or loans which could never be repaid. M'Biye's response to the prosecutor's witnesses was, of course, that 'these people are lying.' The jury chose, instead, to believe that *he* was the liar and he was found guilty," his attorney concluded.

From several hours spent interviewing M'Biye and many of the people associated with him, I am struck with the similarity and "style" between this grand impostor and many of those described elsewhere in this book whose difficulties involve disturbances in their sense of self. One striking similarity is Honoré M'Biye's use of splitting, which, I believe, forms the basis for his uncanny ability to switch from one role to another while appearing absolutely convincing during each performance. At a given moment, he is totally immersed in the character that he is portraying. All aspects of his past are excluded, split off from his consciousness. The future, too, is unavailable, at least in terms of any appreciation of future consequences.

For example, two years before his arrest, M'Biye had sent a cable to a Parisian bank requesting the transfer of funds to the Chemical Bank of New York. At the conclusion of his directive for the funds' transfer appears the request that the Chemical Bank call his secretary "when the funds have been received by you." At this point, not only was there no money in the account but M'Biye's writing of bad checks had established in Paris a debt sufficiently large that the bank there was considering taking legal action against him. (They eventually did follow this course and he was found guilty in absentia.)

The brazenness of such a request for funds that didn't exist amazed the jurors and M'Biye's attorney as well. How could a man ask a bank to inform a secretary concerning the arrival of funds which didn't exist and couldn't, by any stretch of the imagination, be forthcoming? It is this type of logical inconsistency that has led many observers to conclude that the impostor is basically insane and suffers from a delusion. I think that a better explanation is provided by considering the impostor as capable of such a profound degree of splitting that he believes the consequences of his actions can be indefinitely postponed.

Firmly entrenched in the identification of the moment, M'Biye became, in his own mind, a man who actually possessed funds in a foreign country and makes the perfectly reasonable request that these funds be transferred to him. The alteration in belief is not so much a delusion as it is a heightened involvement with the situation and persons surrounding him at the moment. Dressing as a wealthy man, visiting expensive restaurants, driving an elegant car —these are the momentary realities that M'Biye uses in order to fashion a sense of self. Surely such an esteemed individual could not be doubted, not be forced to explain his behavior. In a sense, *appearing* as a certain individual becomes equivalent, in M'Biye's mind, to becoming that individual.

"M'Biye always skirted the naked edge of truth weaving a pattern of marginal credibility," commented his attorney after the trial. "Separating truth from falsity was always a difficult, tortuous process with him, and what made it particularly difficult was M'Biye's unfailing sense of what people would believe. He's a master psychologist."

For every confrontation, M'Biye had a new excuse which often required a slight revision from previous explanations. If money was not available, it was "tied up in a foreign bank." When the foreign bank cabled that no funds existed, M'Biye claimed that "there must be some mistake." When pushed further, matters could always be settled by writing a check. By the time the check "bounced," M'Biye was in a "conference" or an important meeting and would call back. Naturally, the return calls never came.

Coupled with splitting is a chimera-like capacity for imitation. Throughout his career, M'Biye never failed to carry off the identity that he claimed at the moment. Among lawyers he talked and acted like a lawyer. While at the World Bank he successfully affected the manner and diction of a diplomat and specialist in African affairs. For every doubt that surfaced, M'Biye provided an explanation. When pushed to the ultimate at the end of his trial, he claimed that his problem stemmed from his earlier membership in an organization dedicated to the overthrow of the government of Zaire. To get revenge, the government, so M'Biye claimed, had trumped up all the difficulties leading up to his arrest. He was unjustly accused and "not guilty of anything." "At all times during the trial, he exhibited an intense pride and firm belief in his own self-righteousness," said his attorney.

M'Biye's exit from Washington was as dramatic and maddeningly preposterous as his initial arrival. I heard about it several weeks later secondhand from a U.S. marshal assigned to escort M'Biye to the Federal Prison in Danbury, Connecticut. En route, the marshal acceded to M'Biye's request for writing materials so that he could write a letter. Unknown to the marshal, M'Biye slipped the letter into the hands of a flight attendant. It read: "Please help me, I am a member of the Royal Canadian Mounted Police. This man has stolen my gun, uniform and identification. I am now his prisoner. If you or anyone working on this plane can disarm him, I would be most grateful. This man is dangerous!"

Over the next several months, as a result of my experiences with Honoré M'Biye, I began studying the literature on impostors. Rather than being rare, comparatively inscrutable self disorders, impostors are unbelievably common within our culture. I easily discovered examples of impostors pretending to be doctors, lawyers, diplomats, policemen—an impostor journalist at the Washington *Post* even turned up who, on the basis of falsified credentials and a fictional story of an eight-year-old heroin addict, was awarded a Pulitzer Prize.

Impostors are everywhere. Few are unmasked, however, as long as their pretentions are kept within reasonable bounds and their escapades remain within the law. But breaking the law and engaging in the most outrageous charades against other people's sensibilities are part and parcel of the impostor's way of life. They derive pleasure as well as identity from bamboozling others into accepting their pretentions.

In 1958 psychoanalyst Phyllis Greenacre wrote a now-classic review article on impostors. "An impostor is not only a liar, but a very special type of liar who *imposes* on others fabrications of his attainments or worldly possessions." She referred to the impostor's pretensions as a "plagiarizing on a grand scale" but noted, at the same time, a discrepancy between the impostor's skills in certain areas concerned with his deception and a rather striking and inexplicable naïveté in areas ordinarily considered matters of "common sense."

"The investigation of even a few instances of impostors—if one has not become emotionally involved in the deception—is sufficient to show how crude, though clever many impostors are, how very faulty any scheming is, and how often in fact, the element of shrewdness is lacking. Rather, a quality of showmanship is involved with its reliance all on the response of an audience to illusion."

At the basis of the impostor's pretensions is a need for the approval of others, a need that can reach the intensity of an addiction. This is combined with a flair for showmanship and melodramatics. In addition, there is the satisfaction that comes from fooling others. "The impostor seems to flourish on the success of his exhibitionism. Enjoyment of the limelight and an inner triumph of 'putting something over' seems inherent," according to Greenacre.

A goodly portion of the impostor's credibility depends on the degree of confirmation that he receives from the people that he's fooling. They provide him with confirmation of his own fragile sense of self. "It seems as if the impostor becomes temporarily convinced of the rightness of his assumed character, in proportion to the amount of attention that he is able to gain from it."

This need for confirmation of self partially explains the puzzling and maddening aspects of the impostor's behavior. In instances where he has been found out, as with M'Biye, the impostor seems unable to relinquish the assumed role. Under the circumstances where most people would realize the game was up, the impostor continues to persist in his preposterous claims.

M'Biye never admitted to me or anyone else that he was neither a diplomat nor a lawyer, but, instead, continued to act out the role of an aggrieved victim with aplomb and, at times, hilarious dramatics. His attempt to trick me into providing him with a character reference, his ludicrous note to the flight attendant enlisting her aid in disarming the marshal—these are the acts of comedians, the kinds of bizarre situations portrayed by zany comics throughout history. In such instances, audacity and showmanship are combined for the purpose of outwitting and humiliating the opposition. In all cases, an audience is absolutely essential.

An impostor without an audience is, in fact, impossible. It is the approval and admiration of other people which fuels the impostor's efforts at manipulation and control. An impostor is, above all, a variety of manipulator. The concerns which we have discussed throughout this book are highlighted, taken to extremes as it were, in the life histories of impostors. At all times their efforts are directed at an audience which can be manipulated.

"It is from the confirming reactions of the audience that the impostor gets a 'realistic' sense of self, a value greater than anything else he can achieve," wrote Greenacre. "It is the demand for an audience in which the (false) self is reflected that causes impostors often to become of social significance. Both reality and identity seem to the impostor to be strengthened rather than diminished by the success of the fraudulence of his claims."

To the impostor, truth is a matter of the confirming presence of others. If he can get others to believe in him, he can believe in himself. Despite the fantastic nature of such an approach to reality, there are historical examples to prove that the impostor, if confirmed by others in his false pretentions, can sometimes progress to real accomplishment.

No less a figure than Samuel Johnson was taken in by the impostor George Psalmanazar. In his youth Psalmanazar had pretended to be a theological student and pilgrim who traveled throughout Europe begging alms from priests, with whom he conversed in impeccable Latin. When the disguise was found out he fled to Germany and pretended to be a Japanese convert to Christianity. He invented several Japanese religious rites and lived for a time on a self-imposed regimen of roots and berries. After a while, he altered his pretentions somewhat and played at being a Formosan. On the basis of this new identity—no one in the London of the early 1700s had ever seen a Formosan—Psalmanazar wrote a thick book about his imaginary birthplace. Although it was entirely fictional, the work was accepted by scholars and, later, even included in a compendium of travel literature.

Psalmanazar's imposturing included an imaginary language written out in an alphabet of his own invention. He obtained a post at Oxford University, where he taught the language to missionaries who intended to travel to remote corners of the world. To support his imposture of scholar and savant, he left a candle burning all night in the window of his room as a means to impress passersby with his dedication to scholarly pursuits.

After reading a religious tract in the 1720s, Psalmanazar was "converted" and relinquished his identity as a Formosan. He then entered the literary world, where he established himself as a linguistic genius of sorts who, from all contemporary records, seems to have possessed an impressive command of several languages.

The most interesting aspect of the final stage of Psalmanazar's life, however, was his ability to win over a man as intensely scrupulous as Samuel Johnson. Probably his identification as a literary figure was as intense as his earlier pretentions that he was a theological student, a Japanese and a Formosan. Johnson was so impressed by Psalmanazar that he once declared that he would "as soon of thought of contradicting a bishop." Perhaps because of Johnson's evaluation of him, Psalmanazar was spurred on to real accomplishments for the first time in his life. He contributed sections on ancient history to a large publishing project and went on to help Johnson with the compilation of his famous dictionary.

Most impostors are far less successful than Psalmanazar and eventually are found out. This failure to maintain their false selves is partly the result of the compulsiveness that they demonstrate in their pretentions. Without exception, impostors demonstrate what Greenacre calls "an urgency to perpetuate fraudulence."

Each claim, if successfully believed, is followed by increasingly extravagant claims. Eventually the utter audacity of the impostor's pretentions lead to investigations which trip him up. For instance, M'Biye's successful pretense of being a lawyer and employee of the World Bank led to increased boldness in the manipulation of his finances; an enhanced ability to imitate; extremely acute perceptions of style and dress; an entirely convincing manner—all are combined in the impostor with inexplicable lapses of judgment.

If the impostor is clever enough to imitate the style and manner of a diplomat, for instance, how could he be so "stupid" as to ignore the obvious consequences of writing bad checks? Such contradictions have led many of those who have studied impostors to conclude that they suffer from a peculiar defect in their reality sense.

"The overall utility of the sense of reality is, however, impaired," says Greenacre. "What is striking in many impostors is that, although they are quick to pick up details and nuances in the lives and activities of those whom they simulate and can sometimes utilize these with great adroitness, they are frequently so utterly obtuse to many ordinary considerations of fact that they give the impression of mere brazenness or stupidity in many aspects of their life peripheral to their impostures."

An alternative explanation postulates in the impostor a heightened, more intensely focused interest in playacting and enhancing the self through gaining the admiration and approval of others. It is as if all of the impostor's energies are expended in the area of personal aggrandizement with nothing left over for everyday considerations. In a way, the impostor is similar to the idiot savant whose impressive and bewildering accomplishments in certain specialized areas are accompanied by failures in other activities most people hardly have to give a thought about. This corresponds to Cleckley's view that the psychopath—and by implication the impostor, who is a special variety of psychopath—suffers from a defect in his reasoning sense, in essence, suffers from a special, only partially "masked" form of insanity.

M'Biye's imposturing represents the combination of a flawed identity, a highly developed sense of entitlement and a flair for the grandiose. By pretending that he was a diplomat, his own insignificant accomplishments were thereby enhanced. Throughout it all, he began to believe in the reality of the fictional personality that he had constructed. This is what makes an impostor such as M'Biye so convincing. In a sense, the pretentions are accepted after a while by the impostor himself. He truly believes in the truth of the "propaganda" he has created about himself. Thus it is not surprising that many skillful impostors are able to successfully pass lie detector tests. Since they are lying not only to others but to themselves as well, the test often fails to detect them.

Before saying more about the impostors here, let's move on to a man whose whole life is based on imposturing and whose behavior forms a direct continuum with the criminal psychopaths we will discuss in the later sections of this book.

Doing the Razzle

Not long ago I encountered in my waiting room a thin, spare, aesthetic-looking man of about forty-five, dressed in a Roman collar. According to the referral slip, the Reverend Robert Wain had recently been involved in a traffic accident in which he suffered a concussion and was now referred to me for evaluation of headaches.

My first suspicion that things were not as they seemed occurred in the examining room when I observed a series of scars on the reverend's arms. I had noted similar scars on other patients in the past—the short, brutish incisions performed by unskilled operators when removing tattoos.

A clergyman with tattoos was such a sufficient rarity that I inquired about their origin. The reverend then launched into a spirited account of his "rebirth" after living a life of aimless wandering followed by a "conversion" and life-style change, including the removal of his tattoos. He then produced from a leatherette briefcase a pile of testimonial letters from several prominent Washington politicians extolling his years of service as a missionary in a small province in India. After several years, it seems, the reverend had returned to the United States for the purpose of raising funds and, during one such errand, was involved in the auto accident which resulted in his referral for my professional evaluation.

Three days later, I was called by a psychiatrist friend who works on the wards of St. Elizabeth's Hospital. Dr. Robert Torrance is a specialist in forensic psychiatry, the evaluation of criminals for the purpose of determining sanity and responsibility. He told me of a patient presently on the ward for mental evaluation in regard to embezzlement and extortion who had forged my name to a prescription. Dr. Torrance then asked if it was agreeable to me for a detective to come to my office so that I could verify that the signature in question was a forgery. The alleged forger, I was informed, was not only taking the medication himself but was selling pills to other inmates.

Curious about how an inmate confined for mental observation could have obtained one of my office prescriptions, I asked for his description. It took me several minutes to realize that the cleric I had examined three days ago was the same person accused of forging my prescription. I was even more startled later, after a quick review of my notes revealed that the prescription was not a forgery after all, but had been written by me at the clergyman's request for the relief of "tension." Too late, I realized I had been taken in by a psychopath who had been shuttling back and forth between the wards for the criminally insane and my office—with stops along the way to beguile public officials into writing expressions of support for his missionary work. My curiosity was whetted even further when I reflected on similarities between Reverend Wain and the Reverend Jim Jones, the deranged engineer of the Guyana massacre. I will return to this intriguing parallel shortly.

Over the next several months Reverend Wain returned to my office on many occasions. On the first revisit, I told him I was now aware of his true situation and that I would not write any more prescriptions; otherwise I would be willing to continue to treat him for his headaches. Wain agreed.

Free of the need to continue his pose any further, Wain stopped talking about fund raising. Instead he tried to interest me in joining him in a scheme to defraud the insurance companies: he would submit bills for office visits, collect from the insurance company and then "we'd split it up, fifty-fifty, you understand?" When I refused, he became abusive—genuinely outraged that I wouldn't go along with his fraud. When he calmed down after a few moments and accepted the fact that I couldn't be manipulated into illegal actions, he asked if I'd be willing to listen to his "life story" for the purpose of "helping me straighten out my life." I made no promises, but agreed to listen.

I obtained further background on Wain from law-enforcement officers and other psychiatrists who had tried to treat him over the years. What emerged is a profile of a middle-level psychopathic impostor who has learned the "system" so well that he has been able to manipulate a string of psychiatrists into certifying his insanity. In addition, the utter chaos and confusion of his life-style, as presented in his own words, provides a marvelous example of profound disorganization which prevails in the personality of the psychopath. And throughout it all is the recurring refrain of manipulation.

Born into an unstable family (his mother had tried unsuccessfully to abort him and his father died after spending the last nine years of his life in a mental hospital), Wain was in trouble by the time he was a teenager. Placed in a reform school at age fifteen, he was released two years later but arrested almost immediately for stealing a car. He spent three more years in prison. Upon his release at age twenty he "suddenly got smart."

Over the next several years, Wain learned the tricks of the confidence man. He worked for a while as a translator and roustabout with a traveling carnival in Puerto Rico, where he learned the razzle and the other carnival games which have provided him with a living at various times throughout his life. He also learned, along with sleight-of-hand tricks, a dedication to what he repetitively refers to as "my profession."

"You're a professional and have acquired a lot of specialized knowledge, Doc. So have I. I'm a professional too. I've learned the tricks of putting it over on the other guy without giving away the gaff." Wain's identity is tied up with deception. Fascinated by sleight of hand and illusion, he punctuates his conversation with repetitive references to "putting it over" on others. On those rare occasions when he laughs, it invariably involves recollections of the stupefied expressions which his deceptions have elicited from his victims.

Eventually, Wain moved to Los Angeles, where he set himself up in a luxury apartment and began counterfeiting watches and diamonds and playing what he refers to as the "skips game." He would buy up a huge number of airline tickets by credit card, sell them at a discount to cash-paying victims and then cancel the reservations. The victims thus were left holding worthless tickets. When things began heating up, Wain skipped town and fled to the Bahamas.

Upon his arrival in the Bahamas, Wain set himself up as a clergyman in charge of a missionary church. He also met and married his fourth wife without, incidentally, ever bothering to go through the formalities of divorcing any of the previous three. Within weeks he established a payoff arrangement with a local disk jockey who, for a percentage of the take, offered to broadcast Wain's appeals for money to support his church. At one point, according to Wain, the disk jockey took the money, refused to broadcast the speech and "laughed in my face." Angered, Wain assaulted the disk jockey and was arrested.

In jail, he spoke of the disk jockey playing songs on the air which referred disparagingly to him. Apparently he was able to feign the symptoms of a persecutory delusion well enough to convince the authorities that he wasn't responsible for his acts. He was transferred to a psychiatric facility, where, within a few days, his "delusions" cleared and he was released. Over his lifetime, he has perfected his simulation of mental illness. There is a pattern of arrest, delusional claims of persecution, a psychiatric referral and subsequent release.

"What other way to appear crazy than to have persecutory delusions?" he has commented to me with laughter on several occasions. His ability to mimic serious mental illness has fooled psychiatrists on several continents, a record he's proud of.

"For a while I lived with a guy who was a Ph.D. clinical psychologist. I read all his books on mental illness and learned all the symptoms. I've gotten so good at it that sometimes even *I* believe I'm crazy."

Psychiatrists who have treated Wain are less certain that his insanity is feigned. At a commitment hearing, one psychiatrist described in vivid and repulsive detail how Wain smeared his feces over the walls of the observation cell. The description is that of a profoundly regressed, distraught man who has been driven to the outer limits of his psychic endurance. But Wain, sitting quietly and comfortably in my office, gives another version of the event:

"They had me that time and I realized I might be sent up for quite a stretch. So, once again I went the nut route. You should have seen their faces"—he guffaws—"when they saw me smearing my shit over the walls of my cell. Next thing I knew I was in the psych unit. It's incredible how quickly a 'crazy man' can get cured in one of those units. Two days later I was saner than most of the staff."

Throughout his conversation, Wain frequently refers to the "stupidity" of his doctors and lawyers. Judges, too, are "idiots." His favorite phrase for those who are in conflict with him—which includes an appalling number and variety of people—is "the filthy lepers." Rather than speaking in anger as one might expect, however, Wain utters the phrase with the utmost disdain. His grandiosity and superiority—demonstrated by his repetitive razzles, coupled with his capacity to successfully feign mental illness on demand—provides Wain with an identity. He is the intelligent, skilled professional. The authorities, in contrast, are the dupes, the "lepers" who combine incompetence and malevolence in a failed attempt to contend with his superior intellectual endowments.

Wain's relationships with me follow similar patterns. I have always maintained an active interest in swindlers and confidence men and, as a result, have assembled over the years a small coterie of them. Some of these patients come and go freely while others, such as Wain, are "on the lam." Since his escape from St. Elizabeth's, the mental hospital in which he has resided for a number of years, Wain has drifted about. He calls me collect on odd occasions from telephone booths from across the country and we talk. When in town he never makes an appointment because he still doesn't trust me. "You may call the cops and I'll find them waiting for me in your office," he says. Typically, he arrives in my reception room unannounced and I try to find ways of slipping him into the schedule. His letters, which arrive every few weeks, provide lessons in mental sleight of hand. A typical one is postmarked Portland, Maine, but was written on an envelope from the Watergate Hotel in Washington, D.C. Inside is a letter composed on stationery from the Breakers Hotel in Palm Beach, Florida. The letter concludes with the information that I should respond "within the next ten days" to an address in Burlington, Vermont, and the letter would be forwarded. So where is the reverend? The numerous addresses are metaphors for the reverend's multiple identities.

Even more fascinating is the reverend's attitude toward my professional charges. After spending an hour detailing to me how he has swindled someone out of several hundred dollars (he is currently dealing once again in fake diamonds), he mentions that he will send me a check for the visit. At such times, his expression is one of mock seriousness. Meeting him for the first time at such a moment, anyone would be entirely convinced that he was a clergyman who had forgotten his checkbook. On other occasions, when he is once again trying to "sting" one of the insurance companies, he will write and ask my assistance in forwarding a medical report. "The sooner you act, the sooner you get paid," one of his letters concluded. When I refused again to "act," the reverend called me long distance and berated me: "What's your game, Dr. Restak? Are you going to put me in one of your books or something?"

On many occasions, we've spoken about his attitude toward the confidence tricks he employs. To him the process is a game in which he outwits and thereby deprecates his victims. Not only is he gaining money but, by successfully pulling off a scam, he "feels good." His sagging sense of self-esteem and lack of personal integration are counteracted by the euphoria which results from a successful manipulation or swindle. And there's a depth to this stage acting and imposture which can't be fathomed even by him. If caught there's the option of taking the nut route and conning a psychiatrist into accepting his staged behavior (feces smearing, phony delusions and so on) as evidence of insanity. Even when temporarily confined, the tricks continue: while hospitalized at St. Elizabeth's, he ran a numbers game; volunteered to assist the chaplain, whom he then successfully impostured; attempted to elicit my help in swindling the insurance companies. Throughout all this, Wain maintains a thoroughly "professional" attitude. He's proud of the sleight-of-hand tricks he's learned—he could undoubtedly make a living performing as a magician—and he possesses a sure sense of what to say in order to stimulate another person's greed. "The con man is only successful because there's a little bit of psychopathy in everybody," Wain says. "In order to pull off a successful scam, you first must convince the victim he's going to be getting something out of it which he isn't entitled to. The totally honest person can never be victimized by a confidence man."

Along with his "professional attitudes" toward his activities, Wain is familiar with the literature. From him I first learned about Melville's *Confidence Man.* Some of Wain's favorite passages include: "What are you? What am I? Nobody knows who anybody is. The data which life furnishes, towards forming a true estimate of any being, are as insufficient to that end as in geometry one side given would be to determine the triangle."

And: "Would you, in your present need, be willing to accept a loan from a friend, securing him by a mortgage on your homestead, and do so, knowing that you had no reason to feel satisfied that the mortgage might not eventually be transferred into the hands of a foe? Yet the difference between this man and that man is not so great as the difference between what the same may be today and what he may be in days to come."

My contribution to this literary dialogue consists of bringing to Wain's attention some of the thinking on imposturing and psychopathy which writers and psychiatrists have done over the years.

Confessions of Felix Krull, Confidence Man

The best fictional account of a person who is both a psychopath and impostor is found in Thomas Mann's *Confessions of Felix Krull, Confidence Man.*

Krull, the son of a Rhine Valley winemaker, demonstrates at an early age a love for what he calls "games of make-believe." Sitting in a go-cart he imagines himself the Kaiser and is greeted by the amused cheers of his family who call out, "Look, there he goes, the old hero." Rather than a passing phase, however, Krull's interest in make-believe continues into his teens as he regularly fantasizes himself in the role of a prince or a person of great wealth and influence. Attitudes of contempt and superiority toward his friends and classmates accompany these episodes:

"The other boys of the town seemed to me dull and limited indeed, since they obviously did not share my ability and were consequently ignorant of the secret joys I could derive from it by a simple act of will, effortlessly and without any outward preparation."

Comparing himself with the other boys of his age, Krull discovers within himself an active, fertile and imaginative talent for make-believe, along with a voice with "an ingratiating tone" that could "fall so flatteringly upon the ear."

Apparently other people were also affected by Krull's voice. "Your personality makes a pleasing impression," a priest tells him while discussing funeral arrangements for Krull's father. "And I would like to praise you in particular for the agreeable quality of your voice." The pleasing effect on this occasion apparently worked its purpose, since the priest finally gives in to Krull's request that Krull's father, a suicide, be given a Catholic burial.

Once again, Krull's success is accompanied by a sense of superiority. The priest's comments serve as a confirmation of Krull's belief that he is "made of superior stuff, or, as people say, of finer clay."

Krull's favorite youthful pastime involves posing as a model for his godfather, the artist Schimmelpreester. Krull is thrilled with the opportunity of "dressing up" in costumes of different ages, and his skillful performance earns him the accolade "a natural costume boy." But Krull's talents extend far beyond merely standing and posing.

"My godfather even asserted that with the aid of costume and wig I seemed not only able to put on whatever social rank or personal characteristics I chose, but could actually adapt myself to any given period or century."

Krull's enthusiasm for this kind of mimicry soon becomes the prevailing theme which he is to develop over the remainder of his life. And, like that of real-life impostors such as the Reverend Wain, Krull's everyday existence is colorless and unfulfilling in comparison with his fantasy life. "Ah, those were glorious hours! But when they were over and I resumed my ordinary dull dress, how indescribably boring seemed all the world by contrast, in what depths of dejection did I spend the rest of the evening!"

To the impostor, the real world eventually becomes almost unbearable, a reminder of his own lack of personal identity. Various images frequently express this loss of the sense of self, often felt as a strange lack of completeness.

While living with his mother in Frankfurt, Krull stands on one occasion watching a brother and sister who are looking down from a balcony during an afternoon snowstorm. While both are attractive persons, Krull is moved by the peculiar sense that "beauty here lay in the duality, the charming doubleness."

A similar sentiment is evoked on the occasion of his sister's wedding. Krull is both fascinated and jealous that his sister will soon take on another name, another identity, and will be able to sign herself with a new name.

"That fact alone possessed all the charm of novelty. How tiresome to sign the same name to letters and papers all one's life long! The hand grows paralyzed with irritation and disgust—what a pleasant refreshment and stimulation of the whole being comes, then, from being able to give oneself a new name and to hear oneself called by it!"

In these early years, Krull also develops an attitude toward lying and deception which is characteristic of psychopaths and impostors down to the present day. He disdains "a barefaced lie" which is "by that very fact so grossly palpable that nobody can fail to see through it." Only one kind of lie has a chance for success: that which is "the product of a lively imagination."

Lying and deceit thus become matters of creative performance, a form of artistry in which only the superiorly talented can hope to compete. Thus, according to the impostor's inverted logic, only those of a "superior clay" are capable of pulling off deception in ways that are sufficiently clever to avoid detection. The artistry consists of elaborating everyday truths in such a way that deceptions can be created and perpetuated by a kind of verbal sleight of hand.

"Although it is true that I was a sturdy boy, who, except for the usual childhood ailments, never had anything serious the matter with him, it was nevertheless not a gross deception when I decided one morning to avoid the painful oppressions of school by becoming an invalid."

To accomplish this, Krull practiced disarranging his hair, slanting his mouth, drawing in his cheeks and holding them in with his teeth—all directed toward giving the "appearance of having grown thin over night." Such performances, the impostor will tell us, requires talent: "To counterfeit illness effectively could never be within the powers of a coarse-grained man," Krull assures us.

Most interesting and characteristic of all, however, are the reasons that are put forth to justify Krull's exercise in deceit. On the subject of his "invalidism": "For why should I subject myself to such treatment when I had in hand the means of neutralizing the cool powers of my intellectual lords and masters?"

Furthermore, his reactions to school were so intense as to provide, in his mind, a "condition that created a sound basis of truth for my behavior." Once again, to impostors such as Krull, M'Biye and the Reverend Wain, deception becomes a fine art, a form of embroidering in which the artist alternates truth with deception: a skein of truth here interwoven with strands of cleverly reasoned falsehoods there.

Another characteristic of the impostor reveals itself in Krull's ethically overwrought but nonetheless specious distinctions on moral matters. While serving for several months as a combination pimp, adviser and voyeur to a prostitute he meets in a bar, Krull nonetheless rejects the obvious implications of his actions. Once again his sensitivity lifts him above the common lot into a kind of rarefied spiritual atmosphere in which he experiences a "refinement through love."

"One might well be tempted to apply a short, ugly word to my way of life at that time. . . . Whoever thinks that actions make people equal may go ahead and take refuge in this simple procedure. For my own part, I am in agreement with folk wisdom which holds that when two persons do the same thing it is no longer the same; yes, I go further and maintain that labels such as 'drunkard,' 'gambler,' or even 'wastrel' not only do not embrace and define the actual living case, but in some instances do not even touch it."

To Krull, as well as real-life impostors, things are never what they seem and the obvious implications of a person's actions must often be rejected. Actions are not to be judged, says the impostor, by fixed standards which are applied to everyone; there are always many "special" cases. In the instance of "one made from finer clay," for instance, the judgments can only be made by the impostor himself. Thus Krull becomes the final arbiter of his relationships with the prostitute Rozsa; their sordid affair is interpreted by Krull as a preparation for Krull's later "successes of the heart."

"For I know from the very bottom of my being that I could never have borne myself with so much subtlety and elegance in the many vicissitudes of my life if I had not passed through Rozsa's naughty school of love."

Such moral judgments, which are rare even among people given to rationalizing those aspects of their affairs which cause embarrassment or shame, come naturally to the impostor as a result of his underlying narcissism: others don't really exist as independent people, but only as participants in a form of shadow play, a make-believe drama in which the only real actor is the impostor himself.

Krull, on his initial meeting with Rozsa: "It was without introduction, this conversation, it was without polite conventions of any sort; from the very beginning it had the free, exalted irresponsibility that is usually characteristic only of dreams, where our 'I' associates with shadows that have no independent life, with creations of its own, in a way that is after all impossible in waking life where one flesh-and-blood being exists in actual separation from another."

This concentration on the self in which others appear only as dream figures emerging out of a psychic wasteland reaches its full expression in the phenomenon of autoscopy: the impostor actually encounters a vision of himself seen with full clarity walking along the street, or perhaps sitting across from him in a restaurant. Although the experience is rare and by no means confined to impostors (it is more frequently encountered in forms of organic brain disease), its occurrence in the neurologically well is most frequently seen in cases of heightened narcissism. As with the king in Ionesco's drama: "I see myself. Behind everything I exist. There is nothing but me everywhere. Am I in every mirror or am I the mirror of everything?" When narcissism is developed to such a degree, the impostor may actually see himself as a projected participant in an inner dream theater which constitutes his version of reality.

At all times, reality remains something that is to be interpreted rather than simply perceived. Nothing is as it appears but rather the end result of a combination of circumstances and the impostor's intentions. Within such a world *things* can sometimes take on a life of their own in ways that exonerate the impostor from the consequences of his actions.

While repacking his bag after a customs search, for instance, Krull tells us that a small Morocco case belonging to a wealthy woman "unexpectedly slipped into my little bag. . . . This was an occurrence rather than an action and it happened secretly; the case simply smuggled itself in, so to speak, as a byproduct of the good humor that my friendly relations with the authorities of this country had produced in me."

Krull didn't steal the case, he would have us believe, and in truth believes so himself, but rather an "occurrence" took place, almost a form of magic in which the bag "simply smuggled itself in" resulting in Krull's reference at a later point to its "accidental acquisition."

In this instance of what most of us would unhesitatingly label a petty theft, the meaning of Krull's stealing the case is determined once again by an internal feeling state: "A byproduct of the good humor that my friendly relations with the authorities of this country had produced in me."

In a word, events are shaped according to the impostor's manipulation of the people and circumstances he encounters. "The same situations are not the same for everyone, and general conditions, so I would maintain, are subject to extensive personal modification."

This theme of the shifting nature of the self as well as surrounding circumstances determines the impostor's attitude toward life as something which must be created and restructured according to his individual desires. Thus, reality is similar to a stage in which the impostor is free to change roles or alternate his performance at a moment's notice; rewrite the script according to his whim; and even take an active role in directing the performance of other people. The goal throughout all this is ultimately a theatrical one: to replace the absence of an inner self with a performance which will bring success, admiration and, most of all, a temporary sense of identity. "The important thing is to construct out of a total lack of materials, something that would be at least momentarily dazzling," Krull writes in his diary.

To the psychopathic impostor even momentary identifications are total and entirely self-convincing. When Krull is asked if he speaks Italian, he instantly becomes an Italian: "In place of soft-voiced refinement I became possessed by the fiercest of temperaments. There happily rose up in me all the Italian sounds I had ever heard. . . ."

This capacity for instant and total identification, while reaching its highest and most refined development in psychopaths and impostors, can also be found among people engaged in imaginative professions. Actors, particularly mimics and impersonators, impress others, even their intimate friends, as "masks." (*The Mask Behind the Mask* was the title of Peter Evans' biography of the actor Peter Sellers.)

On a "Muppet Show," Peter Sellers' dialogue with Kermit the Frog hints at just such a situation: "Just relax and be yourself," says Kermit.

"No," replies Sellers, "that would be altogether impossible, I could never be myself."

"Never yourself?"

"No, you see there is no me. I do not exist."

"I beg your pardon?"

"There used to be a me, but I had it surgically removed."

This confusion on the matter of *who* one actually is often extends to the impersonators themselves. Peter Sellers reportedly told the novelist Jerzy Kosinski, "My whole life has been devoted to imitating others. But it has been devoted to the portrayal of those who appear to be different from what they are. If I were to tell you that Chauncy Gardiner Chance was the ultimate Peter Sellers, then I would be telling you what my whole life is about. If I don't portray him, he will ultimately portray me."

Sellers' devotion to imitating others has also, on occasion, involved him in amusing episodes of masquerade. In a 1962 interview with the London Sunday *Times*, Sellers describes how he obtained his first job with the BBC.

"I simply couldn't get work with the BBC. I knew that I could do impersonations but nobody would give me a chance. It was the time when 'Much Binding in the Marsh' was a successful show on radio and I thought that people might listen to Kenneth Horne. So I rang up one of the BBC producers in Kenneth Horne's voice. I got through to the producer and said that he should see a young man called Peter Sellers. So he saw me. When I got into the room he said: 'Kenneth Horne has spoken to me about you.' I know, I said, that was me on the telephone."

All of this is in no way meant to imply that Peter Sellers was anything like the persons we are discussing in this book, but it does illustrate the continuum that exists between imitation, impersonation and masquerade, which presumably, as in the cases of Mr. Sellers and others, can be seen in otherwise "normal" personalities. Indeed, the pathological aspects of these behaviors consist in the adoption of the role of an impostor in order to make up for a deficient sense of one's own self-identity. More specifically, most impostors have a need to be recognized as unique, geniuses, people whose special qualities deserve to be hailed by the general public.

In the 1950s, a master impostor named Ferdinand Demara successfully adopted the roles of a psychologist, a monk, a soldier, a sailor, a law enforcement officer, a surgeon and even a psychiatrist —always under a false name. Demara's own evaluation of his personality gathered from several interviews is that he was a genius who didn't require the extensive training necessary to become, for instance, a doctor, but was able to achieve specialized knowledge on a day-to-day basis thanks to his innate talents.

Unable to accept his comparatively humble position in life, Demara embarked on a lifelong pursuit of an identity worthy of his narcissistic vision of himself as a genius, a process which thereby served to deny his real identity: a rather ordinary man whose talents were unlikely to extract him from what he perceived as the mire of mediocrity.

This denial of one's everyday "normal" identity and its replacement by an assumed grandiose identity is symbolized by the impostor's fascination with changing his name. Krull envied his sister's change of name upon learning of her impending marriage and looked forward to the day when he could lay aside "like a soiled and worn-out garment the name to which I was born." The name here, of course, is a substitute for Krull's identity as a defective, unpleasing and ultimately unsatisfactory person (a soiled and worn-out garment). For this reason, he assumes at a later point in his life the name (identity) of a wealthy and distinguished prince.

As a prelude to this, Krull works as a waiter in a fashionable Parisian restaurant. There, his obsession with duality inspires in him the fantasy of an interchangeability between the guests and the servants, who, he believed, are separated only by an "accidental and interchangeable aristocracy."

"With a change of clothes and makeup, the servitors might often just as well have been the masters, and many of those who lounged in the deep wicker chairs, smoking their cigarettes, might have played the waiter. It was pure accident that the reverse was the fact, an accident of wealth."

As a response to this reflection, Krull strikes up a friendship with a wealthy, "engaging young cavalier of airy and carefree manner" who is studying at a nearby academy. From the first moment of their meeting, the nobleman provides Krull with the opportunity to achieve an identity capable of doing justice to his lifelong conviction of being constituted of "finer clay." On one occasion, the nobleman observes to his girlfriend that she wouldn't mind if he and Krull were to change places. "How strange that he should have put into words the preoccupation of my leisure moments, my silent game of exchanging roles," observed Krull.

Eventually the exchange of roles takes place in order that the nobleman may remain in Paris with his girlfriend, while Krull assumes his identity and embarks on a lengthy round-the-world trip planned by the nobleman's parents as a way of breaking up their son's romance. Thus, what started out as fantasy becomes reality: Krull assumes the identity of a nobleman he had been admiring at a distance. And just as quickly as the bargain is agreed upon, Krull slips comfortably into the aristocratic role.

"It was the change and renewal of my worn-out self, the fact that I had been able to put off the old Adam and slip on a new, that gave me such a sense of fulfillment and happiness. I was struck, though, by the fact that in this change of existence there was not simply delightful refreshment but also a sort of emptying out of my innermost being."

Such statements are common among psychopaths, particularly impostors. Basically, the impostor lacks a sense of self: a conviction of being one person born at a certain time who possesses certain abilities along with an inevitable number of liabilities and deficiencies. Seeking for perfection in the form of an idealized self

and failing to find it, the impostor searches for ways of altering external reality in order to create and stage-manage situations in
which, finally, the impostor's talent, beauty, genius, etc. can be
recognized.

The Psychology of "As If"

The psychoanalyst Helene Deutsch treated for many years an impostor whom she called Jimmy. In a paper written in 1955 she speculated on the childhood influences that are likely in later years to produce an impostor. "Jimmy," like the fictional Krull, was born into a wealthy family and suffered the loss of his father at an early age. In both instances, grief was superficial and short-lived, followed by an increasingly rich fantasy life. Daydreams of heroic deeds, great talents and unusual exploits served as substitutes for the normal play activities with other children.

"His narcissism did not permit him to be one of many; his self-love could be nourished only by feelings that he was unique," Deutsch writes. Rather than stimulating a withdrawal from others, however, Jimmy's desire for uniqueness led him to imagine the world about him as a "stage on which he was destined to play the leading role with the rest of humanity as an admiring audience."

Jimmy's search for narcissistic gratification led him to adopt several different roles during his treatment by Helene Deutsch. At one time, he was a "gentleman farmer" dressed in an elegant country outfit, complete with dyed blond hair and eyebrows, who would, on occasion, visit his friends in New York, where he would sit for hours at a time in fashionable restaurants, all the while declaiming on the merits of "country life."

Later, he presided over a "literary salon" and identified himself as a short-story writer. Always generous, almost profligate in matters of expense, Jimmy was able to entice several established writers to join the circle. Finally, after his own stories were the object of critical appraisal, the "salon" was disbanded.

A similar situation developed shortly thereafter when Jimmy relinquished his "literary career" to become a movie producer. After losing thousands of dollars on various Hollywood projects, Jimmy traded in his Hollywood identity for that of an "inventor," eventually managing to persuade a well-known physicist to collaborate with him on several inventions. Through skillful manipulation, Jimmy was even able to convince the physicist that several of his own achievements were actually due to Jimmy's inspiration.

Recalling in later years her experiences with impostors, Helene Deutsch writes of one of them: "Reading his life history one sees that he was perpetually in pursuit of an identity which would do justice to his narcissistic conception of himself in terms of 'I am a genius' and which, at the same time, served to deny his own identity. This denial of his own identity seems to be the chief motive for his actions, as is true in the case of other impostors."

As a result of her experience with Jimmy, Deutsch stressed the impostor's use of fantasy life in order to make up for real or imagined personal deficiencies. "I believe that all impostors have this in common: they assume the identity of other men not because they themselves lack the ability for achievement, but because they have to hide under a strange name to materialize a more or less reality-adapted fantasy." Parenthetically she adds, "It is interesting to observe pathology in what is commonly agreed to be normal. The world is crowded with 'as-if' personalities and, even more so, with impostors and pretenders."

Helene Deutsch's reference to "as-if personalities" dates to an original and highly influential description she had written thirteen years earlier, in 1942. Although the as-if personality isn't exactly an impostor, the similarities are striking.

"The first impression these people make is of complete normality," Deutsch writes. "They are intellectually intact, gifted and bring great understanding to intellectual and emotional problems."

Closer experience, however, reveals certain personality failings which are often difficult to define. Typically gregarious and socially responsive, the as-if personality demonstrates a lack of inner warmth and a loss of genuine emotional contact with people. The expression of feelings is formal but superficial: friendships and romances end suddenly, resulting in a host of different people replacing each other in rapid succession. Throughout all this—and most characteristic—the as-if personality takes on the qualities, traits and beliefs of the person important to him at the moment. His relation to life involves, in Deutsch's words, "a completely passive attitude to the environment with a highly plastic readiness to pick up signals from the outer world and to mold oneself and one's behavior accordingly."

This capacity for identification with other people is combined with a heightened suggestibility, "an automaton-like identification." Lacking a sense of individuality or identity, the as-if personality molds his thoughts and behavior to other people's expectations, resulting in a form of emotional mimicry, lacking depth and genuinely experienced feelings: the as-if quality of their behavior as described by Deutsch.

"All relationships are devoid of any trace of warmth," writes Deutsch. "All the expressions of emotion are formal . . . all inner experience is completely excluded. It is like the performance of an actor who is technically well trained but who lacks the necessary spark to make his impersonations true to life."

This emphasis on the self as an "actor," the "world as a stage," is, of course, not unique to as-if personalities, but rather appears in one form or another in all of the personalities we are discussing in this book. If personality is principally a matter of shifting roles —the rapid and volatile identification of the as-if personality—then the mask is the most suitable vehicle for the expression of whatever "self" is in command at the moment. Further, the person's identification not only shifts from day to day but at any given moment the as-if personality is capable of forming multiple and often contradictory identifications. Since there is no stable and consistent self existing over time, inner conflicts don't exist. Rather, conflicts are projected into the environment.

"The scene of all conflicts remains external like the child for whom everything can proceed without friction, if it only but obey," according to Deutsch. "Both the persistent identification and the passive submission are expressions of the patient's complete adaptation to the current environment, and impart the shadowy quality to the patient's personality."

The preponderance of the as-if personality in our present culture is, of course, almost impossible to gauge. The genuineness of other people's feelings, the depth of their convictions, even the continuity of their personalities, are not easily measured. But by 1955, thirteen years after she had first described the as-if personality, Deutsch was sufficiently impressed with the extent of the problem to remark, "The world is crowded with 'as-if' personalities and even more with impostors and pretenders. Ever since I became interested in the impostor, he pursues me everywhere. I find him among my friends and acquaintances, as well as in myself."

A Meeting with the Master

Reverend Wain exists at the extreme of the continuum of self disorders. He possesses the narcissist's grandiosity and self-absorption along with the borderline's intolerance of intimacy and inability to trust. In addition, due in part no doubt to environmental circumstances, he's carried his need for recognition to the point of criminal activity. He is, in short, a criminal psychopath whose profound disturbance has cut him off from what he contemptuously refers to as the "straight" society.

In Reverend Wain the playacting of the as-if personality is carried to its inevitable conclusion: instead of merely taking on the character of those he associates with, Wain selects a role, in this case that of a clergyman, and acts it out as one might act out a role in a play. This role, in turn, provides some confirmation of an identity.

To the psychopath, appearances are the most important element in an identity. If one looks and acts the part, then, by a strange inner transformation one can become convinced of the reality of this assumed identity. The more grandiose and impressive the impostural role, the greater the degree of personal satisfaction. In addition, the psychopathic impostor eventually gets caught up in the role he's selected. For this reason, Reverend Wain places himself in the middle echelon of con artistry. He has spoken to me frequently of men who are, in his words, "already legends." Like a teenager discussing a favorite sports hero or rock star, the Reverend Wain at such moments becomes energized. "There's one guy in particular you should meet," he said at one point in one of our conversations. "His name is Frank Abagnale, Jr. Maybe something can be done to arrange a meeting between you two."

Three weeks later at 11:10 A.M. I was interrupted by the intrusive buzz from the intercom on my desk. Like most other doctors, I don't relish phone calls while I'm with a patient and I therefore reacted with annoyance and curiosity to this intrusion on my patient's time and my own concentration.

"Yes, Marissa," I said in a tone which conveyed, "This better be good."

"Sorry to interrupt, Dr. Restak, but there's a Mr. Frank Abagnale on the phone from New York. He said he was told to give you a call."

Without a pause I pushed the flashing red hold button: "This is Dr. Restak."

"I understand you want to see me. I'll be in the Tavern on the Green for lunch today at two-fifteen. Can you make it?"

Three hours later, after some frantic schedule changes and a hair-raising cab ride from LaGuardia, I was standing in the crowded foyer at the Tavern on the Green looking for the man who has been billed as the greatest con artist in modern times.

When Frank Abagnale walked in, there was no mistaking him. As the media people would say, he projects an image. Of moderate height and in his early thirties, wearing a dark-blue, perfectly tailored suit, with a diamond lapel pin in the form of the letters F.W.A. and displaying a tall, exquisitely tanned brunette on his right arm, Abagnale is strikingly impressive. He projects exactly the right image of a confident, capable, unhurried and obviously successful young executive.

"Frank Abagnale? I'm Richard Restak."

"Hi . . . this is a friend, Sally." The voice is soft, almost undulant, the gaze penetrating but curiously passive and nonthreatening.

Abagnale turned and inquired about our table, previously reserved for a party of three in the Crystal Room, where, through a canopy of glass, I could see in the late-afternoon sunlight yellow and orange leaves perfectly highlighted against a cloudless blue autumn sky. Abagnale seemed pleased: the ambiance of crystal and glass; an attractive woman at his side; an interviewer with pen and notebook ready to take down his every word. We followed the maître d', Abagnale moving slowly, gracefully and with total assurance. And the maître d' responded accordingly. We were moved to the head of a short line and seated immediately.

"And what would you like to talk to me about?" he asked quietly, his eyes meeting mine.

Abagnale is the perfect interviewee because he does something that no one seems to have time for anymore: he really pays attention to what goes on around him, while remaining totally tuned in to the other person's reactions to him. He reminded me of a languorous jungle cat awaiting its moment to pounce. As he explained it at a later point in our conversation: "A lot of people think that I plan my capers well in advance. Nothing could be further from the truth. I remain alert at all times for the opportunities of the moment. I size up the other person and proceed accordingly."

I was conscious, while formulating a reply to his request about my purpose in talking with him, that Abagnale was stealthfully sizing me up. Who is this doctor from Washington? And, more importantly, what does he want?

I told Abagnale of my interest in impostors and my "admiration" for his work. As I had hoped, the word "admiration" activated the right circuits: Abagnale began speaking and here are some of the things we talked about:

"As a con artist, the money is less important to me than the challenge of outwitting people. You have to be flexible to be able to size up the other person and hit him with just the right approach. On occasion, if you're on the alert, you'll find the other guy is trying to con you in some way. I get a great thrill out of outsmarting such an individual."

Abagnale's talent for "outsmarting" the other individual resulted in his successful impersonation of a Pan Am pilot, a pediatrician, a sociology professor, a federal prison inspector, a lawyer and an FBI agent. According to the indictment against him, Abagnale cashed $2.5 million worth of fraudulent checks, a figure Abagnale says "sounds reasonable." Known to the police in all fifty states and twenty-nine foreign countries, Abagnale jetted back and forth during his career among the world's largest cities living the life, in his words, of "a successful sophisticate." Along the way, he accumulated millions of dollars in assets and forged over seventeen thousand checks. Today, after imprisonment in France, Sweden and the United States, he's on parole, serving as a consultant on white-collar crime and obviously loving every minute of it.

"Let me give you an example of what I mean when I say the con artist often competes against the con man in perfectly ordinary people. Several weeks ago, I was in a southern city to give a talk on white-collar-crime prevention. I was met at the airport by two bank presidents and, on the way back from the airport, we stopped in a service station for some gas. I was just sitting in the back seat thinking of nothing in particular when the gas attendant came over and, in a low voice, asked me if I wanted to buy some stereo equipment. He obviously meant 'hot' stereo equipment. I told him 'sure' and indicated in a louder voice that all three of us would like to see the stuff. Within seconds he produced about two thousand dollars' worth of equipment and said he'd take eight hundred dollars for it. I pulled out eight one-hundred-dollar bills and said: 'Before giving you the money, I'd like to see the receipts you have on all that stuff.' The guy laughed nervously and replied: 'What do you want that for?' I then slowed everything up by pausing just a split second before replying, 'Because we're police officers. Now put that stuff in the trunk of our car and follow us in your car to the police station.'

"Ten minutes later, as our limo approached the police station, the car behind us *mysteriously* made a wrong turn and we wound up with two thousand dollars' worth of stereo equipment free." Frank smiled at this point, a soft, reptilian sort of smile, his eyes unblinking and cold. "You understand, of course. The guy was trying to con me and therefore was vulnerable to a real con man. Best part of it all"—again with the smile—"he wound up thinking he had outsmarted *us:* how could *we* be so stupid as to think *he* was going to follow us to the police station?"

"Wit," "verve" and "style" are words frequently employed by Abagnale to describe his scam schemes. He also apparently operated without the need for violence. He retains to this day an avowed dislike for engaging in any flimflams in which "the little guy gets hurt."

"I don't like ripping off small stores, for instance. In most instances the employees have to make up for the losses or, even worse, they lose their jobs."

His concern for "the little guy" is perhaps reflected by his own physiognomy. Minus the six-hundred-dollar suit, the diamond cufflinks and the alligator shoes, Abagnale's appearance is that of a not unpleasing but in no sense out-of-the-ordinary thirty-year-old. He could be a schoolteacher, a lawyer, a doctor. And it is this very anonymity and free-floating identity that enables Abagnale to successfully impersonate the large cast of different characters he has assumed over the years. Despite their variety, all have one thing in common: the challenge of "putting down a scam."

"There's a type of person whose competitive instincts override reason. He is challenged by a given situation in much the same way as a mountain climber is challenged by a tall peak: because it's there. Right or wrong are not factors, nor are consequences. Such a person looks on crime as a game, and a game is not just the loot, it's the success of the venture that counts."

Success is a word that recurs repetitively in Abagnale's conversation. He now feels that he has finally achieved the success that he's craved. But he's done so in a way that is paradoxically ironic.

"People now are thrilled to make the acquaintance of a con man. When I travel around the country talking on white-collar crime, people want to meet me. They ask me out, provide me with all the tokens of success that are usually associated with doctors or lawyers or whomever I have pretended to be over the years."

Abagnale is most proud of a recent appearance on "The Tonight Show." As well as a confirmation of the "success" he's craved all his life, it also provided him with an insight into one of the reasons he's been able to pull off so many capers.

"Carson told me I could have been a comic. It's all based on timing, he said, and my timing is absolutely perfect," Abagnale recounted, his face frequently freezing into a perfectly executed impersonation of Carson's mixture of sardonism and patronizing dismay when performing before an audience which isn't quite quick enough at catching one of his jokes. Abagnale's imitation, though it lasted only a split second, was indeed a confirmation of Carson's verdict on his performance: perfectly timed and executed. Then Abagnale reverted to the cooperative, engagingly charming but at all times essentially serious and restrained demeanor of a public figure responding to the queries of an interviewer.

"After playing so many different roles, who are you really, Frank?"

"A lot of people have asked me that. I guess maybe they suppose I thought I really was a Pan Am pilot or a doctor or whomever I was impersonating at the time. But that's not true. I've always known who I was no matter what I was pretending to be." He paused as if emphasizing his next few statements. "A psychiatrist who examined me in prison concluded—correctly, I believe —that I'm really an introvert rather than an extrovert. Behind all the masks that I've worn, there is the real Frank Abagnale who watches and judges the performance. Believe me, I've always known who I was."

After receiving parole for a twelve-year prison sentence (originally seventy-two years, after he was tried and found guilty under rule twenty of the U. S. Penal Code, an act that covers "all crimes known and unknown") Abagnale wrote down some of his experiences. Published in 1980, *Catch Me If You Can* contains some of Abagnale's reflections on his identity. "I was a swindler and poseur of astonishing ability. I sometimes astonished myself with some of my impersonations and shenanigans, but I never at any time deluded myself. I was always aware that I was Frank Abagnale, Jr."

On all occasions, Abagnale insists on the *Jr.* behind his name, and speaks with a mixture of pride and pity for his father, the victim of Frank's first operation. At age sixteen, Frank parlayed his father's gasoline credit card into $3400 in cash, obtained through talking gasoline attendants into advancing him money against phony purchases of tires and oil.

"Once again, it was my con artistry taking advantage of the con artist in other people. If a set of tires cost a hundred and sixty dollars, I'd settle for ninety dollars in cash, sign the credit receipt and the owner would bill Mobil for the entire hundred and sixty. Best of all, he never had to part with the set of tires. He ripped off Mobil for seventy dollars and I got ninety—not bad for just shoving a piece of plastic in somebody's face and signing your name on a credit slip."

The ultimate victim of Abagnale's credit card scam was, of course, his father. In a curious lapse of logic, Abagnale maintains to this day that he didn't foresee the consequences that his credit card rip-off would have. "It hadn't occurred to me that Dad would be the patsy in the game." Nor has it occurred to him that his father, now dead, would probably not be proud of his son's career. *Catch Me If You Can* is dedicated simply "To my Dad."

"I was confused and bored at home. Depressed at what was happening to my father. He and Mother were divorcing at about this time when I was fourteen. He wanted her back so desperately but she wouldn't hear of it. Once she made up her mind and left him, she never could be talked into going back. I was part of Dad's campaign to win her back. 'Talk to her, son,' he'd ask of me. 'Tell her I love her, tell her we'd be happier if we all lived together. Tell her you'd be happier if she came home . . . that all you kids would be happier.' He'd give me gifts to deliver to Mom and coach me in speeches designed to break down my mother's resistance. But my mother couldn't be conned . . . she divorced Dad when I was fourteen."

After the divorce, Abagnale decided to live with his father because "Dad needed one of us." The elder Abagnale, a small-time New York politician, spent a lot of time in "some of New York's finest saloons," an education his son greatly took advantage of. "After hanging out with Dad for six months I was streetwise and about five eighths smart." At about this time, Frank Abagnale, Jr., also began playing hookey from school and hanging out with what he now calls "loose-end kids from my neighborhood."

"These are just guys with a screwed-up family situation trying to get attention from someone, if only the truant officer. Maybe that's why I started hanging out with them. Perhaps I was seeking attention myself. I did want my parents together again, and I had vague notions at the time that if I acted like a juvenile delinquent it might provide a common ground for reconciliation."

Today, Frank Abagnale, Jr., is a curious amalgam of his father's habits and values: flashy cars ("I remember that I was sixteen when Dad had two big Cadillacs"); diamond stickpins adorning expensive suits; and, one suspects, an unending stream of female companions. But there are also traits so diametrically opposed that one suspects they, too, have been adopted in a defiant response to Frank's relationship with his father. For instance, while the elder Abagnale was a "two-fisted drinker," Frank Abagnale, Jr., has always remained a teetotaler. "I don't drink because I don't want to take even the slightest risk that I'll lower my mask even for an instant."

While Frank, Sr., was a dedicated family man whose life "came apart" at the time of his divorce, Frank, Jr., remains unattached. "The blurb on my book jacket claims I live in Houston with a wife and daughter, but that's a scam too. Many of my talks are given to family people and I want to come across as one of them."

Most of all, the younger Abagnale has retained throughout his adult life a grim determination never to suffer the personal and financial setbacks which plagued his father's later years. "While I was in reform school"—after the gasoline credit card caper—"Dad went into financial difficulties and lost his business. He was really wiped out. Forced to sell the house, his two Cadillacs, everything. In the space of a few months, Dad went from living like a millionaire to living like a postal clerk."

After running away from home and setting up in New York, the younger Abagnale finally settled on his lifetime goal: to be a success.

"I did have a definite goal. I was going to be a success in some field. I was going to make it to the top of some mountain, and once there no one was going to dislodge me from the peak. I wasn't going to make the mistakes my Dad had made. I was determined on that point."

Frank Abagnale, Jr.'s, relationship with his father is most interesting in the area of personal success. After suffering severe financial losses, the elder Abagnale was, in his son's words, "wiped out." Forced to sell his expensive cars, he drove a "battered old Chevy" and lived in a small apartment. Once when asked by his son how he felt about his reverses he replied: "That's the wrong way to look at it, Frank. It's not what a man has but what a man is that's important. This car is fine for me. It gets me around. I know who I am and what I am, and that's what counts . . . as long as a man knows what he is and where he is, he'll be all right."

"Trouble was," the younger Abagnale wrote in *Catch Me If You Can*, "at the time I didn't know what I was or who I was." But within three years, Frank, Jr., assures us, he finally knew who he was: "anyone I want to be."

Frank, Jr.'s, odyssey of impersonation was spurred on by his need to achieve and retain the kind of success his father had so ignominiously lost. His first and most frequent impersonation was that of an airline pilot, whose uniform "marked the wearer as a person of rare skills, courage or achievement." In another age Frank might have selected knight errant or entrepreneur. The details are less important than the image and the prestige. "A man's alter ego is nothing more than his favorite image of himself," says Abagnale. "The mirror in my room in the Windsor Hotel in Paris reflected my favorite image of me . . . a darkly handsome young airline pilot, smooth-skilled, bull-shouldered and immaculately groomed.

"It was heady stuff and, in fact, I became instantly addicted. During the next five years the uniform was my alter ego. I used it in the same manner a junkie shoots up on heroin. Whenever I felt lonely, depressed, rejected or doubtful of my own worth, I'd dress up in my pilot's uniform and seek out a crowd. The uniform brought me respect and dignity. Without it on, at times, I felt useless and dejected. With it on, during such times, I felt like I was wearing Fortunatus' cap and walking in seven-league boots."

Today, sitting with an attractive brunette amid the hustle and ambiance of the Tavern on the Green, Frank appears a successful, self-assured man of the world. One has no difficulty imagining him in an ad for Chivas Regal or Rolls-Royce, or maybe American Express.

"A couple of months ago the American Express people approached me about doing one of their ads. I'm sure you've seen them. 'You don't know me, but wherever I travel I'm never without my American Express card,' and I pull out the American Express card from my pocket, winding up with ten or twelve cards in my hand as I look around for the cops," Frank says with a laugh, once again mimicking Johnny Carson playing at being outrageous.

"You do that Carson thing so well, Frank," I said. "Your impersonation just made me think of something I never realized before: Carson is kind of a con man, isn't he?"

"Exactly! Now you're getting to what imposture is all about." Abagnale paused, his gaze intent and serious for the first time. "Now let me ask you something, Dr. Restak. When I first went public and admitted I was an impostor, I expected that people would hate me and show me nothing but contempt. But they didn't. Soon I got up the nerve to do some public speaking. The same thing happened: no hecklers, just people who couldn't wait to meet me. And now my book is on the best-seller list. Now for the question: Why are people so interested in impostors? Why is the con man of such interest to so many people?"

Suspecting that Frank had the answer to the question he had just asked and being more interested in hearing his ideas and speculations on the matter than my own, I replied: "I haven't any idea."

"Well, I have. The impostor is the hero of our age. We live in the era of the rip-off artist. Everybody's ripping off the little guy: the government, the oil companies, people's banks. As a result, the little guy is ecstatic when he reads about an impostor or a con artist ripping off these huge megalithic organizations which seem so impregnable. What can the ordinary person do about taxes or high interest rates or expensive gasoline? Nothing. So isn't it fun to read about somebody who stings these organizations!

"Another thing. Consider how many people are involved in jobs that are essentially nothing more than scams of one sort or another. Many lawyers, most public relations people, a lot of middle-level managers—they're all con artists. It's all based on impressing people—asking them to believe something about you that you want them to believe. If you can impress somebody you can also intimidate them."

Although he didn't discuss the matter in psychological terms, Frank Abagnale, Jr., impresses me as a man with a deep split in his personality. A lifetime fascination with mirrors; his frequent references to "image" and techniques ("I learned early that class is universally admired; almost any fault, sin or crime is considered more leniently if there's a touch of class involved"); his references to masks behind which he hides to observe and comment on the "style" of his own performance; his ability to coolly size up the opposition; the use of imposture to shore up a flagging sense of identity—all point to a fundamental disturbance in the self. His present identity as an expert on white-collar crime serves the same purpose as his previous impostures. "I'm still a con artist," Frank said at one point in our conversation. "But now the game is a legal one. Now I get the recognition, money and success within the law that I had to commit crimes for in the past. All in all, I think I'm pretty lucky."

With the luncheon finished, Frank called for the check and, after barely glancing at the total, he flipped the waiter a gold American Express card. "A few years ago these people wanted me in jail," he said with a flashing smile. "Now that I'm making it they only want my business. So who's the con artist and who's the victim?"

Frank Abagnale, Jr., and the Reverend Wain are worlds apart on the continuum of manipulative confidence men. While Wain is a plodder, Abagnale is an inspired con man's con man: smooth, articulate and possessing an exquisite sense of presence and timing. They share similar dynamics, however: confusion early in life regarding who they "really are"; the overweaning need to be "important" without investing the requisite time and effort for legitimate accomplishment; the grandiosity which fuels an increasing ambition to "be somebody." But the "somebody" is always evaluated by the imagery of video: flashing cars, exotically beautiful women, luxury apartments.

Conjure up in your mind all the images of the American success story and you can picture Frank Abagnale, Jr., occupying it with aplomb. As we'll discuss in more detail in the last portion of this book, psychopathy and contemporary life symbiotically support each other. A culture where "appearance" is everything breeds personalities who take their sense of self from the things they can accumulate. When one's identity is inextricably bound up with externals, there is no real need for an inner life. The psychopathic impostor is a robot who programs himself early in life and then careens out of control for the next thirty or forty years. Further, his identity is tied up with outfoxing the rest of us. To this extent, the impostor is an extreme competitor. He is out to show the rest of us how stupid or incompetent we are compared to his own cleverness and adaptiveness. Cynically aware of the petty larceny which is at the basis of everyday social life, the impostor enthusiastically throws himself into the roles we have all come to admire. Loving the "little guy," excited about the possibility that, on occasion, great institutions can be brought to their knees through the efforts of single individuals, we're natural patsies when it comes to people like Abagnale. We not only endure such impostors, we positively encourage them. Who doesn't feel a nagging sense within his own heart of hearts that he is not, to some extent, an impostor? "Show me a man who is not an impostor at least in little ways and I'll show you a failure," Frank Abagnale told me. "We're all impostors and our greatest fun comes from finding each other out."

Given the present state of things in the United States, we can probably expect the number of full-fledged impostors to increase. Certainly the number of impostors within the business and academic community is on the increase. The Harvard Business School, for instance, receives four or five fraudulent requests a week for transcripts and recommendations. Typically, an impostor will call the school giving the name of a bona fide graduate and requesting a copy of his transcript. Once received, the name on the transcript is altered and the document included in a portfolio sent to prospective employers.

In an interview with the New York *Times* on the subject of impostors, Robert Houghton, Associate Registrar at Stanford University, said, "the number of inquiries we're getting from companies and the number of fraudulent cases have both more than doubled in the past five years." Houghton estimated that Stanford also detected about four or five impostors per week.

This increase in impostors, although deeply disturbing, shouldn't come as a surprise. Imposture is the natural consequence of a society in which the appearance of success is as important as success itself. Further, impostors are charming, they're ingratiating, they are simultaneously gratifying to our senses of amusement and cynicism, etc. Most important, they play within the rules set down by a success-oriented, materialistic society. In a world where there exist deeply felt but unexpressed feelings of inadequacy, what greater way to overcome these feelings than through imposture?

Who hasn't experienced the transformation which can be brought about by throwing worries aside, dressing up for an evening and going forth to meet the world with a brazen insouciance? With the impostor, life itself is a matter of dressing up for the dual purpose of elevating his sense of personal integration and imposing a self-constructed persona upon others. At some point, however, the imposture breaks down and the borderline is crossed into a violent, even murderous grasping for those things that can't be wheedled by charm and manipulation. In the next section we'll explore the outer limits of psychopathy through an examination of several murderers.

VII

The Destroyers

"In the blindest fury of destructiveness the satisfaction of an instinct is accompanied by an extraordinarily high degree of narcissistic enjoyment . . . owing to its old wishes for omnipotence."

Sigmund Freud

Homicidal Rage: The Ultimate Manipulation

In the New York subway system during 1980, a series of sudden, seemingly spontaneous knifings occurred: People chosen at random were brutally assaulted with a knife wielded by an unknown assailant who fled, only to reappear a day or two later and repeat his performance. In response to such "insane" happenings, many people shake their heads in dismay and frustration. They feel that no one can ever explain such bizarre attacks.

Theories have abounded in the past which purportedly explain why some people kill others, seemingly without motive. Freud, for instance, related criminal behavior to an unconscious sense of guilt. A variation of this envisioned violent behavior to be an expression of an unconscious need for punishment. Combining these views with yet a third view results in an explanation which postulated that homicidal assault represents (1) an attack on an ungiving persecutory environment, (2) a mechanism for the alleviation of guilt, and (3) an unconscious demand for punishment. Despite the superficial appeal of such explanations, they really provide little in the way of understanding past homicides or preventing future ones.

In recent years, attempts at psychological understanding of the dynamics of violence have centered on issues regarding personal integration—in essence, disorders of the self. In contrast to facile references to "unconscious guilt," contemporary workers are concentrating on investigating the extent to which youthful offenders envision themselves as independent and worthwhile individuals in their own right, separate from parents and other family members. In many instances, this separation is faulty and results in incom-

plete or pathologic development in the self. According to the formulation as discussed earlier (enter Dr. Kohut), such individuals
retain a *self-object merger*. Oftentimes, the object part of this
merger is a hated, resented figure, for instance, a mother who is
perceived as unavailable or rejecting. This "negative" object is
often repudiated by projecting it into other people in the environment. Thus the potential juvenile murderer splits off the unacceptable part of himself and attributes it to the victim, who is
thus depersonalized. In a typical instance, the victim is responded
to in a way which corresponds to the murderer's perception of his
parent: cold, unreasonable and hostilely rejecting. Only in this instance, the rage response isn't inhibited as it would be with the
parent; instead, it is acted out in a murderous frenzy.

The second indication of the importance of narcissistic issues in
homicidal behaviors comes from the study of sudden murder, single, isolated, unexpected episodes of violent, impulsive behavior
which is not premeditated and occurs without obvious purpose,
such as profit or other personal advantage. From a study of over
forty sudden murderers, a composite picture emerges of an individual suffering from a deficient and distorted sense of self. In
most instances, the killers, all of them male, exhibited a lifelong
helplessness in controlling their own identity. They were dependent on others, primarily parents or spouses, but at the same time
deeply resented the dependency. Typically, the murder took place
in a setting of rejection. Many of the killers studied seemed unable to accept the dissolution of a relationship. One man who
pleaded unsuccessfully for his wife to reunite with him arrived at
her apartment with a rifle which he had hastily purchased. "Come
back to me or I'll shoot myself," he cried. She responded, "Who
cares, go ahead." He then fired three shots into her head.

Another murderer, formerly addicted to alcohol and narcotics,
went back to work as a laboratory technician, discontinued all
drugs and reestablished a marital relationship described by his psychiatrist as "superficially good." At this point, the wife indicated
that she was leaving him, a course of action she had considered
for several years, but felt she could only carry out now that her
husband was "adjusting so well." This threatened abandonment

and rejection stimulated a brutal rage which culminated in a particularly gruesome mutilation-murder.

Behind these separate murders lurked a fear of a loss of control, either of the self or of some part of the environment, as perceived by the attacker. Self-esteem issues loomed large in all instances. Threatened with further deterioration in the sense of integration, filled with a sense of personal inadequacy, helplessness and frustration, the murderers lashed out in an attempt to repair the loss of the sense of self. Typically, there was an absence of regret and remorse regarding the murder. Many of the murderers studied continued to feel that their behavior was justified on the basis of the deep sense of betrayal they had experienced.

Psychoanalyst James B. McCarthy, writing in the *American Journal of Psychoanalysis,* describes his conclusions after examining ten adolescent murderers: "In my view, their expression of the homicidal rage can be understood as an attempt at reparation of the self." In each case the murderer failed to experience himself as an independent individual. The self-concept remained merged with that of fearsome, frightening persons in the environment (often rejecting parents). Self-esteem fluctuated wildly from grandiose self-sufficiency to the depths of vulnerability and helplessness.

Fueling these rapid shifts in self-esteem regulation was a predominant emphasis on *shame* rather than *guilt* as a regulator of behavior. In each instance, something had happened immediately prior to the murder which resulted in a severe blow to the narcissist's self-esteem. A powerfully destructive rage was set off against the individual who had inflicted the narcissistic wound. This was a feeble attempt to repair a fragmented identity. Within such a setting the personality of the victim is irrelevant: in all cases, the youths showed no remorse over the murder and continued to voice anger and violence toward their deceased victims. In their own minds, the narcissistic injuries that they had experienced justified the extreme measures that they had taken. The murder, in fact, confirmed their sense of reality and personal integration. "Homicidal acts or explosively violent assaults can be understood as attempts at redress of a common narcissistic vulnerability," writes McCarthy.

Despite the importance of McCarthy's findings in regard to narcissism and murder, it must be pointed out that each of the ten murderers came from extremely chaotic backgrounds (in nine cases the parents had deserted); they were not, in other words, typical of the kinds of narcissistic manipulators I've described throughout this book. Nevertheless, the importance of narcissistic issues in provoking a murderous onslaught, particularly the reparative effect on self-experience brought about by homicidal attack, is worthy of note. These people killed in order to retain some semblance of self-integration. The extent of this fury (one youngster brutally slashed his mother with a kitchen knife), along with the absence of any remorse, underscores the power of narcissistic rage. There isn't the slightest doubt that these young murderers thought themselves entirely justified in what they had done. They reacted, in fact, as if their murderous assault had been provoked in self-defense, and, in a way, this was true: their self-integration, their experience of themselves as separate, distinct and worthwhile individuals, had been threatened.

In each instance, there was a glaring gap between real accomplishment or potential and the murderer's self-concept. The boy who slashed his mother to death was seventeen, of dull normal intelligence, at a third-grade reading level but with a fantasy life that included a vision of himself as a world-famous archeologist. In order to maintain this grandiose vision of himself as a special person, he had taken to carrying a knife with him at all times. Soon, his self-esteem and personal integration became dependent on violent, antisocial acts which culminated in the rageful murder of his mother.

If narcissistic rage can lead to acts of murder, how does it differ from simple aggression? Dr. Kohut pointed to a "specific psychological flavor" of the aggression of narcissistic rage. In instances of simple aggression, the violent or hostile act is directed toward a fairly limited objective. The offender is reacted to as a specific individual who has done something that, in the aggressor's mind, is deserving of hostile action. Overall, though, the process is a limited one. Not so with narcissistic rage.

"The need for revenge," said Kohut, "for righting a wrong, for undoing a hurt by whatever means, and a deeply anchored, unrelenting compulsion in the pursuit of all these aims which gives no rest to those who have suffered a narcissistic injury—these are the features that are characteristic of the phenomenon of narcissistic rage in all its forms and which set it apart from other kinds of aggression."

Although narcissistic rage is multidetermined, the underlying dynamic seems to rest on shame rather than guilt. It is common among the Japanese, for example, since their society emphasizes—particularly in child rearing—ridicule and the threat of ostracism as social control mechanisms. As a result, there is a need to maintain decorum and dignity at all times. Faced with humiliation or the threat of social embarrassment, an individual may fly into a murderous, rageful assault on himself or others.

In *The Chrysanthemum and the Sword*, sociologist Ruth Benedict describes the narcissistic rage of the Japanese: "Sometimes people explode into the most aggressive acts. They are roused to these aggressions not when their principles or their freedom is challenged . . . but when they detect an insult or a detraction."

A similar process of violent, seemingly senseless paroxysms of homicidal rage is increasingly encountered within our own society. On the basis of "insignificant slights," massive displays of anger and rage are set off, often culminating in homicide. Unless the phenomenon of narcissistic rage is kept in mind, these attacks appear gratuitous, utterly senseless. Yet in a society where shame rather than guilt serves as a motivator and sustainer of self-integration and self-esteem, the propensity for rageful acts will increase. In a society where "appearance" is everything, shame is easily provoked leading to panicky feelings of self-annihilation. Once people cease to derive their sense of self from internal standards they become totally dependent on the confirming responses of other people. They actually become the personality that others create for them via social interaction. Thus, individuals who are attempting to maintain a grandiose self-image (the seventeen-year-old with a third-grade reading level but with fantasies of becoming a world-famous archeologist) exhibit an exquisite sensitivity toward slights and disparagements. In such a mind-set, the world must conform to their distorted or unrealistic self-evaluations. Those who will not conform—the detractors and denigrators—must be utterly destroyed.

"The enemy who calls forth the archaic rage of the narcissistically vulnerable, is seen by him not as an autonomous source of impulsions, but *as a flaw in a narcissistically perceived reality,*" writes Kohut.

The narcissist's grandiosity—the need to maintain an inflated, unrealistic version of the self—is the flip side of a deeply entrenched feeling of worthlessness and inferiority. A narcissistically vulnerable and potentially dangerous individual cannot achieve an integrated experience of himself, but seesaws between inflated, fantastic visions (a world-famous archeologist) and the limitations which will realistically preclude any real achievement (borderline I.Q., third-grade reading level and so on). Unable to reconcile these splits and contradictions, the individual may opt for the grandiosity, thus cutting himself off further from other people to whom such a narcissistically disturbed person is either an object of amusement or dismay.

Homicidal rage is the ultimate measure resorted to in an effort to repair the damaged sense of self. It is the *ultimate manipulation,* in which the victim is depersonalized, reacted to as a repudiated aspect of the self. Thus, murder serves a narcissistic function since the rage is directed not at a person who exists in his own right, but a phantom, a combination of the killer (self) and those people in the environment (objects) against whom he rages: in essence, a fused self object, to employ the term preferred by Heinz Kohut.

In addition, the expression of narcissistic rage restores the sense of integration by restoring some degree of self-esteem. The killer experiences himself as justified in his action; he shows no remorse. The perpetrator experiences a total lack of empathy for the victim. Narcissistic rage involves both a hunger for revenge and a persistent compulsion to pursue it. At the basis of these compulsions are feelings of anxiety, helplessness and inadequacy. The murder quietens these profoundly uncomfortable feelings, thus leading to an increase of self-integration, itself a prerequisite to any form of self-esteem. Given the right circumstances, the process can take place in a short period of time. The presence of overt sadistic or masochistic elements, for instance, permits the eruption of explosive rage to occur with a chilling suddenness. Typical of this was a homicide in the Washington, D.C., area, known as the "Parakeet Murder."

The Murder of a Parakeet

Skip Adams-Taylor, a twenty-year-old homosexual, identified himself as a British subject and a sailor in the Australian Navy. Actually, Adams-Taylor had never been in Australia and hailed from a small town in Georgia. He had served a short stint in the Navy, but the U. S. Navy, since Adams-Taylor was an American citizen and not a British subject, as he claimed. He was, in essence, an impostor, but an impostor with a potential for explosive and murderous rage, as subsequent events were to show.

On the evening of July 25, 1980, Adams-Taylor ordered a limousine driver to take him to a local disco, where he met a woman, Joyce D. Robertson, got "real drunk," according to his own testimony, and left with the woman late in the evening. For the next hour, the two of them sipped champagne and toured Washington while watching "Prisoner of Cell Block 8" on the limousine's color TV. They were then driven to the woman's apartment, where, in Adams-Taylor's words, "they began playing a sex-oriented game with a whip." Adams-Taylor continued to drink more wine and apparently, at some point, passed out on the woman's bed. Here are the events which occurred after that, according to Adams-Taylor's tape-recorded account to investigating detectives.

"The next morning she got out of bed at seven and I was tired and I wanted to just go back to sleep . . . but she wanted to have sex and I didn't.

"All I was thinking was, I have to get out of here . . . After 'Wonder Woman' she got the whip and started hitting me. I was getting tired of getting hit with a whip by a girl, so I suggested we take a shower.

"She wanted to have sex and I didn't want to. I knew she would say, 'Oh, he doesn't find me very attractive' . . . then it dawned on me, I'll make her choke until she passes out and then I'll leave."

Adams-Taylor came up behind his victim as she was lying on the couch with the whip draped around her neck. The whip snapped. "I think she thought I was just playing around," Adams-Taylor recalled. His victim did not resist. He then snatched the sash from the woman's robe, knotted it around her neck and strangled her. At this point, the victim's pet parakeet, freed from its cage, began peeping with this result: "The little bird began to peep and peep and it made me nervous," Adams-Taylor recalled. He grabbed the bird, ripped off its head with his bare hands and tossed it near his victim's body.

Adams-Taylor's defense consisted of the assertion that the murder resulted from a failed attempt to spare his victim's feelings. "She would feel badly, unwanted, rejected," he wished the jury to believe. To spare her these painful feelings he had hit upon a plan of choking her "until she passes out and then I'll leave."

"She'll hate me, but the thing is that she won't be crying and I don't like for girls to cry. I figured [she would pass out] long enough for me to grab all my things. I didn't mean to kill her."

Left at this, the parakeet murder sounds like a case of bad judgment and the misapplication of excessive force. There is little to suggest that the murder resulted from the narcissistic rage that we discussed earlier. A cross examination by a detective who recorded Adams-Taylor's explanation of the events, provided a clue to the killer's true motivation.

"He told me that there were two kinds of women: 'sluts and fishes who were promiscuous and would have sexual contact on the first or second date and sisters, who are somebody nonsexual.'" Adams-Taylor then told the detective that he beat the victim's dead body with the whip while screaming that she was a "no-good slut."

A tentative, more convincing re-creation of events goes something like this: Adams-Taylor's homosexuality and expressed animus toward women (the fish) who are sexually "free" (the sluts) was given dangerously free expression through the use of a whip and the enactment of sadomasochistic fantasies. Although he was the victim—the one being beaten—his own precarious sense of identity (the false British accent, his claim to be in the Australian Navy and so on) coupled with his unwillingness or, more likely, inability to perform sexually, stirred up overwhelming feelings of inadequacy and anger. At this point, his identification with his victim became so complete that he attributed his own sense of personal humiliation and devaluation to her. If he left the apartment, thereby rejecting her, she would begin to experience the narcissistic hurt which he was feeling. "I knew she would say, 'Oh, he doesn't find me very attractive.'" It is likely that his own sense of personal inadequacy coupled with his rage at a woman whose moral behavior he despised, yet was curiously drawn to, provided the setting for murder. The final and necessary ingredient, however, was the whip used in the sadomasochistic sex-oriented game. At some point, the killer began to experience further dissolution, a true splitting within his consciousness.

"I began to panic . . . my subconscious was saying she's dead, but your conscious always tells you things like that and I said, no, she just passed out, she's not going to be asleep very much longer so you better hurry."

This expressed concern for his victim's feelings is followed moments later by the whipping of her now-dead body, accompanied by repetitive recitations that the girl was a "no-good slut."

This reconstruction of events based on Skip Adams-Taylor's own sworn testimony remains nonetheless only a partial account. No one knows for certain what was said or done on the evening of July 25, 1980. The sequence of events, however, bears an eerie similarity to the plot of Judith Rossner's *Looking for Mr. Goodbar*. A comparison of the Parakeet Murder and the fictionalized murder described by Rossner sheds considerable light on the ways narcissism can lead to sudden, brutal murders.

In this best-selling novel the main character, Theresa Dunn, is brutally murdered by a drifter, Gary Cooper White, she picks up in a bar. White's tape-recorded confession of the events leading up to the murder is almost identical in tone to the tape-recorded testimony given by Skip Adams-Taylor concerning the real-life murder of Joyce D. Robertson. But in the novel, the elements of devaluation and narcissistic rage are explicitly spelled out.

In the first few pages the narrator highlights the "most notable quality" of White's confession: "Gary White, who had brutally assaulted and murdered Theresa Dunn a few hours after meeting her in a Manhattan singles spot called Mr. Goodbar, had a very clear sense of himself as the victim of the woman he had murdered." In order to understand how this could be so, we have to delve a little further into *Looking for Mr. Goodbar.* The motivation of the murderer in this novel sheds considerable light not only on the Parakeet Murder, but on the subject of narcissistic rage in general.

Almost invariably, a narcissistic rage powerful enough to lead to murder involves a two-way destructive communication in which one person, the victim, sets out by verbal assault to destroy the self of a narcissistically vulnerable individual. In response to this fragmenting and profoundly disorienting experience, the devalued person lashes out in a vengeful attack which culminates in murder. To this extent the murderer and the victim each suffer from the consequences of a distorted narcissism.

Theresa Dunn's background includes a case of polio contracted as a child. Later, the muscular imbalance in her back leads to scoliosis (a bending of the spine). The effect of this physical deformity is exceeded only by the emotional scars which it creates. Theresa experiences permanent feelings of rage toward her parents. If the scoliosis had been diagnosed early enough, casts probably could have prevented the deformity—or, at least, so she believes. In addition to the resentment which Theresa feels toward her parents because of their failure to prevent her deformity (a mild one, it seems, since few people in the novel are even aware of her limp), she is also displaced in her parents' affection by an older sister, Katherine, who is treated "like a movie star" by the rest of the family. Out of this complex background of physical deformity, anger, guilt and jealousy, Theresa fashions a false self much in the manner of the false selves described by Laing in the earlier chapters of this book.

As an adult, Theresa takes on a hard, cynical image in which sexuality is split off from all tender feelings. When others love her, she only despises them for their weakness. Throughout it all are rare insights into her lack of personal integration created by the maintenance of two separate selves:

"Actually, when she thought about it all, she didn't really feel that she *had* a life, one life, that is, belonging to a person, Theresa Dunn. There was a Miss Dunn who taught a bunch of children who adored her ('Oh, that's Miss Dunn,' she heard one of her children say once to a parent. 'She's one of the kids. A big one.') and there was someone named Terry who whored around in bars when she couldn't sleep at night. But the only thing those two people had in common was the body they inhabited. If one died, the other would never miss her—although she herself, Theresa, the person who thought and felt but had no life, would miss either one."

This split within Theresa's personality—between two separate, paradoxical but, most of all, contradictory selves—is expressed even in her living arrangements. The furnishings in the apartments she has lived in most recently have a dissonance about them that reflects the dissonance and splits within her own personality. "Her old possessions were there and she still loved them . . . But the things she had added . . . they didn't look as though they belonged in the same apartment with the other stuff. As though two people with different tastes and personalities had pooled their belongings in one room."

And there are other similarities between Theresa's feelings about her apartment and her feelings about herself. Just as an apartment is separated into different rooms, Theresa's inner life is divided into nonconnecting "compartments," only some of which are "real." Theresa's relationship with a lawyer friend who is crazy about her is "real" but, at the same time, is marked by cynical, hurting barbs which Theresa launches in order to keep him at a distance. "She'd had to constantly define her boundaries for fear of his stepping over them." But with the pickups she meets in bars, this process of defending isn't necessary. She can merely withdraw into herself, view her body in the act of making love in a curious, detached way.

This split within Theresa is most apparent in the division she has set up in her mind between love and sexuality. As part of her hard, cynical other self she revels in episodic, anonymous trysts with "lovers" she can discard in the morning. Any efforts to establish more stable, affectionate relationships, however, result in the emergence of her hurt, fragile self whose existence she refuses to acknowledge. "There is no point to this kind of talk," she says to the one man who loves her but whose love frightens and angers her. "You have the misery once and then if you talk about it again you have it again."

Theresa lives within a falsified world in which all tenderness and all possibilities for commitment are denied. In addition, it's a world without hope or purpose. She is cut off from her past by anger and guilt, with the future equally inaccessible to her. Theresa illustrates better than any other character in modern literature the lack of continuity, the loss of self which results when inner splitting is used to resolve emotional distress. She is a borderline personality whose everyday functioning is successful except for when it comes to managing affection or aggression. These emotions can only be handled by "splitting" herself into a hard, cynical self and a frightened, fragile self whose feelings can't be expressed or even talked about lest the feelings become overwhelming. "If I don't talk about it, I don't feel it," she responds when asked why she chooses not to talk about her feelings. This split within herself leaves her drifting without a sense of purpose or identity, never really knowing what she wants.

"What *did* she want anyway? She tried to think of some specific thing she wanted, in the present or in the future. She'd never really thought in those terms and it was a problem for her to do so now . . . You could only know who you were and what you wanted *now*. How could you be so sure you would exist in a year, much less that you would want what one year back in time you'd thought you would want?"

Theresa's response to her helplessness is a deepening capacity for anger and sudden senseless outbursts of stinging verbal hostility. It's this periodic accumulation and discharge of rage that eventually leads to her death. It also accounts for the murderer's perception of himself as Theresa's victim.

Gary Cooper White, Theresa's murderer, shares her propensity for splitting the self into compartments. A fugitive, with a pregnant wife in Florida, he fled to New York some weeks before the murder and took up residence with a homosexual. In his tape-recorded confession, the contradictions which result from his fragmented sense of self appear in the explanations he offers for his relations with the homosexual. At first he states that he was unaware that his benefactor was a homosexual who was attracted to him. Later he admits to knowing that the man was gay, but expresses confidence that he could "handle it." At a later point in the confession, he experiences genuine surprise when the police ask him about money sewn into the hem of his coat. Weeks earlier, he had put it there with the intention of mailing it to his wife; he then promptly "forgot about it." Evidently, the splits within White's personality extend even to his memory for real-life events.

With this as a background it's possible to discern the striking similarity between the fictional killing of Theresa Dunn and the real-life killing of Joyce D. Robertson. Both murders followed rejections. After sex, Theresa demands that White leave her apartment: she can't stand the thought of facing him "over coffee in the morning." Her insistence that he leave incites White to a narcissistic rage. Like Skip Adams-Taylor, he claims in his later confession that he only intended to temporarily restrain his victim. He begins muffling her cries with a pillow. She bites and kicks at him, screaming all the while for help. Finally, in a fury he smashes her skull with a lamp.

"I pulled the lamp off the table and smashed it down on her head. It was like I wasn't thinking. I swear to God. It was like someone else was doing it. I remember I'm looking down at her just before I bring it down and I'm looking at her face . . . she's so scared . . . but it's like I had nothing to do with it. It's like I'm a million miles away."

Each of the perpetrators in these two murders experiences a momentary identification with his victim. Adams-Taylor murders to spare his victim's feelings. "She would feel badly, unwanted, rejected." In fact, it was he who felt rejected and humiliated, culminating in his whipping of her body after the strangling.

In the fictional *Looking for Mr. Goodbar* (based loosely on a real-life murder in Manhattan) both victim and murderer experience a momentary identification with each other. Theresa, moments before her death, lies "on her side without moving, facing his back, barely breathing for fear that he would become aware of her awareness. As ashamed as though it were *she* doing this disgusting, humiliating thing in the bed next to someone else."

After the murder, White rushes from the apartment only to discover that his leg hurts and he must limp in the manner of Theresa. "I don't know what she did to me," he cries out. In each instance, these momentary identifications serve as a stimulus for rageful vengeance directed at parts of the self which are perceived as shameful and humiliating. Theresa is terrified at her realization of the basic similarity between herself and White. She rebels against this "bum with a record" and lashes out in an angry demand that he leave. To White, already humiliated earlier by Theresa's assertion that he was a "queer," her angry demand incites the fearful rage that he was barely capable of suppressing up to this point.

An examination of these murders reveals that each of the participants employed internal splitting operations. The most conspicuous split involves the separation of sexuality from tenderness or love. In those instances where the integrity of the self is split, expressions of sex and aggression become dominant controlling forces in the personality. Theresa experienced sex the way a drug addict experiences heroin: an overwhelming, increasing and unreasoning need. It is as if the sexual aspect of her personality were somehow split off from the rest of her being.

At night when alone in her apartment she is overcome with a restlessness and desperation which drives her into bars looking for a man, any man who can quiet this craving for raw sexuality. Her "lovers" must be anonymous and must treat her with the requisite contempt. It's their coldness and indifference mirroring similar feelings in Theresa which she finds so attractive, which "turn her on." "The whole thing was strange. Here was this strange man being nasty and buying her drinks at the same time . . . the strangest thing was that she was feeling very sexy."

After a time, sex and aggression become fused, almost inseparable. In instances such as Rhonda, whom we met on page 166, the fusion can become so extreme that pleasure can be gotten only from the experience of physical pain. With Theresa, the pain is that of humiliation: men being "nasty" and, at the same time, paying her attention. She then becomes sexually aroused.

But sexual arousal can quickly turn to disgust and rage at those aspects of the self which are perceived in the other person. It's as if the fear of "lost boundaries" which tortured Theresa all her life finally took place. She was, in a sense, White, this "bum with a record" who wouldn't get out of her bed or her apartment on command, wouldn't disappear into the anonymous, hostile void from which he had come. He, in turn, was forced to confront—in Theresa's physical repulsion to him, her sadistic biting insults, her own self-righteous fury—a shameful and devalued self. He was worthless, still only a "queer" despite his heterosexual performance with her. Each of the participants in this deadly drama was forced to confront within the other individual aspects of their selves which couldn't be endured. As a result they lashed out at each other in narcissistic rage.

In the Skip Adams-Taylor case, the dynamics are similar. He, too, was a man of uncertain sexual orientation whose lack of sexual identity was confronted and ridiculed. In addition, there was the merging identities, the loss of self boundaries: he wanted to spare *her* feelings by strangling her till she "fainted" and then flee from the apartment. But when the strangling began, Taylor's pent-up fury burst forth into a murderous rage as he began beating his victim's body with a whip. This split in the self can be discerned in the stream-of-consciousness narrative Taylor provided after the murder during the taping of his confession. He began to "panic," one part of himself saying she was dead and another claiming that she had "just passed out."

The participants in the Parakeet Murder and the semifictional death of Theresa Dunn exist within the borderline-psychopathic range of the continuum we've discussed in this book. Although narcissistic issues are prominent, Theresa Dunn's underlying personality is essentially borderline. Her incapacity to sustain a consistent self ("She didn't really feel that she had a life, one life, that is, belonging to a person"), coupled with her lifelong underlying rage at her family as well as her succession of "lovers," marks her as suffering from a borderline disorder.

The murderers, however, both White and Adams-Taylor, exist more in the psychopathic range. The drifting from place to place; the problems with the law; the identification with fringe elements of society—these traits are typical of psychopathic personalities with some borderline features. The essential component which escalates aggression into murder is the psychopath's lack of conformity to the law. To him, murder is just one acceptable option among many.

Narcissistic rage provides the key to understanding many aspects of contemporary life which at first appear inexplicable. The killings of Joyce D. Robertson and the semifictional Theresa Dunn are less "senseless" when viewed within the context of what happens when people suffering from self disorders are thrown into conflict along issues of love and aggression.

Throughout this book I've concentrated on individuals with self defects involving narcissism. Most of these individuals are unlikely to become violent or do anyone harm. In those instances where the self disorder is more deep-seated, however (Skip Adams-Taylor), the distorted narcissism can explode into fury and destructiveness. Ridicule and belittlement cannot be tolerated by such people, simply because they are already unsure of who they are and must seek confirmation of their worth from those around them. When that worth and esteem isn't forthcoming from others or, even worse, is replaced by contempt or ridicule, those suffering from a serious self disorder may erupt into a murderous fury.

Our understanding of this process can provide some hope for the prevention of similar episodes in the future. Disparagement, irony, ridicule, are dangerous attitudes to express toward individuals who, we reasonably expect, may be suffering from a self disorder or other forms of distorted narcissism. This insight follows from our understanding of the dynamics of the manipulative personality, principally those individuals within the borderline and psychopathic ends of the spectrum where splits within the fabric of the self are coupled with conflicts around aggression and tenderness.

A particularly ominous addition to these features is the desire for *power*. This can set the stage for narcissistic rage on a grand scale. The greatest example in our time of the truth of this formulation is Jim Jones, the demonic architect of the horrors of Guyana.

Jim Jones: The Outer Limits of Manipulation

Although it's always hazardous to speculate about the mental condition of a person one hasn't met, Jim Jones appears to have represented at various times in his career the full continuum of manipulative behaviors. Starting out as a child with a precocious interest in fundamentalist religion, Jones was noted from his earliest years for carrying a Bible and lecturing schoolmates in a garage set up as an imitation church. But even at this early stage in his career, he demonstrated internal splits and contradictions, what one reporter who studied Jones's life describes as his "Jekyll and Hyde" personality.

At one moment preaching or baptizing other youngsters in the local creek, Jones could change, instantly, into what a former neighbor called a "mean little six-year-old, the Dennis the Menace of Lynn, Indiana." Given to theatrical gestures and grandiose rituals, Jones presided over elaborate funeral services for dead cats. While his youthful congregation looked on, he would preach about the dead animals. Despite his seemingly sincere expressions of sympathy and regret, it was suspected that Jones obtained stray cats which, according to rumor, he used for sacrifice. This coincided with a period when Jones's home was overflowing with injured or stray animals.

Whatever other purpose these stray animals may have served, they gave Jones a sense of purpose, a feeling of companionship and camaraderie with the rejected and isolated, an orientation which Jones put to good use in later years when he enlisted the poor and the outcasts of his temple. But behind this expression of sympathy existed a grim and sadistic exploiter of human frailty and weakness.

During his childhood garage "sermons" Jones would strike out at members of his congregation who seemed inattentive or in some way weren't going along with the mock rituals. Later, he would exploit these terror tactics to the ultimate in his "mass suicide" exercises, the last of which ended so insanely.

At every point in his career Jones expressed internal splits in his self. He was grandiose, yet expressed profound interest in the poor. He was fanatically religious, yet given to heterosexual and homosexual excesses as a means of controlling erring members of his congregation. Although he favored peaceful demonstrations, he could turn brutal within minutes and deliver long harangues about persecution and the imminent destruction of his "dream," the People's Temple. Throughout it all, the manipulative nature of Jones's appeal was spoken of repeatedly by those closest to him.

"It's hard to describe the attraction," said a fifty-four-year-old former follower in a newspaper interview, "but he had a way of convincing people that he was something that he wasn't. He was pleasant and well-spoken; appealing. He was dynamic in voice and gesture and imposing in appearance. He knew when to shout or when to lower his voice."

Throughout his career—except, of course, during his final moments of madness—Jones seems never to have lost his power to manipulate others. One former cult member, a chairman of a social action committee prior to joining Jones's People's Temple, recalls his first impression of Jones.

"Jones was so charismatic that he could talk at one meeting to very religious people about healing, and at another to very political people about justice."

Jones possessed considerable talents for manipulating persons of power and influence. At the height of his career, local as well as national political figures came as a matter of course to Jones's temple, a buff-colored converted synagogue in the Filmore district of San Francisco. Governor Jerry Brown came. So did Mayor George Moscone. Even soon-to-be First Lady Rosalynn Carter joined Jones on the speaker's platform on the occasion of her visit to San Francisco to open the city's Democratic Campaign Headquarters for her husband. Jones's ability to charm and ingratiate himself with persons in power resulted in hundreds of signatures from people who might later prove useful to Jones. In a letter to Mrs. Carter—a letter to which she responded thanking Jones for his suggestion that the United States ship urgently needed medical supplies to Cuba—Jones wrote expressing his "support in the quest for a new moral tone that your husband is so valiantly attempting to bring to this country."

Later, after the events of Guyana, questions would be raised concerning Jones's sanity. Several psychiatrists have declared him a psychotic. Although Jones was undoubtedly psychotic during the paroxysms of his final days, this is not the whole story by any means. Jones was successful at winning over politicians, inducing educated, intelligent people to join the temple, even impressing media personalities with the strength of his convictions and the soundness of his principles. Such feats do not suggest the psychotic as much as they do the smoothly calculating manipulator. At all times he seems to have retained the ability to coolly appraise just how much he could get away with. Even his expressions of paranoia have a playacting quality about them.

"To understand the magnetism of Jones, it is necessary to see how he wove together with artful phrases his appeals to the humanitarian yearnings, the politics and the physical vanities of his constituents," wrote Charles A. Krause, the reporter who covered the Guyana massacre for the Washington *Post*.

On the subject of Jones's sanity or insanity, a former temple member, eighteen-year-old Deborah Blakeley from Berkeley, California, who joined the cult to "bring structure and self-discipline to my own life," speculated about Jones's attitude toward what others described as his "delusions."

"When I first joined the cult, Reverend Jones seemed to make clear distinctions between fantasy and reality. I believe that most of the time when he said irrational things, he was aware that they were irrational but that they served as a tool for his leadership. His theory was that the end justified the means."

At some point, however, Jones's manipulations became so grandiose, his own image of himself so overpowering, that he shifted positions from master manipulator to a ruthless, frenzied fanatic.

Throughout his career, Jones exemplified the cunning, conning manipulator who could turn every occasion into an opportunity for personal advantage. His skills at recruiting other people, often people of intelligence and discernment, seem unbelievable in light of later events at Guyana. His grandiosity and megalomania, instead of alerting others to his dangerous potential, were taken up and further elaborated upon. "Let me present to you a combination of Martin Luther King, Angela Davis, Albert Einstein and Chairman Mao," were the words of introduction describing Jones at a testimonial in his behalf in 1976 at the People's Temple.

Eventually Jones was able to obtain the endorsement of prominent political and media figures: Hubert Humphrey, Roy Wilkins, Jane Fonda. He met with Walter Mondale on Air Force One, attended a private dinner with Attorney General Griffin Bell on the occasion of Bell's visit to San Francisco. Most interesting of all, however, was Jones's ability to manipulate the press. The editor of the San Francisco *Examiner*, who at one point attempted to kill the story of the abuses at the People's Temple, wrote after Guyana: "Jones was a very exciting, very impressive person who said all the right things, possibly the most fascinating person I've ever met." The editor's attempt to stop his reporter from investigating Jones failed, however, and the story was transferred to *New West Magazine*, where it was eventually published in August 1977 as "Inside People's Temple."

Partly responsible for Jones's success at manipulating others was his discernment of how his own ambitions could be successfully advanced through public relations and political maneuvering in the support of social and national politicians. Hundreds of children were available on short notice to work tirelessly for whatever political figure Jones was supporting at the moment. Both Governor Brown and Mayor Moscone took advantage of Jones's talents for assembling large and enthusiastic crowds, as did Rosalynn Carter on the occasion of her 1976 campaign visit to San Francisco. During the campaign itself, more than 10 percent of the entire state's volunteers were members of the People's Temple, most of them senior citizens who could be relied upon to turn out in large numbers for the central committee's get-out-the-vote-for-

Carter drive. Under the guise of philanthropy, Jones was able to convince others of his humanitarian interests. But behind the front of benevolence and activism in support of the downtrodden lurked an addiction to power.

Much has been written about the influence on Jones's development of Father Divine, the megalomaniacal black preacher whose divine peace mission provided a model for Jones's People's Temple. From Father Divine, Jones learned the ability to convince others that their own ideals could be realized by allying themselves with a powerful figure who could combine religion with a concern for improved social welfare for the downtrodden.

Nor was it accidental that Jones's temple was opened in California. The San Francisco Bay area was a refuge for people disenchanted with the system, cynical about the possibility of social change. In place of the fervent optimism of the early sixties, the social climate of the San Francisco to which Jones moved in 1971 was one of cynicism and despair. The system was unresponsive to people's needs and there was little indication that things were going to change in the near future. Jones was able to manipulate the situation and convince a cross section of the population that a powerful cult figure would be able to succeed where ordinary political activities had failed. While the emphasis was political and social, the style was grounded on Jones's appreciation that a leader must be ruthless, brutal and, if necessary, homicidal. Half of the books in Jones's small private library at the People's Temple are on Adolf Hitler. Another Jones hero was Charles Manson, the madman responsible for masterminding the Tate–La Bianca murders. On several occasions, Jones spoke of his admiration for Manson.

Since Guyana, there have been many theories about Jim Jones and how he was able to convince so many people to join an organization that, retrospectively, was obviously so exploitive and destructive. Since Jones left few written records, any theories about his mental state must remain speculative. My own interpretation of the Jones phenomenon is that he wasn't initially psychotic. He was intelligent, ambitious and driven to the realization of narcissistic grandiosity through religious fundamentalism. I think it's highly likely that, initially at least, Jones truly believed in the doctrines he was preaching. By allying himself with social and ethnic minorities, he was able to achieve benefits for others along with an affirmation of his own power. Within a society such as ours, that places such a high priority on image, he was able to manipulate the media in ways that depicted him as a savior. Later, as his grandiosity became more openly expressed and out of control, he no longer required or tolerated the controls which membership in a commune offers to its members, i.e., group identification and shared interests and goals. Jones had truly become a deity himself.

"Too many people are looking at this and not at me," he shouted one Sunday in the temple as he threw a copy of the Bible to the floor. It was shortly after this that Jones demanded that his followers stop employing the informal "Jim" as a form of address and replace it with "Father."

Rather than suffering from an outright psychosis, it's more likely that in the last years of his life, Jones became increasingly helpless in integrating the diverse and contradictory aspects of his personality: the concerned social activist; the megalomaniacal power seeker; the smooth public relations manipulator—each of these separate selves came into increasing conflict with the other. As the conflict intensified, Jones's behavior became more bizarre: homosexual and heterosexual affairs; sadism; child abuse; increasing drug use; the lengthy harangues which he delivered to his congregation at all hours of the day and night. With increased drug use, particularly the amphetamines which one temple member cited as "burning out the cells in his brain," Jones's identity fragmented even further. He was experiencing each of these different and irreconcilable selves, absent the sense of contradiction or fragmentation which seems so obvious yet inexplicable to the impartial observer. Eventually, it is likely that the final madness of the mass suicide appeared as a logical option, a reasonable response to the persecutions that Jones felt would result in the destruction of his church. "I don't know what else to say to these people. But to me death is not a fearful thing. It is living that is cursed. It's not worth living like this," Jones shouted to his followers a few minutes after some of them had begun drinking the poison.

At this point Jones's insanity is unquestionable. He had spoken many times before about the importance of mass "revolutionary suicide" as a means of "integration," a fitting word which mirrors perfectly, I believe, Jones's perception of the splits within his own personality which eventually resulted in a total fragmentation. At the end, the drive toward destruction had become paramount, resulting in "rehearsals" starting back as far as 1975 for the final "White Night."

This phenomenon of destruction and violence preempting other aspects of the personality is frequently observed among individuals with fragmented selves. Mark David Chapman, the murderer of Beatle John Lennon, captured the essence of this matter moments after shooting the rock star. "Most of me didn't want to do it, but a little of me did. I couldn't help myself." At a certain point, the failures of synthesis and integration within the personality result in the eruption of murderous or suicidal impulses, extreme forms of the narcissistic rage described earlier. In such a state of mind even death is preferable to giving up the dream of omnipotence and power. The need for a confirmation of worth is so overpowering because the self is experienced as essentially worthless. Thus seemingly trivial occurrences can serve as the triggers for violence. For instance, Chapman complained moments after the shooting that he didn't like the way Lennon had autographed a record album six hours earlier. This served as the immediate stimulus for Chapman to return and murder the rock star.

In Jones's case, his narcissism was attacked by the questions of the reporters who, during the visit of Congressman Leo Ryan to Guyana, challenged his grandiose claims that the members of the People's Temple were happy and wished to remain in their isolated jungle compound. Jones's fragmentation reached psychotic proportions. "So my opinion is that you be kind to children and be kind to seniors and take the potion like they used to take in ancient Greece and step over quietly, because we are not committing suicide, it is a revolutionary act. We can't go back, they won't leave us alone. They're [Ryan and his party] now going back to tell more lies, which means more congressmen, and there is no way, no way we can survive."

Jones provides a worst-case scenario of the manipulative personality. When narcissism escalates into a feeling of omnipotent grandiosity, the failing sense of self begins to depend for its support on the creation of an increasingly private world, where the distinction between fantasy and reality are blurred.

Beyond this, Jones represents the logical but hopefully not necessarily inevitable product of a culture which encourages fragmentation within the self. With the failure of "liberal" political ideologies to solve social and economic problems, there's always the danger that more authoritarian, more rigid and repressive influences will be *freely* selected.

All the members of the People's Temple originally joined of their own free will. Although coercion and intimidation eventually became the modus operandi of Jones and his hand-picked lieutenants, the initial appeal was an opportunity to counter the materialistic, uncaring social system that was responsible for Vietnam, three political assassinations, the upsurge of drug use, despair and ennui among the nation's young. Jones, by means of his radical separation from the establishment and his avowed dedication to human rights, promised his followers a better life through the relinquishment of private possessions, but even more importantly, *private identity*.

Through identification with the People's Temple, its members could collectively embark on creating on a minor scale a kind of society which was impossible within the United States in the 1960s and 1970s. This is basically similar to the "tune in, turn on and drop out" philosophy of Timothy Leary and the flower children of the sixties, but with the important difference that, in place of drugs, the followers of Jones substituted a mixture of fundamentalist religion and social activism. In both instances, the person—the individual self—is less important than the collective identity. Vast numbers of people thought of themselves as members of a "family" with their primary allegiance to Leary, Jones or other contemporary charismatic figures. It's not accidental that the Manson group also identified themselves as a "family" headed by a profoundly disturbed "father." In this instance, sinister and destructive forms of paternalism were freely selected by large numbers of people (at least in the case of the People's Temple) as preferable alternatives to the wider managerial and bureaucratic society. It is for this reason that I believe Jones isn't just an anomaly or a temporary aberration. Rather, the frustrations that large numbers of people are today experiencing within our society in regard to achieving a sense of social equity provides and will continue to provide the driving force for them to identify with absolutist and authoritarian leaders.

Through their membership in the People's Temple, many people were not only able to provide a meaning for their lives but also to carry out the kinds of caring activities which were individually impossible for them. For instance, the People's Temple was initially involved in providing food and shelter to disadvantaged blacks and Chicanos in California. Only later, as their leader's grandiosity and narcissism became completely uncontrollable, did the emphasis shift toward more malignant forms of manipulation and control.

The difference between Jones and previous charismatic leaders stems from the psychopathology shared between him and his cult members. Jones and others like him utilized manipulation in order to forge for themselves a grandiose identity which could bolster their deeply ingrained sense of fragmentation. He literally attempted to become the god he initially planned on serving. With each step toward greater manipulative control over larger numbers of people came an increase in the grandiose identity. Eventually, as members of the People's Temple remarked, Jones became unable to discern between where reality left off and fantasy began.

But the phenomenon of Jonestown cannot be laid entirely at the hands of a deranged leader. If this were so, phenomena such as Jonestown would have occurred frequently in our history. In fact, such catastrophes are extremely rare and something as horrific as Jonestown totally unique to American life. (Even though the Jonestown disaster occurred in Guyana, Jim Jones and the People's Temple were an American phenomenon, a point which the Guyana authorities have rightly insisted on all along and which President Carter attempted to obscure in his remarks that "I believe that we don't need to deplore on a nationwide basis the fact that the Jonestown, so called, was typical of America, because it is not. It did not take place in our country.")

In addition to a narcissistic leader, it was also necessary that the cult members share a devalued identity, a feeling that they were somehow incomplete and deficient. A cross section of the views of the surviving members of the People's Temple reveals individuals with pervasive feelings of frustration and dissatisfaction with the system. They speak of experiencing themselves as cut off from the family or the community along with a deep sense of unworthiness and worthlessness. Typical of this view is the comment made by a sixteen-year-old People's Temple member, "I was like a simple ant in the whole world. I was nothing, going nowhere. I was bored and unhappy at home. Jones made me feel like I was someone. Just the sound of his voice made you feel like you had power."

In a sense Jones and his followers exhibited interacting pathologies. The cult members needed and demanded a leader who provided the cohesion within the group that the members, individually, so sorely lacked. Jones, in turn, required the acquiescence of other individuals in order to realize the omnipotent fantasies that he had created by his own deranged narcissism. The meeting point of these interactive pathologies was Jones's skills at manipulation and control.

Combining a natural talent for deception, intimidation and a dedicated study and familiarity with the mechanisms of brainwashing and thought reform, Jones was able to create within his followers a state of total acquiescence, an acquiescence so firm that large numbers of cult members willingly cooperated in an orgy of self-destruction.

Could such a course of events happen again? I believe that it can and will. Jones, like Manson before him, represents a personality type which flourishes within our society. Within limits, manipulative and exploitive individuals are the ones who are best able to adjust to our culture, where the emphasis is on materialism, one-upmanship, increased mobility, the loss of the sense of community, the need for accomplishment and the expression of charm combined with ruthlessness in dealing with others. The emphasis on image and personal magnetism to the exclusion of inner conviction or personal ethical resources provides the optimal circumstances for the rise of charismatic leaders marked by their brutality and inhumanity.

On a television interview, Jeannie Mills, a former People's Temple member, appeared with another guest, a former Manson family member. The moderator inquired of Mills whether, if Jim Jones were to return from the dead, people would once again follow him. "Absolutely," she responded. "He had charisma." The former Manson family member agreed.

With Jim Jones we reach the outer limits of the continuum of self disorders. Mark and Sonya, whom we met in the early chapters, illustrate the disturbance at its mildest. Mark (p. 27), for instance, is overly conventional and his suffering affects principally himself. When he is not involved in a relationship which calls forth feelings of intimacy, he is perfectly normal. But whenever he begins to move emotionally closer to someone, his personality, his selfhood, begins to crumble and fragment.

Sonya (p. 35), presents a similar situation, but in her case her self cohesion is more precarious. She reaches out blindly for experiences which will give her life a sense of direction. The diversity of these experiences (nude model, architect) involves her in conflicts which further distort her feelings of who she "really is." As a result, even though she is well into adulthood, she still thinks of herself as "fluid," "unfinished," her future full of vague potentialities for "fulfillment."

Although Mark and Sonya differ in the directions that their lives have taken them, they are both fairly "conventional" people whose self disorders and need to manipulate are under control.

Jonathan's (p. 136) needs for integration are so great that he requires another person's presence in order to feel real and alive. His inability to tolerate loneliness drives him into repetitive, compulsive, manipulative efforts to gain the attention and attendance of other people. In his own words, he is "addicted" to people the way a drug addict is addicted to drugs: as a means of quieting anxieties and uneasiness. Little happiness or comfort is derived from these exploitive relationships, however, and Jonathan is further driven into compulsive attempts to quell his "performance anxiety." Because of his basic dependence on others in order to realize his own personal worth, Jonathan is deeply resentful and, as a result, infuses into his relationships sadistic, degrading features which "punish" the people on whom he is becoming so dependent for his self-definition. Basic to Jonathan's personality are overwhelming narcissistic requirements for approval and admiration coexisting with a derogatory inner image which he's constructed about himself as a "splat on the wall." His needs are so great that he experiences a "burning feeling to call somebody; grab a girl; nothing else counted, no pride, no dignity."

Jonathan's personality is basically split: his grandiose, narcissistic demands for admiration are generally in conflict with the angrily aggressive and sadistic features of his personality which require the degradation of the person he allows himself to "fall in love with." On the whole though, Jonathan, like Mark and Sonya, plays out his emotional conflicts within a conventional setting in which, for the most part, social and legal standards are lived up to.

With Anita (p. 147), the first borderline individual we encountered, we begin to witness a breakdown of social standards and ethical barriers. Her fragmentation is clearly within the pathologic range. Hedonistic pleasure-driven excursions into the hinterlands of sensuality propel her into situations when not only her marriage and reputation but her safety as well are at stake. Her personality is so severely fractionated that one lover after another simply "disappears" like a ship sailing over the horizon. Soon, even her judgment and expectations are disturbed and she expects to discover "real love" within sordid and perverse affairs which, to her, are meaningless and evanescent. Most important for our consideration, however, is the tendency for Anita's fragmented self to bring her into conflict with social mores.

With Lynn (p. 174), this conflict is carried even further. She is well aware of the consequences of her drug use should it be found out. But her deep, existential insecurity and suffering drive her toward a chemical solution to the anguish she feels. Her narcissistic requirements for other people's approval create within her feelings of shame, anger and frustration which she assuages through sexual degradation: being "used" by another person. We also encounter for the first time within Lynn the tendency to fractionate sexuality and its component parts, a process which corresponds to the splitting and lack of integration within her self. Thus, various sexual behaviors which customarily are part of foreplay become the totality of the sexual act. Biting, smelling, sucking, chewing and fellatio, rather than being a part of sexuality, comprise its total experience. This tendency to fractionate complex experiences into their component parts and then substitute one of the components for the total is one expression of personality fragmentation.

With the psychopathic personality, we encounter individuals whose narcissism is so extreme and grandiose that they exist in a kind of splendid isolation in which the creation of a grandiose self takes precedence over legal, moral or interpersonal commitments. These individuals are also much more deeply disturbed than the people we've previously encountered. In their lives, fantasy is the predominant motivating force, with reality providing only a kind of stage setting in which they can act out their narcissism.

M'Biye (p. 206) and Robert Wain (p. 222) have crossed into the borderland where the requirements of realistic appraisal are suspended and other people exist only as "bit players" to be manipulated in the creation of a fantasy existence of nearly infinite power, might and influence.

Finally, with Jim Jones the more malignant manipulator emerges whose narcissism is laced with destructiveness, hate, rage and overwhelming hostility. Murder becomes the ultimate manipulation in which another person's life can be extinguished without remorse or compunction. In the case of Jones, at least, the other previously described elements of the manipulative personality can be clearly discerned: showmanship, exploitation, concentration on media and image—all the elements of the narcissistic personality. Later, as his self disturbance became more grave, borderline and psychopathic features came to predominate: cunning evasions of legal and ethical principles; increasing grandiosity; sexual identity disturbances; profound regressions into the depths of hypochondria with its concentration on *parts* of the body to the exclusion of the whole; the appropriation of the temple members' money and possessions; the fraud schemes; the increasing drug usage; the sadism in which people were required to perform sexually degrading acts in order to maintain the "love" of Father Jones—all these characteristics involve the interpenetration of borderline-psychopathic features into what formerly had been a typical narcissistic disturbance. Jim Jones provides within one individual a whole range of manipulative behaviors. He also serves as a warning of the outer limits of destructiveness to which unrestrained narcissism may extend.

With the psychopath, we reach the outer limits of our continuum. Along with an overriding narcissism and a loss of self boundaries which the psychopath shares with the borderline personality, his self disturbance also includes a readiness to break the law, to lie and steal, to murder if the circumstances seem to require it. While each of these personalities is different, they are also uncannily similar. Each is affected by a schism within the self. Each experiences himself or herself as basically divided, unwhole, fragile—the terms may vary, but the "flavor" is one of incompleteness and insufficiency. In order to counter these feelings, other people are reacted to as *things*. A great emphasis is placed on pretense (the impostor exemplifies this in its purest form), image and the outward show of feelings which are not experienced.

At this point, I'm going to attempt a word sketch of the manipulator. It will incorporate all the insights we have gathered from our observations of the various personalities described throughout this book. In contrast to these earlier studies of "real people," this description will be a composite, an overall impressionistic sketch of the manipulator. No one individual could possibly display all the traits I'll mention. In short, there is no Manipulator any more than there is a Typical American or an Average Consumer; the individual that we are describing, who suffers from a primary disorder of the self, may display only a few of the traits. All manipulators display some of them.

VIII

The Manipulator

"The entrepreneur is often someone who doesn't know what to do, who doesn't have a vocation and sometimes can't find a job. And very often I know that most entrepreneurs will agree that the real turning point in their lives, the very important turning point, is the moment they will share with no one—the moment in which they were humiliated and they feel bad and they said 'I'll show you.'"

Diane Von Furstenberg, president, DVF, Inc.

A Short History of Just About Everybody
You're Likely to Meet These Days
(Present Company Excepted, of Course)

Basically, the manipulator suffers from a defect of the self. This may be as subtle as the minor setbacks to self-esteem that we all experience from time to time or, on the extreme end of the spectrum, the manipulator may be a sick individual indeed, lacking a cohesive self and reacting to every situation with rage, envy and fragmentation as with the borderline and the psychopath. This variation in the intensity of disorders of the self accounts for the fact that the manipulator can be found both in the boardrooms of our nation's corporations and the disturbed wards of hospitals specializing in the treatment of severe and chronic mental illness (Robert Wain). Where the self is fragmented and disunited, interpersonal relationships are equally episodic and discontinuous. Survival depends on gaining one's ends by manipulating people and the environment. This orientation can be recognized by certain characteristics.

In the mildest sense, the manipulator is troubled by a vague sense of inauthenticity or phoniness, a feeling that she's not quite "put together." Accompanying these feelings are uncomfortable sensations of boredom and ennui. Life often seems to lack a purpose; actions are divorced from any overall plan. Things seem at times simply meaningless. If these experiences are chronic, then a major disorder of the self exists. Usually, however, the feelings are transient and fit well within the spectrum of "normality."

Oftentimes, the manipulator speaks of herself as existing somehow subtly apart from her body. She envisions herself as basically "living inside" a body which is to be directed by a controlling "me" who oversees and comments upon the self's performance. As a result, the manipulator is greatly concerned with "style" and "flair," speaking frequently about her "image." At all times, she's swayed much more by considerations of shame than of guilt. How do things appear? What would so-and-so think of me if they found out what I'm *really* like?

As part of this concentration on appearances, the manipulator is capable of tolerating contradictions and inconsistencies which would drive her nonmanipulative counterpart to distraction. But to the manipulator, things are what they appear and, therefore, great efforts are expended to "manage" impressions. Easy grace and superficial charm hide a basic insecurity and distrust. Other people are part of the manipulator's stage management of her image and must be coerced into accepting the manipulator for what she *wishes* herself to be rather than on the basis of any judgments of what she actually says or does.

The manipulator's social relations are marked by hypersociability combined with ruthlessness and a predatory instinct. Lacking a fully integrated sense of self, the manipulator is also incapable of empathizing with other people. Combined with this is an interest in technicism, the application of "techniques" designed to anticipate and manage other people's responses. In all instances, people are not so much to be reasoned with or convinced as they are to be ruthlessly exploited. A penumbra of emptiness and loss coexists with a hypertrophied sense of entitlement: other people have the "treasures" that the manipulator knows that she lacks. Furthermore, they possess these treasures unjustly and thus the manipulator feels no compunction or remorse in trying to extract them by guile. Obviously, moral and ethical values play no part here since, in all instances, appearances determine the context in which behavior is to be interpreted and understood.

In the more extreme forms, the manipulator's concentration on image and appearance takes the form of repetitive, compulsive alterations of her body. Plastic surgery is increasingly relied upon by manipulators in order to be able to project the desired "image" of youth and beauty. The severest disturbance of self may entail altering one's sex by transsexual surgery in order to liberate a self which, characteristically, is spoken of as being "trapped in the body of the opposite sex." Milder disturbances may remain confined to obsessive concerns about weight, minor body blemishes or wrinkles. In any case, the manipulator is always aware of something "missing," something not quite right with herself.

Interpersonal relationships must always remain superficial lest the manipulator become overwhelmed by feelings of entitlement, envy or rage. Coexisting with this is an intolerance for extended relationships. Multiple marriages and short-lived cohabitation arrangements are interrupted by breakups marked by emotional storms followed by a relief on the part of the manipulator that she's finally "rid of" the former "loved one." The manipulator typically shows neither regret nor fond remembrance for the person who perhaps only days earlier seemed the most important person in the manipulator's life. Lovers are simply "forgotten" in a chilling absence of recall—almost as if the loved one had simply ceased to exist.

After repetitive breakups, the manipulator is confirmed in her conviction that she's better off not letting things get too "heavy." No one can be trusted because essentially the manipulator can't trust herself and remains persistently unsure of her own feelings.

The manipulator lacks the confidence that most people retain in the permanence of their own feelings. As a rule, most human relationships break down over a period of time. People discover in little ways over many months and years that they and their partners are not right for each other. Not so the manipulator. Who knows, perhaps on a certain day she may awaken to discover that she no longer "loves" the other person. An argument or petty disappointment can set off such a paroxysm of rage and envy in the manipulator that the other person must be eliminated, the relationship destroyed. But since the manipulator poorly tolerates loneliness—requiring, as she does, constant reassurance from other people of her self-worth—she quickly establishes another "intimate" relationship marked by the usual superficiality, mistrust and insecurity.

The manipulator exists in a thousand different disguises and is encountered in every level of society. Through an emphasis on "handling" other people, the manipulator represents the ultimate triumph of function over substance. "There isn't anybody I can't talk into anything," is the essence of the manipulator's philosophy. To the manipulator, problems are mere matters of "perception," and if perceptions can be changed, then the problem can be expected to disappear. Everything is a matter of "presentation and packaging." Change is brought about by altering "attitudes" rather than by addressing issues. Talk to the manipulator about a problem, and within seconds she's shifted the discussion toward the personalities of the people involved. "What's his weak spot? How can I charm him over to my side?" These are the questions the manipulator substitutes for the hard issues of performance. To the manipulator, the bottom line is always one of cajoling, tricking, seducing or otherwise enticing the opposition.

Although the manipulator's style is often a buoyant one, the underlining attitude is cynical and pessimistic: there isn't anyone who can't be persuaded and won over. No one really believes in anything; people are only waiting for the right kind of "stroking," the correct "approach" to be made and, presto, everything will be turned around. Behind the manipulator's charm, buoyancy and generally upbeat approach is concealed a grim-lipped, exploitive cynicism. "If only I can *get* to him I know I can convince him." Only in all instances, convincing is a matter of exploiting rather than explanation.

All of this isn't meant to imply, of course, that a manipulative style can't be extremely useful and effective under the correct circumstances. On occasion, problems arise within any organization which are more a matter of personality conflict and personal philosophy than substantive issues. In such situations the manipulator can be extremely useful. Her easy amiability and insinuative manner can facilitate mutual exchange while doing away with constrictive matters of protocol and precedence. For this reason, manipulators are often extremely successful at arbitrating issues within organizations which are based primarily on "bruised egos" or personality conflicts. But the manipulator's greatest weakness comes from her inability to understand that there really are issues that some people care deeply about. Since the manipulator's personality is basically chameleonlike, changing according to the situation and individuals who are dominant at the moment, she's incapable of appreciating the steadfastness of others. For this reason, despite her claimed "flexibility" in interpersonal relationships, the manipulator's own attitudes toward the integrity of others are cast in granite. If other people are unyielding in their opposition to a measure, the manipulator simply "turns on more charm" and manipulates all the harder.

Since the manipulator is basically a phony, she can't believe that everyone else isn't a phony as well. An unwillingness to "negotiate" an issue must mean, according to the manipulator's convoluted logic, that the requisite price hasn't yet been reached. It never occurs to the manipulator that she may be dealing with a person who is convinced of the rectitude of his position and, consequently, will not budge an inch. In such a situation, the manipulator is totally ineffective and is forced to pull out all stops. The end result is usually a saccharine, cloying performance which barely conceals the manipulator's underlying rage.

According to the psychopathology motivating the manipulator (we must remember that manipulation is a modus operandi for individuals with deficiencies in the sense of self ranging from "normal" to severely disturbed personalities), a full gamut of responses may eventually be forthcoming, ranging anywhere from displays of hurt feelings to outbreaks of murderous rage.

Manipulators, like paranoids, can, under certain circumstances, contribute significantly to an organization's effectiveness. But just as the paranoid can see threats where no threats exist and hence impair everyone's effectiveness, so too the manipulator can completely miss the point of other people's resistance. Her desperate attempts to exploit and cajole the opposition under circumstances where no compromise is possible only serve to worsen a deteriorating situation to the point where not only issues but goodwill are lost as well. When these failings are kept under control, however, the manipulator can make valuable contributions to an organization since, at all times, the manipulator is an extremely keen observer of the "human-interest" side of everything. She also possesses a keen insight into the dynamics of everyone else's personality but her own. This helps to explain why manipulators

often rise within organizations to positions of power and influence. Typically, this occurs in fields where things really do depend on perceptions rather than hard, measurable commodities.
Public relations, sales, politics, management—these are the areas
where the manipulator excels. But the manipulator's influence is
not confined to these areas by any means.

Within any complex society there develops an increasing interdependence which demands from everyone some degree of tact,
diplomacy and basic familiarity with "public relations." Lawyers,
for instance, will be the first to admit that if they make a bad impression on the judge, their chance of success in a courtroom case
is slim. And isn't the "bedside manner" of the physician only a
substitute term describing his skills in dealing with the personalities of his patients? There isn't any line of work that doesn't
demand some interpersonal skill. For this reason, the manipulator
is no longer confined to specific areas but can be found in operating rooms, around oil rigs, on the boards of directors. She's teach-
ing our children, doing our hair, drawing up our wills and cleaning
our teeth. Manipulators are everywhere.

Recognition of the manipulator isn't hard once you're alerted to
her existence. An easy charm and amiability is usually the most
striking personality characteristic. You feel important, *special*,
when you're talking to a manipulator. That's because the manipulator is reading your responses, playing you in such a way as to
set you up for whatever the manipulator has in mind for you at a
later point. The manipulator is totally promiscuous when it comes
to charm. Since she operates on only one wavelength, manipulation, her interpersonal relationships have a sameness about them
that is truly unbelievable. The manipulator tries to charm her
hairdresser, her doctor, her children's teachers. Her tragedy consists in her inability to adopt any different attitude or approach
when dealing with her husband. Manipulators do poorly whenever
it comes to intimate interpersonal relationships simply because,
basically, *nobody enjoys being manipulated*.

At some point, no matter how clever she may be, the manipulator is unmasked for what she is: an insecure, angry, untrusting individual who can only deal with other people on the level of sub-

terfuge and deception. While such an attitude, under certain circumstances, can be successful in the office or at cocktail parties, it's an extreme liability when it comes to intimacy. As a result, the divorce rate among manipulators is astronomical. I've never encountered a manipulator who has sustained an enduring relationship. The manipulator's life is filled with intense but short-lived passions.

Ten minutes after meeting a manipulator, she's acting as if she's known you all her life. Her affections are indiscriminately bestowed on the most casual of bases. It's as if the manipulator is using an on-off switch from her emotions instead of the modulator or fine tuner which most people possess. The level of affection displayed by the manipulator is the same whether she's known you two days or two years. For this reason, the manipulator gives the deceptive appearance of deep and abiding friendships. She's familiar with everyone on a first-name basis. (Historically, the first manipulator can be traced back at least to biblical times: she was the woman who, moments after being introduced to John the Baptist, referred to him ever after as "Jack.")

The real difficulty recognizing and defining the manipulator stems from the undeniable fact that we are all manipulators on occasion. A person who refuses to engage in any manipulative behavior at all would most likely be found living in a cave. But most of us are selective in our manipulation. We recognize ourselves as individuals with certain convictions and principles and, therefore, have little difficulty in ascribing similar attitudes to others. Nor do we get our kicks out of fooling other people. We have acquaintances, friends, relatives, lovers and spouses and our relationship with each has a selectivity about it. We don't ordinarily take the same approach to our dermatologist as we do to our husband. But admittedly, these kinds of distinctions are easier written about than clearly recognized when encountered in real life.

The Failure to Love

The handsome and self-absorbed young man
looked at the lovely and self-absorbed girl
and thrilled.

The lovely and self-absorbed girl
looked back at the handsome and self-absorbed young man
and thrilled.

And in that thrill he felt:
Her self-absorption is even as strong as mine.
I must see if I can't break through it
and absorb her in me.

And in that thrill she felt:
His self-absorption is even stronger than mine!
What fun, even stronger than mine!
I must see if I can't absorb this Samson of self-absorption.

So they simply adored one another
and in the end
they were both nervous wrecks, because
In self-absorption and self-interest they were equally matched.

D. H. Lawrence

The giving and receiving of affection, it turns out, is actually
one of the most demanding tests that can be made of the cohe-

siveness of the self. While everyone, on occasion, is exploitive and manipulative in business or professional affairs, the manipulator extends this pattern to her most intimate relationships. Characteristically, she feels in competition with the "loved one." Anger, envy and a growing sense of futility and frustration lead to the repetitive establishment and subsequent breaking off of romantic attachments. While the manipulator may express a desire for long-term relationships, her behavior precludes even the possibility of such a permanence.

Typically, the manipulator chooses her companion for narcissistic motives. She can't feel any desire for a man unless he's admired and sought after by other women. By appropriating this valued "treasure" for herself, she simultaneously gratifies her wishes for self-enhancement, possessiveness and triumph over her competitors. Yet, by a strange paradox, such a manipulator soon finds that she cannot control her own envy and greed. The fact that the man has accepted her only further confirms her own deeply entrenched feelings of worthlessness. In the end, it's as if the manipulator were condemned to a no-win situation: if she is rejected, the rebuff immediately stirs up her fury and frustration. But if she's accepted, then her need to possess, exploit and ultimately devaluate the partner leads to situations that are unbearable for both parties.

Usually, failures in loving are the result of failures in intimacy. How can you love someone you hardly know? And intimacy presents a particularly difficult problem for the manipulator. Basically unsure of who he or she *really is*, suffering from a failure of the sense of self, the manipulator is also unable to experience another person in an integrated manner. The same tendency toward splitting within her own personality is expressed in the manipulator's experience of other people. Those who are the "good guys" are overidealized—depending, of course, on whether they continue to provide the manipulator with unending approval! Many marriages are based on such one-way love relationships.

We're all familiar with couples in which one member, usually the man, is handsome and charming while the wife comes across as a drab, rather plain nonentity whose only distinguishing characteristic is her total dedication to her husband. Everything she says and does relates to her husband. Her conversation is sprinkled with quotes of her husband's opinion. She unconsciously duplicates his gestures and, on occasion, even takes on his tone of voice or inflections.

Formerly, psychiatrists thought of such relationships as sado-masochistic, in which the sadist enjoys subjugating his masochistic partner to the status of a slave. Now it seems more likely that such relationships are the result of manipulation: one person is the recipient of all the love, but is unable to give love in return.

Intimacy is more than sexuality. If that were the most important component, then this would have to be judged the most intimate generation in history. Today, people are hardly acquainted with each other before they are living together in relationships which, though perhaps sexually satisfying, are often marked by striking failures in intimacy. Both inside marriage and without, sexuality and intimacy are often confused. "Talk to a naked girl for an hour," is the invitation extended on a sign outside a San Francisco massage parlor. Although the sign indicates the undoubted availability of more than just "talk," the come-on nevertheless strikes a receptive chord within those who confuse sexuality with intimacy. "Now that we are finished with *that*, what would you like to talk about, mister?"

This inverse relationship between promiscuous sexuality and intimacy, although often posed in moralistic terms, actually isn't based on morality or ethics at all, but on our own very real need to form and maintain special caring relationships. D. H. Lawrence, hardly a spokesman for middle-class morality, articulated the situation with great insight in his poem "Behavior":

> "If we are properly clothed and disciplined in the dining room or the street
> then the private intimacy of friendship will be real and precious
> and our naked contact will be rare and vivid and tremendous.
>
> But when everybody goes round with soul half-bared, or quite
> in promiscuous intimate appeal
> then friendship is impossible
> and naked embrace an anti-climax, humiliating and ridiculous."

As Lawrence puts it earlier in the poem, "It's absurd for me to display my naked soul at the tea-table."

The greatest obstacle to the manipulator's achieving intimacy and, hence, loving is her inability to manage her overwhelming sense of rage and aggression. As she moves emotionally closer to another person, she fears to "let go" and open herself up to new vistas of experience and emotion. Initially, the interest and enthusiasm of the person creates within the manipulator a sense of excitement. She is turned on to the newness of the other person. Yet, at the same time, the manipulator's precarious sense of self is threatened by feelings of disintegration, a dread of impending annihilation in which she will be irretrievably lost. To surrender herself to another is to lose herself, to merge with a lover in a consummation which, she fears, will ultimately destroy her. The only way to save herself from such a threat is to strike out against the lover, thus reestablishing her sense of self.

Union thus becomes indistinguishable from fusion and intimacy the most potent threat to the manipulator's fragile sense of self. Typically, the threat is met by creating situations which appear to justify the manipulator's increasing rage and hostility. Envy, jealousy, criticism, sarcasm and belittlement mark the manipulator's attempt to extricate herself from the "love" relationship. Often, the lover is accused of selfishness and self-centeredness. Finally, the manipulator discovers that the couple no longer "communicate" and the relationship flounders in the wake of accusations and resentments. All too often, however, the hostility escalates into physical abuse—even, in some cases, murder.

If the manipulator can't live with the other person she often can't live without him either. It's as if the manipulator eventually reaches the point of no return: she has lost whatever sense of self she once possessed and must re-create a new self within the other person. But not surprisingly, the lover, finding such dependency unbearably demanding, attempts to break off the relationship. Then in a final burst of rage, the manipulator destroys the now-hated "lover." Such developments fortunately are rare and occur predominantly among manipulators on the borderline and psychopathic end of the spectrum we've described. Nevertheless, the increasing tendency for "lovers' quarrels" to terminate in violent death underscores the anguish that certain manipulators experience in the face of rejection. They are not simply being rejected; they are literally being destroyed by the lover who, according to the manipulator's frame of reference, has stolen away the sense of self.

In order to avoid this self-annihilation, the manipulator employs a series of techniques aimed at avoiding intimacy and, hence, preserving the precarious self. Interestingly, these techniques have come to enjoy wide popularity in contemporary movies and books as well as exerting great influence on the feelings many people currently experience in relating to people in "real life."

Noninvolvement, coolness, distance, not becoming "hung up," the "love-is-never-having-to-say-you're-sorry" formula—all are manipulative defenses against intimacy.

How can anyone be expected to love another person if love is the equivalent of psychic annihilation? How can it be possible for the manipulator to love when her attitudes toward the lover may abruptly shift at any moment from intense infatuation to an equally intense hostility toward a now-hated enemy?

At all times the manipulator tends to view people and events in extremes. People are either wonderful—representing the "all-good" early object relations—or they are despised, corresponding to the "all-bad" images which haunt the manipulator's perceptions from early childhood and extend throughout her lifetime.

The manipulator is incapable of recognizing that no one is perfect, that people are at all times a mixture of the good and the bad, the wise and the foolish. There aren't, in short, "perfect types" who can be reacted to like characters in a fairy tale. The manipulator never learns that life isn't a matter of witches and goblins, on the one hand, and princesses and fairy godmothers on the other.

In a sense, the manipulator seeks a world without ambiguity. The "good" figures are to be curried up to and overidealized, while the "bad" ones are to be repudiated and destroyed. In order to do this, the manipulator has created a special world within her own psyche via splitting: one part of the self is out of emotional contact with the other. Thus, for example, the manipulator can rant and rave about sexual morality on Sunday and participate in group sex experiences on Friday. In this example, thanks to splitting, the emotional accompaniments of religious self-righteousness are kept separate from the feelings accompanying the sexually polymorphic experience. In a similar way, the manipulator "splits" everyone she encounters into groups with opposite emotional valences. Furthermore, the valence can change unexpectedly, usually toward devaluation and contempt.

We've all discovered, on occasion, that our heroes have clay feet. But to the manipulator, all heroes eventually are devalued since, realistically, they can never be expected to live up to the manipulator's grandiose expectations. The manipulator suffers from an overdeveloped sense of disappointment in other people. She voices frequent regret tinged with sadness that other people aren't quite able to live up to her expectations. Her disappointment is clothed with a brooding irony. Life is sad, people can't be trusted, how wonderful things once were before the other person's larceny destroyed the relationship and so on.

Incapable of true intimacy, the manipulator seeks instead the "images" which she's observed often accompany intimate relationships. The manipulator is ready at a moment's notice to discuss personal and private matters with comparative strangers. Thanks to her extreme self-absorption, there is no more interesting topic to discuss than her own experiences and feelings. But the keen observer of human behavior will note that the intimate details are recited with great self-preoccupation and display. There is a noticeable absence of the reticence most people feel when discussing personal matters with casual acquaintances.

To the manipulator, such self-display serves a dual purpose: it provides opportunity for focusing attention on herself while engaging in pseudo intimacy. With the manipulator to whom the media is the message, the image serves as an effective substitute for reality.

In place of intimate feelings, the manipulator substitutes intimate subjects. She often accompanies such self-revelations with gestures that would suggest intimacy. A cocktail-party acquaintance chosen as the manipulator's temporary confidant may find himself greeted on the next occasion with a kiss or an embrace. (He may, with equal likelihood, be ignored if in the interval the manipulator's envy and rage have transformed him into an enemy that must be devalued!)

Manipulators are given to kissing and hugging comparative strangers as a way of demonstrating affections which they don't feel. Unable to love and confused about intimacy, they mistakenly assume that other people experience the same confusion of feelings toward acquaintances and intimates. Thus, the manipulator may be effusively enthusiastic toward the hairdresser in the morning and in the afternoon find herself unable to summon up more than a hollow "hello" for her husband or lover. The effusiveness is all show, the manipulator is now emotionally depleted, her ration of intimacy used up for the day.

In the absence of a capacity for intimacy, the manipulator must depend on display, making the right sounds at the right time, saying the appropriate words to create the illusion of a closeness and warmth which is not felt. Thus it is not surprising that many people are vaguely uncomfortable around manipulators. Their emotional antennae alert them that something is amiss, but what? Certainly the manipulator says and does all the right things.

Missing from these encounters are the emotional underpinnings which give meaning and validity to human relations. The manipulator's inability to experience the other person as unique and separate along with her feigned emotions and attempts at pseudo intimacy lend a wooden, mechanical quality to the manipulator's personal interactions. Somehow or other people are always vaguely aware that they exist only as extensions of the manipulator's own personality.

Years ago, psychiatrists wrote about "anaclitic relationships." If you've ever collected names for a petition, then you understand what an anaclitic relationship is all about. A name on the line is all that's important. It doesn't matter who the person is: individual and identifying characteristics are irrelevant. All that's needed is a name, somebody's name, anybody's name added to the list.

To the manipulator, all relationships are anaclitic. One person can be substituted for another (assuming, of course, that they're included among those currently enjoying the manipulator's favor).

This interpersonal promiscuity is often associated with sexual promiscuity. The likelihood of such a development is aided by the manipulator's requirement that other people be stripped of their individuality: bodies and minds are equally interchangeable. If other people serve as a means of confirming the sense of self, mere shadow figures, bit players in the drama of the manipulator's grandiose saga, then one sexual partner can easily be substituted for another, just as the extras in a Hollywood production are expendable and can be replaced at a moment's notice.

A particularly attractive and seductive manipulator one day explained to me her attitudes toward her varying and ever-changing sexual partners. "I know better than to get emotionally involved with a married man, for instance. I just wouldn't let myself do that. But sex has nothing to do with *real* involvement. I can enjoy sex with somebody and still hold part of myself back. Just because I sleep with somebody that isn't the same thing as getting involved with them."

Most interesting here is the implication that intimacy, as well as her own feelings, can be controlled and directed, turned on and off as the occasion demands. But eventually, such a manipulator of intimacy is trapped within the web of her own narcissism: her succession of "lovers" can never be experienced in their own individuality but only as extension of her own weakened self. "There's only one man I've really loved . . . he left me after living with me for a couple of years, but I'm still working on getting him back."

"Why was he so special?" I asked.

"With him," she replied, a meaningful surge of spontaneous emotion in her voice, "I once had a mystical experience while we made love."

Although I can only guess as to why her "lover" departed and whether he will return, his flight may have been in response to the threat of being submerged into this woman's perverted narcissism. To her, the "lover" is only experienced in terms of her own feelings and fantasies.

Once again, D. H. Lawrence invoked with uncanny accuracy the inherent narcissism in such "love" relationships along with the accompanying sense of suffocation they induce in others.

> "But why do I feel so strangely about you?
> said the lovely young lady, half wistful, half menacing.
> I took to my heels and ran
> before she could set the claws of her self-conscious questioning in me
> or tear me with the fangs of disappointment
> because I could not answer the riddle of her own self-importance."

The manipulator's sexual life is marked by a need for intense stimulation, heightened eroticism and a primitive primary oral sexuality aimed at merger with the lover. Oral sex temporarily seems to fill the need for bodily union and merger. Psychiatrists who specialize in the treatment of sexual disturbances write frequently that such a person experiences his or her mouth as an organ to devour or consume the lover. Fellatio and cunnilingus satisfy the manipulator's "eat-or-be-eaten" orientation toward sexuality.

Forms of sadism and masochism may occur at a later point and frequently coexist with the request for anal intercourse or, in the more disturbed individuals, group sexuality in which the borderland between self and others is further diffused. Specifically, the strength of the manipulator's sense of self is directly related to the intensity of experienced emotion. When bored she "can come alive" via intense emotional or sexual experiences. When this need goes seriously awry, the expression may take the form of deliberately provoked or self-inflicted painful experiences such as with Rhonda (p. 166). Wrist cutting, drug use, alcoholic binges— these often provide, at least momentarily, a sense of cohesion. Pain and humiliation may coexist with bizarrely erotic performances in which the manipulator simultaneously experiences the "heights" and "depths" of emotionality.

One of my own patients, a married woman in her early forties, would periodically rent a room in a cheap hotel near the docks. There, with her fur and designer dress draping the bottom of the bed, she would take on the whole fleet of arriving sailors from the ships in an orgy of single and group sex. Afterward she would inflict superficial wounds on her wrists, gulp down a sublethal dose of sleeping pills and summon the desk clerk as she sank into a mild drug-induced stupor. For her, these experiences validated her sense of cohesiveness, of being "really alive." This combination of heightened, though perverse, sexuality and masochistic surrender provided a confirming intensity of emotion, a means of establishing and maintaining her sense of self.

But even in instances of less dramatic behavior, the manipulator's sexual orientation is missing the component of tenderness or affection. Thus the manipulator basically does not love herself, feels basically incomplete and worthless. She has trouble loving others. Others exist only as a means of bolstering the manipulator's constantly sagging self-esteem. They are seduced and retained until conflicts eventually arise and the relationship is broken off. Sexuality thus typically exists apart from love.

Freud anticipated the manipulator's peculiar orientation toward love in 1921 when he wrote: "But at this point [when the affectionate, that is, personal, factor of a love relationship gives place entirely to the sensual one] regression has taken place to an early stage of sexual relations at which being in love has yet played no part, and all sexual objects were judged to be of equal value, somewhat in the sense of Bernard Shaw's malicious aphorism to the effect that being in love means greatly exaggerating the difference between one woman and another."

Combined with the manipulator's incapacity for love is her impaired ability to manage her own aggression and anger. To display anger openly is to risk the loss of the other person's supporting and nurturing functions, functions that are so important to the manipulator's fragile sense of worth. For this reason, hostility is expressed passively: rather than denying someone something, the manipulator will delay giving it. Rather than arguing, the manipulator withholds her affection, "freezing" the other person out with emotional coldness, hauteur and distance.

But at some point the manipulator's capacity to contain her anger will fail and her aggression will be expressed in emotional storms or flights into hyperactivity. Often the hyperactivity takes the form of impulsive and hectic "love affairs" which, in turn, end in further storms and renewed hypersexuality. Both desiring and fearing emotional closeness, the manipulator wants to merge with a strong and supportive person who will confirm her ever-dissipating sense of self. But at a certain point, all relationships other than the superficial ones become confining and threatening. The manipulator both desires and fears the loss of self which merger with another person entails. The manipulator impulsively seeks intimacy, particularly intensely erotic, perversely sensual sexual union in which body boundaries can be alternately lost and rediscovered, as with the child playing a game of peek-a-boo before a mirror. But in all instances, the other person is reacted to only as an object which can satisfy the manipulator's need for self-definition and enhancement.

Typically, the manipulator tires of people with the same regularity with which she tires of things. When this occurs, the manipulator defends against her waning interest by creating scenes, uproar, in fact anything which is likely to provide a momentary sense of excitement or stimulation. In this way, the relationship can once again seem real, momentarily liberated from the ennui that threatens to engulf both parties. I believe many a lovers' quarrel is based on this attempt to simultaneously deny and resist the boredom and emptiness that threatens to squeeze the viability out of the relationship. To the manipulator, such a process is inevitably repeated in every "love" relationship. Split off into several fragmented and essentially isolated islands, the self of the manipulator lacks the necessary cohesion to sustain a prolonged relationship. Simply put, everyone eventually becomes "boring." For where there is no sense of personal continuity or cohesion, a long-term relationship is impossible: each of the manipulator's different selves responds at different times and in different ways to the "loved one." Just as no one would want to wear the same dress day in and day out, so the manipulator doesn't want to "wear" the same person. Other people, too, must be changed and altered according to fashions and the opportunities of the moment.

IX

The Manipulator in Society

"My kid can pull off a con job on the other kids that I can't believe. He's so good at it that even I can't tell from one minute to the next whether or not to believe him. But I don't worry about him at all. Within a few years that kid's gonna go far."

A proud parent discussing his son

The Cool Syndrome

In the last section of this book I would like to apply some of the things we've discussed. We've ranged widely over the previous chapters, starting with an examination of the lives of people who fit, albeit uncomfortably, within what most of us would be willing to concede as "normality," and proceeding at the other end of the spectrum toward individuals who are on the brink of outright insanity and criminality.

As I hope I've made clear by now, these assorted and at first glance highly dissimilar personalities can be understood as representing various degrees of disruption within the integration of the self. The relevance of these self disorders within our society springs from their ubiquity as well as the profound effect they have on our culture.

In contemporary America, we experience firsthand the cultural effects of individual and group fragmentation. Our society is at the moment overwhelmed with individuals suffering from self disorders of various intensities. Furthermore, cultural stereotypes, many of them derived from advertising and the media, serve to perpetuate life-styles based on splitting and the absence of personal cohesion. This last section will examine how narcissistic and borderline values, for instance, are becoming assimilated into the mainstream of American life.

The difficulty increasing numbers of people are experiencing when it comes to intimacy; the rise in divorces based on "temporary commitment"; the pervasive loss of individual and national purpose; the preoccupation with national and international events as a form of theater—these are only some of the forces that are producing pervasive and powerful self disturbances within our culture.

With the preceding description of the manipulator as background, I'd like to take up in the last section of the book the issues of: (1) why manipulators are so common within our society; (2) the factors that are responsible for the rise of manipulation; and (3) what, if anything, can be done to stem the tide of further manipulation.

This section is more speculative than the earlier parts of the book, and I don't expect everyone to agree with everything I say. I don't think that anyone could seriously disagree, however, that the manipulator in his or her various guises is becoming an easily recognizable and admired personality type within the contemporary culture (i.e., the recent popularity of J.R. and the "Dallas" TV series with its cast of exploitive, manipulative characters). The disagreement is more likely to involve the question of whether or not the manipulator was present during earlier periods of our history. After all, Herman Melville wrote *The Confidence Man*, the first literary expression of the manipulator, in 1857. But my point is a different one. While the manipulator may have existed at all times and in all levels of society, it is only recently, I believe, that he's come into his own as a much-admired and much-imitated member of society. To this extent, disorders of the self—the essential dynamics that enable us to understand the manipulator—have increased, at least in the quantitative sense. We have more manipulators now than ever in our history. A search for a reason behind this increase leads to some interesting speculations.

• Is it possible that contemporary technological society is itself "splitting"? Certainly people are expected to move facilely from one social and occupational realm to another. In fact, in many of our nation's businesses the capacity for developing and sustaining multiple identities is a requirement for success. "Flexibility" is highly valued even though, basically, it often involves the capacity to shift personal and corporate allegiances with a minimum of fuss and bother. Unfortunately, some people soon become accustomed to walking out on their marriages with the same lack of concern they show when switching from one corporation to another. Husbands and wives are manipulated as skillfully as corporate vice-presidents.

• Mass communication has united people in the world into a kind of pseudo community. While we may know nothing about the customs and cultures of a particular people, we can learn about them through television and be video participants in suitably "newsworthy" aspects of their lives. But the kinds of things we learn about them are often things that demand that we objectify them—in a word, manipulate our concepts in ways that are inherently dehumanizing. For instance, we may witness on TV the aftermath of an erupting volcano. Amid the rubble lie bodies of children. If we actually saw the children dying before us, we would, no doubt, have pity. But how can we have pity day in and day out in the face of hundreds of tragedies that are real to us only through the cold medium of video? We close our hearts and our sympathies: No one except perhaps a Mother Theresa can live every moment of every day in a state of receptivity to the sufferings of others. Those of us who aren't saints close our hearts if not our minds. We "split off" aspects of our consciousness that we can't manage. As a result, we manipulate not only our image of other people, but our own feelings toward them.

• Never before in our history has our society put such emphasis on self-realization, doing one's own thing. As a result, the emotional ties between one person and another have been severed to the extent that no one feels he or she owes anyone anything anymore. Instead, intimacy is sought in "therapy" situations. But increased involvement with encounter groups, therapies and assertiveness-training programs hasn't resulted in people getting on any better with one another. The divorce rate is higher than any time in our history. Partly to blame is the fact that people have stopped considering the possibility that the problems reside within them. Instead, the problems are always considered someone else's and, to make things right, it's necessary only to become more self-assertive, tuned in to one's own feelings and so on. Since people feel they can't change society, efforts are made to develop ways for exploiting and manipulating it. Thus, we have the rise of smooth-talking, likable, white-collar con men. How to fight them? We are advised to outsmart, outcon, and outmanipulate them.

Manipulation is becoming the modus operandi of larger and larger numbers of people. It's also an inherent part of the national character. As a nation we're forgetting that it matters less whether a person is "other-" or "inner-directed," introverted or extroverted, than it does whether a person is capable of engaging in mutually satisfying, trusting relationships. The alternative is incessant exploitation and manipulation: In essence, dehumanization, impersonality and an increase in the very distrust and ennui interpersonal relationships are intended to dispel.

Several contemporary findings within the social sciences suggest that manipulation is fast on the way to becoming a national lifestyle. The basis for this change in attitude is an alteration of the ways many people are beginning to think about the self. In recent years, some investigators are questioning whether our traditional attitudes toward the self may not be illusory.

Normally, we assume that most people possess a fairly stable self identity, and although they certainly may change their minds on certain issues from time to time and behave somewhat differently under varying circumstances, their self is consistent over the long haul: Those who are honest remain honest; friendly people will retain more of an openness in their social relations and so on. But such assumptions may be incorrect. To some people, their personality depends very much on their social situation. Such a person may have not just one but several selves, according to the expectations of the people around them. Furthermore, for such people the self—rather than an integrated internally determined structure—may be the end result of their social interactions.

Dr. Mark Snyder, professor of psychology at the University of Minnesota, believes that the concept of self can best be approached via the study of the techniques different people use to control the impression they make on others ("impression management"). Snyder's research interests are centered on the commonly observed but little understood differences in people's abilities in this area. Some people are exquisitely sensitive to the public impression they are making and can adjust their behavior almost instantaneously if they observe that the impression is not proceeding as they intend.

It's a common observation in business meetings, courtrooms and cocktail parties that some people possess highly developed skills in monitoring the impressions they are making, while others, whom Snyder refers to as "low self monitors," prefer "just being themselves" despite whatever impression they may be making on others. These differences in impression management can also be observed across professions and occupations: Lawyers, politicians and actors are among the "high self monitors." Not surprisingly, psychopaths, confidence artists and as-if personalities also possess highly developed talents for self-monitoring. "He who really loves the world shapes himself to please it," noted Felix Krull. As we have seen, the psychopath and the impostor are virtuosos in the art of "reading" other people's responses for the purpose of altering self performance in the service of deception.

Snyder's research is consistent with the view that psychopaths, impostors and as-if personalities may demonstrate a greater proficiency in self-monitoring and impression management based on the absence of *any* internalized experience comparable to a "self." They are, in a sense, chameleons who can alter their personalities according to the expectations of those around them.

In the case of impostors, there is a need to maintain a fictionalized self and, as a consequence, self-monitoring and impression-management activities are directed toward maintaining their fraudulent identities in the face of potential skeptics.

With as-if personalities, self-monitoring activities are directed toward maintaining behavior and personality characteristics consistent with the identifications currently operative. The important point, of course, is that impression management and self-monitoring are normal processes in which we all engage, but among the types of people we are discussing in this book, the processes are developed to an extraordinary degree. Thus, our concept of the "self" may require some modification in the light of findings among high self monitors.

Snyder and others have found that high self-monitoring individuals have the greatest problem when it comes to simply "being themselves." When questioned about their attitudes toward controversial subjects, for instance, they are apt to respond with a socially accepted response, yet their behavior may indicate just the opposite orientation.

Among white "liberal" undergraduate students at Harvard, for instance, those who went out of their way to avoid contact with black students most often, expressed in an interview enlightened sentiments on the subject of harmonious race relations. They really said one thing and did another. Such flexibility in self presentation, while it often contributes to smooth interpersonal relationships, nevertheless often exacts an emotional price from a high self monitor. "In some circumstances we are persuaded by our own appearances," says Snyder. "We become the person we appear to be." The cost of such self modifications includes a disparity between what Snyder calls the public appearance and the private realities of the self. "High self-monitoring orientations may be purchased at the cost of having one's actions reflect and communicate very little about one's private attitudes and feelings and dispositions."

High self monitors, according to Snyder, partition their lives, carefully separating people and experiences so that there is a minimum of overlap. A high self monitor, for instance, can never give a party and invite all of his or her friends. Too much conflict and role confusion might result. High self monitors fragment their lives, engaging in splitting-type operations in which certain people are chosen only for specific activities. The danger in this approach is, of course, that after a while the high self monitors split their experiences into so many varying and even contradictory ways that a complete paralysis of will can supervene whenever it's time to "relax and be yourself." There seems to be no clear-cut "self" outside of a defining social situation.

What's involved with the high self monitor is not a deliberate attempt to deceive, as seen in the psychopath or impostor. Nor do we find the severe fractionation of the self as observed in the as-if personality. Rather, the high self monitor's skills at impression management make possible a manipulation of the social environment through a series of changing self presentations. To the high self monitor, people are what they appear to be in a particular situation and nothing more. Thus, identity is less a matter of developing an internal consistent and stable self presentation, than it is a process of fashioning the self according to the social demands of the moment. Appearance and image take precedence over feelings and convictions. If one is what one appears to be, then, an acceptable social self becomes inseparable from one's personal identity.

Within such a world, the concept of the person is meaningless without some reference to existing social situations. To ask about the "real self" of a high self monitor is to enquire concerning the existence of a phantom. In a sense, such a person has no self, at least not in the context a low self monitor would understand: a set of enduring and generally consistent attitudes, beliefs and actions that alter very little from one moment to the next and are influenced only minimally by the responses of other people.

The political process, to take just one example, is heavily involved in impression management with our leaders advised on a daily basis on ways public opinion can be manipulated via skilled self presentation. As a first step, media consultants conduct a poll to measure the public's opinion on an issue. Secondly, they advise the candidate on ways he can accommodate himself toward the public's perceptions as revealed by the poll. In this dialogue between candidate and media consultant there is little emphasis on the kinds of questions asked by low self monitors: "What seems to be the wisest course of action in the long run, current opinion notwithstanding?" "What are the qualities of a good leader?" Currently the answers to these questions would be: "There is no best course of action because a leader who ignores public opinion isn't likely to survive long enough to see the result of any overwhelmingly unpopular course of action. Further, a good leader is one who is sensitive to the public's expectations and molds his public self accordingly."

In the past, leadership seems to have largely involved low self monitors who developed their positions from a sense of inner conviction which was firmly held. They pressed on until either their views prevailed or they were replaced by other low self monitors with different but equally tenaciously held opinions. A leader, according to this view, is a person of "principle" and is influenced by "integrity," "honesty" and other internal considerations which, to the high self monitor, have no reality outside of specific situations. In response to each challenge, the leader who is a high self monitor must try to "negotiate" a "compromise" between what he would like to do and what he is told by the polls that the public is likely to approve. A politician's popularity thus becomes a matter of wildly careening fluctuations in the polls resulting from the public's perception of what he is doing or appearing to do at any moment. Success thus becomes a matter of poll results indicating favorable public perceptions of his impression management. Within such a mind set, problems never exist as problems but only in the form of failures of impression management, in short, public relations problems.

Remember Richard Nixon's concern during Watergate whether or not the public was likely to believe the various alternative "scenarios" that he proposed? "How will it play in Peoria?" has in a few short years progressed from a serious presidential inquiry to an amusing catch phrase employed by impression managers everywhere.

This emphasis on the importance of how issues are perceived rather than on any intrinsic merits of the issues themselves provides an explanation for many otherwise puzzling and maddening aspects of contemporary life. If things are nothing more than they appear, then what is a more worthy enterprise than taking the necessary pains to ensure that things appear to be the way one wishes?

A well-known New York advertising agency recently branched out into a separate division dedicated to "image and advocacy advertising and corporate communications for associations and corporations rather than product advertising." One of this agency's "image" accounts was the Three Mile Island Nuclear Generating Plant. The power company, it seems, feels that it received a "raw deal" over the near core meltdown incident in 1979 and hired this nationally known advertising agency to improve its "image." Included among the services provided by the public relations firm are "mock television studios where executives can prepare for interviews by sitting under lights and facing a panel of hostile questioners. The performance is videotaped and criticized."

A similar use of "mock" television techniques in order to evaluate "performance" was a regular feature of the Jimmy Carter White House. For instance, video-taped "trial runs" were studied carefully on a regular basis by Gerald Rafshoon, President Carter's in-house public relations expert, in terms of Carter's "credibility."

In contemporary America day-to-day interaction is becoming a matter of impression management aimed at manipulating the thoughts and emotions of other people. In some instances, moreover, such behavior is a prerequisite for success.

The Harvard Business School course for Negotiating presently takes advantage of the student's willingness to engage in lying and other deceitful practices. Each week the students are paired off by their teacher and instructed to negotiate with each other on "mock" situations. During one week the students may be attempting to reach a compromise on wage disputes, one side negotiating for the management and the other from the labor point of view. Other simulated negotiations include property transfers, personal injury disputes between plaintiffs and the insurance company—in fact, just about any conflict situation in which people might be expected to negotiate or compromise. In all instances, the best grades go to the students who negotiate most successfully: get the best contracts in the case of labor negotiator or, when representing management, holding the workers to the lowest increase or maybe no increase at all.

Although there are many factors that contribute to a successful classroom negotiator, one trait stands out above any other: the student's willingness to engage in what their professor refers to as "strategic misrepresentation." One top scorer in the Competitive Decision Making course explained the process in slightly blunter terms about how he was able to obtain the highest grade: "I've learned to lie to get a better score."

Many of the negotiating situations are designed, the teacher admits, so that the truth teller is at a disadvantage when competing with anyone who lies or engages in gross misrepresentation. Since the negotiating methods employed by the students emphasize face-to-face confrontations, the key element to success often turns out to consist of convincing your "opponent" of your forthrightness at the very moment you are most intensely engaged in "strategic misrepresentation."

For the successful classroom negotiator, the rewards can be sweet indeed: a high grade in an important course in the nation's most prestigious business school. As a further reward for such accomplishment, the student can expect attractive, top-level career opportunities after graduation into the real world where, presumably, similar negotiating techniques will continue.

While most students at the beginning of a semester report uneasiness about bluffing or outright lying as part of their negotiations, the most successful overcome their moral scruples or perhaps are never troubled by them in the first place. "Too much of an issue was made of ethics" recalls the class's highest scorer. "I'm sorry if it made people uncomfortable, but that's the way the world is. I guess that sounds hard-nosed, but if it is better for me I did it. Most people did."

The Competitive Decision Making course emphasizes the personal style that the psychopath and the manipulator employ with natural facility. Like the con man, the negotiator becomes skilled at playing on the other person's credulity; pushing things far enough to attain one's ends; avoiding discovery or arousing anger.

In this process a premium is placed on the capacity for the rapid formation and dissolution of identifications. More than anything else, the skilled negotiator must retain a fluid self concept which, from moment to moment, can reflect back to his opponent as in a mirror those personal qualities he feels are most likely to win over the opponent. Frequently, this entails an intuitive grasp of the other person's capacity for envy and greed. A similar pattern is encountered among successful con artists.

Some years ago a young black girl who identified herself as a missionary visited a ghetto in Washington, D.C., where she spent several hours talking and playing with the children in a neighborhood playground. After learning from the children the names and addresses of several people on the block, she began door-to-door canvassing for contributions for the construction of a "church in Central Africa." Based on the background obtained from her playground informants she was able to "personalize" her appeal.

"Your neighbor Mrs. Smith down the street was kind enough to give me twenty dollars, and she mentioned that you could *probably* see your way clear to contributing as much." Obviously, this ploy was aimed at manipulating her victims while playing on their tendencies to compare themselves on matters of generosity. But, in addition, the "missionary's" talent for deception also included the employment of a more subtle fraud based on her perception that everyone in the neighborhood wanted to get something tangible in return for a contribution.

Each donation would be rewarded, she said, with the receipt of food stamps valued at twice the amount of the donation. The religious organization, she explained, had been given the stamps by the government, and since the church's immediate need wasn't for food but money with which to build the "church in Africa," they were happy to "reward" any acts of generosity with a free gift of food stamps.

Eventually the fraud was uncovered when a potential donor recognized the food stamps as bogus and called the police. Up to that moment, however, the "missionary" was well on her way to fleecing the entire neighborhood via skillful manipulation of her victims' envy and greed: No one wanted to be revealed as lacking in generosity and—after the matter of food stamps was approached—people competed with each other for the opportunity, under the guise of "charity," to get back more than they were giving.

Although this young girl is more apt to be labeled as a con artist rather than a negotiator, she nonetheless illustrates an exaggerated "strategic misrepresentation." The pattern, at any rate, is almost identical: obtain something from someone that they would ordinarily be reluctant to give up (money) by offering them something that would enable them to feel that *they* are coming out the winner (phony food stamps which they believe could be redeemed at twice the amount of money expended). The negotiator, as with the con artist, depends for success on arousing his opponent's latent psychopathy: the "victim" is only a victim because at some moment, however briefly, he sees himself as the victimizer.

In a similar way, the negotiator, driven as he is to obtain a resolution favorable to himself without any more regard for the other person's point of view than is absolutely forced upon him, is in constant danger of being duped by means of his own greed. If neither side of a negotiation is concerned with anything beyond self-interest, then the process becomes one of getting as much as possible, giving up little or nothing and, most importantly, doing so by tricking the opponent into thinking he is pulling off something. The process that is common to all of this and is the hallmark of both the con artist and the negotiator is, of course, manipulation.

The increase in the number of high self monitors within our society corresponds to an uncanny degree with an increase in the number, or at least the visibility, within our culture of psychopaths, impostors and as-if personalities. These extreme and pathological character disorders represent the ultimate in impression management and high self monitoring. But there is other evidence which can be cited indicating that we are becoming a society of manipulators.

Several contemporary findings within the social sciences suggest that manipulation is fast on the way to becoming a national "life-style." The basis for this change in attitude is an alteration in the ways many people are beginning to think about the self.

Several years ago, American social psychologist Richard Christie presented a paper at the American Psychological Association drawn from a lifetime study of the writings of Niccolò Machiavelli. Christie's interest stemmed from his attempt to develop a hypothetical role model of the contemporary Machiavellian. Christie was convinced that Machiavelli's treatise *The Prince* was more than just an interesting historical document; on the contrary, it continued to exert a profound influence on present day life. Using Machiavelli's own words, suitably modernized, Christie developed a twenty-point Mach Scale. "The best way to handle people is to tell them what they want to hear," would be assented to by a high Mach, while he would reject "honesty is the best policy in all cases." Christie based his highly discriminating test on a hypothetical role model of the Machiavel based on four characteristics:

1. A relative lack of affect in interpersonal relationships: Manipulating should be enhanced by viewing others as objects.
2. A lack of concern with conventional morality: Regarding lying, cheating and deceit in general, manipulators should have a utilitarian view of interaction with others.
3. A lack of gross psychopathology: The manipulator is hypothesized to take a rational view of others and is in contact with objective reality.
4. Low ideological commitment: He is more interested in tactics to an end than in inflexible striving for an idealistic goal.

Among Christie's four items, some are obviously easier to test than others. A "lack of affect in interpersonal relations," for instance, is likely to impress many people as hopelessly subjective, given existing cultural attitudes concerning open expressions of anger and affection, to say nothing of other primarily emotional matters. But lying and cheating are more objective.

In several tests (which were rather Machiavellian themselves!) Christie's subjects were unaware of the purpose of the experiment, which was aimed at discovering how the subject would respond when caught cheating. From the beginning, all the participants were subtly encouraged to cheat on the tests, and did so, but with one highly revealing difference. When confronted, the low Mach had difficulty looking the examiner in the eye. The high Mach, in contrast, was able to maintain steady eye contact while vehemently denying any deception.

In an even more Machiavellian experiment, the participants were requested to play the role of "experimenter" themselves and administer a test, but with the additional instruction to do everything possible to distract their subjects and, hence, lower their performance. Since the general procedures of test taking are rather standardized and include little interference on the part of the administrator, this was a true measure of the ingenuity of the high

Mach. In such a situation which emphasized subtlety, cleverness and the maintenance of a pleasing but nonetheless annoying and distracting façade, the high Mach outscored the low by a ratio of over two to one. In addition to outperforming their low-scoring counterparts, the high Machs enjoyed the experiment, most particularly the deployment of those manipulating devices which confounded his unsuspecting test subjects.

What emerged from these early experiments of Christie was the profile of an individual (the High Machiavel or High Mach) with little concern for conventional moral standards who camouflages amorality with a manipulative manner along with a highly developed capacity for maintaining innocence in the face of overwhelming evidence of duplicity. Left at this, the high Mach's effectiveness at manipulating other people would be sharply precluded. Once a high Mach was recognized, other people could protect themselves from him either by simply limiting their contact with him or, when this was not possible, remaining on guard against further deceit on his part. But Christie's subsequent experiments demonstrated that the high Mach's blandishments aren't so easily resisted.

In an experiment called the Ten-Dollar Game, high-, middle- and low-Mach scorers were seated randomly in groups of three around a table on which were placed ten one-dollar bills. The instructions were simple, terse and diabolical: the money was to be divided between any *two* subjects who could agree on how to do it. This fiendishly clever experiment excluded the obvious and most morally neutral approach of simply giving everyone three dollars and assigning the odd dollar by some form of chance, i.e., flipping coins with the odd person pocketing the dollar. But since only *two* people at the table could divide the money, all three had to engage in bargaining, negotiating and, most important, manipulating the two other persons at their table. At the seven tables of three persons each, the high Machs were able to come to some agreement and wound up with the greater portion of the money. High Machs averaged $5.57 in winnings, middle scorers $3.14 and low Machs only $1.28.

In the Ten-Dollar Game, the high Mach was forced to engage

in some form of cooperation with another person and did so with striking success. Since the rules precluded any assignment of the money to a single individual—even if such a highly unlikely agreement were to take place—the high Mach had to play two individuals against each other with sufficient cleverness to entice one of them into an arrangement which left the third person with nothing.

To the casual observer, the Ten-Dollar Game suggests that the high Mach is capable, when the occasion demands, of empathizing with others. But to assume this would be a dangerous oversimplification. There are other experiments carried out by Christie and his associate, C. Geis, which suggest rather, that, to the high Mach, the other people in the experiment are only "things" which are as dispensable as dollar bills.

In an arrangement in which two players were requested to cooperate in a test of manual dexterity, high Mach scorers tended to be unaffected by the abilities of their partners. In each pairing, the high Machs' performance, good or bad, remained about the same. The low Machs' performance, however, seemed to be affected by the interaction created between their partners' ability and their own. Sometimes they played better, sometimes worse, depending on their dynamic interchange with other persons. From these findings, Christie concludes: "Low Machs treat others as persons; highs treat them as objects . . . Encounter prone, lows know others by moving into contact with them. They do not stand off . . . but open up to and get carried away by the influence of the other."

After ten years of experiments with the Mach tests, a profile emerges of a high Mach which is disturbingly similar to behavioral observations of the kinds of manipulators described throughout this book: they are self-centered, charming, deceptive, relatively unconcerned with others, exploitive, capable of maintaining deceit in the face of confrontation, oriented toward individual performance, "using" others in cooperative measures only as a last resort and then only as objects no different from the nonhuman environment. What makes this parallel particularly important are the conclusions that Christie and Geis reached: "If our speculations are correct, modern society is becoming increasingly more similar in structure to the kinds of laboratory situations in which high Machiavellians win. Available evidence also suggests that individual orientations towards manipulations are increasing."

Our present social structure is evolving toward the time when Machiavellianism, if not outright psychopathy, may be an absolute requirement for success. In business, entertainment, politics and the media, topheavy bureaucracies are emerging in which highly structured authority networks are giving way to looser, more "interactive" methods for reaching decisions. For instance, increasing numbers of meetings are becoming routine within organizations that involve more and more people who, realistically, often have very little to contribute on the matters under discussion but whose presence is required in order to maintain at least the appearance of coequal participation in the decision and policy making. In such settings, the quip, the finely turned phrase, the timely compliment, may do much to advance one's position in a firm or organization. This isn't to argue that industry and business should return to the days of tyrannic moguls, nonunionism and fourteen-hour work days, but it does suggest, on the basis of the Christie-Geis findings, that our present social structure is beginning to resemble more and more the kinds of experimental situations in which high Machs and manipulators can be expected to perform exceedingly well.

"The more similar to the non-laboratory world the experimental situation was, e.g., face-to-face contact, greater latitude for improvising behaviors, the more affectively complex the situation, the greater was the relative advantage of the high Machs."

In a study published in 1978, Dr. Robert J. Smith and James E. Griffin, of the University of Maryland, compared Christie and Geis's Mach IV scale to the MMPI psychopathic deviation scale, a standard measure of psychopathic trends within the personality. They found a significant correlation between these two scales, suggesting that "psychopathy and Machiavellianism are converging dimensions."

Society is becoming increasingly accepting of Machiavellian values. We are encountering on a daily basis individuals displaying what Christie and Geis termed the "cool syndrome": psychological standoffishness with the emphasis on personal rather than group values; deficient empathy for other people's feelings; behavior which occurs independent of, and even in direct contradiction to, espoused beliefs and values; the capacity to successfully argue positions different from one's own; the ability to lie and deceive without any outward signs of uneasiness—these are the personality characteristics which, though attributed to the Machiavellian, actually are encountered more frequently among manipulators, particularly those at the psychopathic end of the spectrum. The manipulator is, in essence, an extension of the Machiavellian personality. Further, Machiavellianism provides a "rational" orientation toward achieving success.

The manipulator is the natural consequence of a society which rewards material success, outward "image" and competitive strivings for status. Increasingly, pathologic manipulators can be expected in the near future that range from the impostor to the con man to, at the extreme of the continuum, the murderous psychopath. In each instance, the driving force is the same: construction of a coherent identity (self) through the manipulation of the environment, particularly the responses of other people.

There are indications that the manipulator's style and absence of values have already exerted a corroding effect on our attitudes. For instance, during 1980 eleven public officials charged with criminal matters were up for reelection. Seven of them were reelected to office. In various parts of the country, a comparatively invariant scenario was enacted: a well-dressed, articulate, totally "credible" candidate swore his innocence before TV cameras and promised that the judicial process would vindicate him. The performances were skillful and often utterly convincing. We bought their version of what had transpired only to later discover, after their convictions, that their protestations of innocence were pure flimflam. We were taken in by the "image of innocence."

In a world where everything is ultimately a matter of "performance" the psychopath or impostor is in a position to provide the most convincing performance. Thus we increasingly encounter on the six o'clock news the suave, likable, totally believable, manipu-

lative white-collar criminal who's out to convince us, as he's convinced himself, that his problems are ultimately due to a bad
"image." If he can but look the part of an innocent party then,
according to his logic, his innocence can easily be established in
court. It's all a matter of "presentation," "packaging," projecting
the right "image."

What does the word "image" evoke in your mind? As a
starter, the word can refer to mirrors and self-reflection. But the
more contemporary use of the word evokes the *video image*. It's
from this source that the manipulator takes his origins and is sustained in his deceptions. An understanding of manipulation, as
well as any action aimed at decreasing its prevalence within our society, depends on our ability to understand the pervasive effect of
video imagery on the shaping of character. As I'll show in the next
chapter, it's not a coincidence that the rise of the manipulator co-
incides with the establishment of video imagery, particularly television, as the most pervasive instrument for social conditioning in
our time.

The Modular "Me"

In Samuel Beckett's play *Krapp's Last Tape*, the reclusive and malevolent Krapp has, over his lifetime, recorded each year's events on an annual tape, one of which, as the play opens, he plays over in the isolation of his "den." Now sixty-nine, Krapp ranges thirty years into the past and selects a tape recorded on his thirty-ninth birthday when he was "sound as a bell" and "intellectually, I now have every reason to suspect, at the crest of the wave or thereabouts."

The thirty-nine-year-old Krapp—his voice resounding strongly and pompously on the tape—speaks of listening, some moments before, to a still earlier Krapp recorded at about age twenty-seven. Krapp and the audience are thus simultaneously experiencing two of Krapp's former selves, both rendered physically "present" thanks to the technology of tape. The thirty-nine-year-old Krapp (the voice on the tape) speaks to the sixty-nine-year-old Krapp and the audience of his estrangement from the self aged twenty-seven. "Hard to believe I was ever that young whelp." He laughs at his earlier idealism, the "aspirations" and "resolutions" that seem so comical to the pompously cynical Krapp at thirty-nine. While the tape plays on, the "real" Krapp, who stares from the stage out at the audience, experiences a similar discontinuity. Abruptly he switches tapes and begins speaking into the recorder: "Just been listening to that stupid bastard I took myself for thirty years ago, hard to believe I was ever as bad as that. Thank God that's all done with anyway."

Krapp's self, as presented to the audience, is a house of distorting mirrors, each mirror reflecting a strange, contradictory and discontinuous vision of Krapp.

Is he the cynical thirty-nine-year-old sophisticate who on the tape mocks the idealism of his twenty-seven-year-old predecessor? Or is Krapp "really" the sixty-nine-year-old hermit who sits before the audience and attempts to extract comfort from the thought that at least he's now smarter than "that stupid bastard" of thirty-nine? The mind boggles as it envisions the possibility of an infinite regression of Krapp's: a twenty-seven-year-old Krapp expressing his estrangement and contempt for a still-younger twenty-one-year-old Krapp who, in turn, spurns the teenage Krapp and so on. In each instance Krapp is discontinuous, each self morbidly engaged in "self-conscious" reflection ending in a repudiation of all earlier feelings and expressions. At the conclusion of the play and as a final indication of Krapp's discontinuity, he discovers to his horror that he's unable to make his last tape. There is simply no present life, no self to record, merely a morbid preoccupation with an endless series of former Krapps preserved by a means of the impersonal technology of tape. Krapp, in the final moments of the play, is revealed as a man who *has no self*.

In *Krapp's Last Tape,* the tape recorder provides Krapp with a means of encountering his multiple selves. But the continuity in time provided by the series of yearly tapes stands in stark contrast to Krapp's personal discontinuity. To Krapp, the voices he hears on the tapes belong to persons with whom he feels no connection, people whose existence, in fact, serves only to annoy: "a young whelp," a "bastard." The tapes, rather than providing Krapp with the creative powers he desired earlier in life—his one novel has turned out a failure—serve only to entice him from real-life, flesh-and-blood encounters which might provide the raw materials necessary for artistic creation.

Technology, particularly the technology of communication—the tapes hoarded by Krapp—can be broadening and educational or, as with Krapp, ultimately fractionating. Thanks to technology, we experience so many points of view and encounter so many diverse and contradictory phenomena that we too can end up like Krapp unsure of "reality" or even who we are. I've discussed this on several occasions with media professionals. Jay Bobowitz, an independent television producer, articulated the dilemma most clearly.

"We can't really measure the impact TV, for instance, is having on our sense of who we are. Isn't it interesting that the first generation raised with TV has become so preoccupied with identity? But I think this is understandable. Television affects all of us by forcing us to confront aspects of ourselves that we would have little or no contact with otherwise. I'm thinking, particularly, of the 'real life' aspects of television: scenes of disasters or wars, for instance. They may be having a splintering effect on us as we try to force out of our consciousness certain perceptions and feelings that we refuse to acknowledge.

"Formerly it was easier to avoid such confrontations with ourselves. We could stop reading newspapers, for instance. But how can anybody possibly get away from the effects of TV? You go out to a bar to have a drink and you find yourself exposed to pictures of somebody's house burning down, all presented in 'living color' on the bartender's portable TV. After ten or twenty years of this kind of experience I think it natural that people begin to wonder who they are, even in some instances suspecting that they may be several selves all at once."

Social commentator Alvin Toffler in *The Third Wave* points to a similar diversification of identity brought about by the mass media:

"The de-massification of the media today presents a dazzling diversity of role models and life-styles for one to measure oneself against. Moreover, the new media do not feed us fully formed chunks, but broken chips and blips of imagery. Instead of being handed a selection of coherent identities to choose among, we are required to piece one together: a configurative or modular 'me.' This is far more difficult, and it explains why so many millions are desperately searching for identity."

Although it's always hazardous to blame complex problems on solitary causes, the prevailing disturbance in the unity of the self which many people experience is at least partially caused, I believe, by the fractionating effect of media imagery. It is virtually impossible for anyone in our culture to avoid measuring his own sense of identity according to media-derived stereotypes.

For several years now, social commentators have noted that

television serves to provide a confirmation of what is and is not "real." Joel Swerdlow, coauthor of *Remote Control: Television and the Manipulation of American Life,* says: "Television is the great certifying agent of our time. Most Americans do not believe in the reality of any event or emotion that they have not seen at one time or another on television."

A sense of personal identity may also be constructed around video imagery. New York talk show hostess Nikki Haskell describes the reaction of patrons at the Underground, a disco near Union Square.

"Listen," says Nikki, "when the TV lights go on, people go crazy. They love it. I don't care *who* they are, how famous, how rich, how beautiful. If they say they don't want to be photographed, I know one thing about them: They're liars. *Everyone* wants to be on TV. Of *course* they say they don't come for the Friday night cameras. But when those lights hit, they're like flies near honey. And *somehow* even the most camera-shy celebrity manages to position himself right smack in front of my camera.

"Even the crowd on the dance floor! I keep a cameraman down there with a monitor so the dancers can see themselves. What energy they create—just to be on a TV monitor! You have to see it to believe it."

But the transforming effect of video imagery on personal identity isn't limited by any means to recreational pursuits. In my own medical practice, I am constantly caught up in the web of mutual expectations existing between me and my patients. For one thing, patients have definite expectations of how a doctor is "supposed" to talk and act. For the most part, these expectations are based on television and movie experiences. They affect not only my patients but me as well. "Media" depictions of doctors are constantly exerting an influence by consciously or unconsciously influencing my responses. For example, certain questions and comments, formerly unheard of, are now almost routine in a hospital waiting room. "I don't want him kept alive by machines," is a frequent statement made by relatives. Inquiry often reveals that the relatives rarely have any idea just what kind of "machines" are capable of prolonging life. Their descriptions are based on images and dialogues that they have seen and heard on TV. Furthermore, their statements are made with the disconcerting mixture of blandness and emotional distancing you would expect from someone reading a script.

The public's encounters with doctors, lawyers and policemen—to mention only three professionals often depicted on television—frequently are based on expectations created by television. The client or patient brings to the relationship a certain expectation and fashions his behavior accordingly. The professional, in turn, responds to the "script." As Swerdlow points out in his book, these mutual expectations—based as they are on fantasies and fiction gathered from TV—can lead to disastrous consequences. A doctor who fails to heal his patient *à la* Marcus Welby, M.D., may find himself the object of a malpractice suit.

Television not only creates certain expectations within people, but is capable of modifying their personality in fundamental ways. It is even possible for television, in fact, to create and sustain certain selves.

In Jerzy Kosinski's *Being There*, the main character (Chauncy Gardiner Chance), a retarded and socially isolated gardener realizes his own existence, literally creates a self out of the myriad images he sees every day on his TV. "By changing the channel he could change himself. He could go through phases, as garden plants went through phases, but he could change as rapidly as he wished by twisting the dial backward and forward. . . . By turning the dial, Chance could bring others inside his eyelids. Thus he came to believe that it was he, Chance, and no one else, who made himself be."

Chance's perceptions resemble television images, rapidly replacing each other without leaving a trace except in the memory of the viewer. "As long as one did not look at people, they did not exist. They began to exist, as on TV, when one turned one's eyes on them. Only then could they stay in one's mind before being erased by new images."

Chance's attitude toward himself also is based on his experiences with television. "By looking at him, others could make him be clear, could open him up and unfold him; not to be seen was

to blur and to fade out." Along with supplying Chance with a
self, television provided him with a repertoire of behaviors gleaned
from the images he's seen over the years on TV and stored in his
memory.

When asked by an attorney to sign a form renouncing all
claims on his former employer's estate, Chance can't admit his inability to read. "On TV programs people who did not know how
to read or write were often mocked and ridiculed." To avoid this,
Chance calculates the time needed to read a page. "On TV the
time it took people to read legal papers varied." He finally bluffs
his way by imitating the manner of a TV actor faced with examining an important legal document. Chance's performance
proves only too successful. When he informs the attorney handling the estate, "I can't sign it," his reluctance is interpreted as
an unwillingness to relinquish a claim on the estate rather than a
description of his inability to write or sign his name.

Chance's perceptions remain linked to the images he's seen on
TV. After leaving his house for the first time in thirty years, he's
surprised to discover that "the street, the cars, the buildings, the
people, the faint sounds were images already burned into his
memory. So far everything outside the gate resembled what he
had seen on TV."

Social relationships, too, are modeled on encounters Chance
remembers from TV. At one point he carries on a discussion by
imagining his companion "as if she were on television." In the
style of a TV interviewer, he repeats back portions of other people's sentences, a practice which soon earns for him a reputation
as a discerning and sympathetic listener. Later, when invited to
dine with an elderly businessman and his young wife, Chance "in
deciding how to behave chose the TV program of a young businessman who often dined with his boss and the boss's daughter."

On the basis of scripts memorized from years of television viewing, Chance creates a pseudo world in which television images
provide meaning and continuity. His reliance on television even
makes possible the elaboration of a "philosophy" with which to
face the perils and uncertainties of the world Chance can neither
understand nor anticipate: "as on TV, what would follow next was

hidden; he knew the actors on the new program were unknown. He did not have to be afraid, for everything that happened had its sequel, and the best that he could do was to wait patiently for his own forthcoming appearance."

Although Chance is a fictional character, he nonetheless represents in exaggerated form something that all of us have experienced at one time or another. "It's unreal," we comment in response to something highly unpleasant, embarrassing or traumatic. And although we don't deny that the event happened, our comments suggest that its unreality places it within the realm of something that we might have seen on television. Businessmen discuss "scenarios" at their morning conferences before rushing off to keep an appointment with their media consultant, who may tell them ways of appearing more "credible" or "sincere." Thus sincerity—traditionally understood as a strict correspondence between intention and actual performance between what one does and what one intends—has become, through the intermediary of technology, the cunning construction of a visual image designed to persuade.

Throughout all this, the media have brought about a fundamental schism in our emotional lives. What we "think" and "feel," how we evaluate the world around us, the basis for our beliefs as well as the measure of our opinions of other people—all are increasingly dependent on our experiences with video imagery.

A marvelous insight into the effects of video technology on personality was provided several years ago by Kosinski, who, prior to writing *Being There*, taught elementary school.

Kosinski invited students between ten and fourteen years of age to be interviewed. He said to each one, "I want to do an interview with you, to ask you some very private and even embarrassing questions, but I won't record our conversation or repeat to anyone what you tell me. To start with, do you masturbate?" When the children reacted with embarrassment and shock, Kosinski followed up with "Do you steal often? Have you stolen anything recently?" Again the children floundered, almost speechless with embarrassment. At this point Kosinski revealed the true nature of his experiment. "Now I'll tell you why I asked you all these questions. You see, I would like to film the interview and show it on television. . . . Your parents, your friends, strangers, the whole country would see it." The students agreed. Here are the results of the experiment in Kosinski's own words:

"Once the equipment was installed, I started the video camera and it was time to address my first 'guest.' 'Now tell me,' I asked . . . 'do you masturbate? If you do, tell our audience how and when you do it.' The boy, suddenly poised and blasé, leaned toward me. 'Well yes, occasionally I do. Of course, I'm not sure I can describe it. But I can try. . . .' An inviting smile stolen from 'The Mike Douglas Show'. . . . After Tom described all, leaving nothing to the public's imagination, I changed the subject. I said, 'Everybody will be interested in your experiences as a thief. Have you ever stolen anything?' Pensively, as if recalling a pleasant childhood incident, Tom said, 'Every once in a while when I go to the Five and Ten, you know, I like to pick up something. . . .'"

In an attempt to further gauge the effects of TV on social behavior, Kosinski staffed a classroom with a TV camera and monitors so that the children could either watch him directly or turn their attention to the monitors and see him on television. As part of the experiment, Kosinski arranged for a man to suddenly enter the classroom and start an argument which soon escalated into shouting and, eventually, pushing and shoving of Kosinski. While all of this was going on, a concealed camera recorded the children's reactions. In almost all instances the children watched the assault on the TV camera rather than the "real thing" and never raised any protest or appeared alarmed. Later when questioned about their behavior, the children spoke in video terms. "You looked so scared and he was so mean," one child reported. "You could see *everything* on those screens. They are great."

Commenting on the experiment, Kosinski told an interviewer, "The children sat transfixed, as if the TV cameras neutralized the act of violence. And perhaps they did. By filming a brutal physical struggle from a variety of viewpoints, the cameras transformed a human conflict into an aesthetic happening, distancing the audience and allowing them an alternative to moral judgment and involvement."

The capacity of video to offer an alternative to moral judgment explains, I believe, some of the phenomena which we have all become accustomed to by this time. Consider again the suave, well-dressed, unflappable white-collar criminal who stands outside the courtroom in front of the TV cameras, calmly maintaining his innocence in the face of overwhelming evidence to the contrary. Such an individual's self-expression is based on *how he imagines himself to appear on a TV monitor*. Once again, the process is one of image simulation: look the part of the innocent victim, continue to deny responsibility. This, of course, is the modus operandi of the psychopath to whom truth is always a matter of "projecting the right image."

Video imagery thus encourages the expression of psychopathic and manipulative values within a society. The fascination of the children watching Kosinski being beaten up; the suspension of moral judgment; the emphasis on performance and unflappability under pressure; the suppression or extinction of all emotions as a response to a reality perceived through the artifact of visual imagery; the splitting of one's own consciousness so that one is always aware of the "impression" being made (the "image" being projected)—these aspects of the manipulative personality are associated with video technology. They are also actively nurtured within our society, where greater numbers of people are experiencing their own lives in terms of what they have seen on television or in movies.

"Credibility" and "believability" are increasingly associated in our minds with imagery from video technology. People and events are "believable" depending on the "image" which they project. A split is thus created between inner and outer reality. Such a situation is one in which the manipulator positively shines. Skilled in the art of projecting images in place of convictions, the manipulator is able to appear entirely convincing in almost any situation. Since the manipulator actually *becomes* the part he's playing, there is never the opportunity to unmask him as a hypocrite. In a sense, the manipulator isn't a hypocrite: he is so involved in projecting impressions and images that, at some point, he becomes totally identified with his current "role."

The intrusion of the media into world affairs has resulted in the substitution of images for reality. For instance, the distinction between news and entertainment has become blurred, with history reconstructed according to dramatic needs of video imagery.

For the past several years we've had TV "docudramas" of the assassination of J.F.K., the Bay of Pigs invasion, the political career of Joseph McCarthy. As of this writing, a docudrama is under way about the Iranian crisis and the release of the American hostages. It seems that not only the present but the past is now considered ripe for "public relations" approaches. History is to be rewritten complete with "enhanced dialogue"—the standard disclaimer at the end of a show which serves as the only reminder that the dialogue is a product of the imagination of television writers rather than the actual words used by the historical personages.

Reality is becoming programmed, the distinction between the real and the fictional merging in a hybrid docudrama: when real life isn't exciting enough it can be hyped up by dramatic techniques. The danger of such a phenomenon is that, after a while, it becomes almost impossible to tell what is real and what isn't. The "image" is a unified one with fact and fiction blended to the point that, after a while, even the writers and producers themselves aren't sure what "really happened."

Most important for our purposes, though, is what such a development pretends for the manipulators in our midst. Since they believe that everything is essentially an "image" problem, the only way to make up for real-life failures is to develop the appropriate docudramas that will portray the correct images. Along with the confusion and distortion that this approach engenders in the rest of us, it also creates a generalized feeling of helplessness and despair. After a while we feel, "What's the use?" If history is always reconstructed, what benefit is there in studying the experiences of the past? Under the leadership of the manipulators and minor psychopaths within the television industry, our history is now under threat from the kind of "revisionism" which has gone on in Russia for the past fifty years.

With the passing of each premier, Russian history books have been rewritten and events reinterpreted according to the needs of the moment. A similar process is under way in the contemporary United States, only in this instance, it is being carried out by video. Manipulation is the key to the process. Thoughts, ideals, interpretation of history, judgments of the performance of our leaders—all of these separate but interrelated issues can be "interpreted" by means of specially constructed docudramas and other "re-creations." And who do you think will be most involved in this trend? None other than the manipulator. To him, there is no historical continuity, no truth, no ideals. Events mean nothing in themselves, but must be "interpreted." Only, in all instances, the "interpretation" is a matter of projecting the correct "image." The distinction between news and entertainment, between reality and fantasy, is being broken down in the interest of rendering reality more interesting and entertaining. It is small wonder then that larger numbers of people are beginning to experience themselves as part of a television drama; are wondering, in fact, whether they are, indeed, real. Chauncy Gardiner Chance may well go on to become the hero of the age where manipulators vie with each other in a competition to make fiction more "realistic" than reality itself.

Left at this, television and video technology could only be accused of contributing to a furthering of less malignant forms of manipulation (narcissism, mildly antisocial trends: lying, deception and so on). But I think the indictment can be extended a good deal further. TV has brought about a fundamental schism in our emotional lives. Bombarded as we are with scenes of violence, both "real-life" and fictionalized, our nervous systems are threatened with overload. As a result, curious splitting maneuvers have become common, indeed necessary, for psychological survival.

We sit before our television sipping a cocktail and discussing our day in the office while our attention drifts to a newscast showing the bloody body of an eight-year-old boy found murdered in a woods somewhere in Georgia. After a while, we learn to respond to such horrors as if the boy weren't "real," as if the grisly scene that's thrust upon us is only a "fiction."

In the aftermath of the assassination attempt on President Ronald Reagan, the television news shows replayed again and again in slow motion video tapes of Reagan being pushed into his limousine and press secretary James Brady falling on the pavement, blood pouring from the wound in his head. Close-up views of the policeman shot in the neck revealed the panic and utter psychic disintegration of a man openly weeping in fear, pain and bewilderment.

After the first few hours, the films were condensed so that the "drama" could be shortened and "enhanced" for maximum impact. On several stations, the pictures were accompanied by a musical background. It was the most powerful and impressive *show* in town.

After about the third viewing of the Reagan assassination attempt, I found myself privately engaging in comments about how "good" the pictures were and how well the Secret Service men had "performed." A real-life struggle in which four men almost lost their lives became submerged in a fantasy in which real life became indistinguishable from fictionalized drama. In discussing this with colleagues I learned that they had experienced similar reactions. The whole event was simply *unreal.*

Exposure to events of emotional significance within the "cool" medium of television results in a blunting and deforming of our sensibilities. As with the children witnessing Kosinski's being "roughed up," the television monitor provides a means of distancing one's self from one's own emotional reactions. Emotional responses and intellectual perceptions become "split off" from each other.

We register the events of a president wincing from the pain of a bullet wound but do so absent the emotional responses that ordinarily accompany such perceptions. Eventually, thoughts and feelings become disconnected and we lose our sense of proportion of what is and isn't emotionally important.

At this point, as the result of video experiences such as the Reagan assassination attempt, we are turning into a nation of emotional cripples. It's not that the emotions aren't there; it's rather that they become distorted as we become distorted into creatures who can no longer empathize. Life under such circumstances becomes a docudrama and we react to a fallen president with the kind of morbid admiration that is usually expressed toward the televised interaction of a hit man and his victim. "Great camera work!" "An impressive action sequence!" "Really an incredible performance!"

Television captures our interest by applying a well-known principle that our nervous systems respond preferentially to the most extreme of several competing stimuli. The loudest noise, the brightest color, the most outrageous statement—we instinctively turn our attention toward these extremes. Within the emotional sphere the extremes are horror, fury, murderous rage, uncontrollable passion—in essence, the conflict areas of the borderline personality.

Through television, borderline values and concepts are presented as if they were the everyday concern of the average citizen and since, as Oscar Wilde pointed out, "life imitates art," rather than the other way around, "real life" soon begins to take on a borderline flavor. The increase in violence, particularly sadistic, sexually tinged violence, is at least partly due to the increased representation of these offenses in the media.

The English psychologist H. J. Eysenck, in his book *Sex, Violence and the Media,* coauthored with D. K. B. Nias, recently summarized the matter: "There is no doubt, as we shall see, that the increase in crime, violence, and vandalism and what might be called unorthodox or unusual sex practices, over the past twenty or thirty years has been paralleled by an increase in the portrayal of violence in the media, particularly films and TV, by a similar increase in the number of pornographic publications, films and books, and by the greater explicitness of portrayal of sexual behavior in the media and literary publications."

While Eysenck carefully qualifies his statements, saying that a correlation does not necessarily argue a causal connection, his conclusions, at least in the case of violence, are unambiguous: "It is particularly convincing in our view that different methods of investigation all point to an association between viewing violence and subsequent aggression." Included under the effects of pornography Eysenck includes the promotion of antisocial sexual behav-

ior, marital maladjustment, the modifying of fantasies and attitudes toward one sex partner. "There is even evidence that it may
lead to aggression and violence."

The combining of sex and violence, so prominent a feature of
our culture at the present time, is only one manifestation of the
prevailing ethos of the borderline personality whose self disorder
revolves around the issues of anger and aggression.

Probably at no time in history have individuals with recognizable and identifiable mental disorders had so powerful an
influence in the shaping of a culture as borderline personalities
have today. The borderline character has become a "life-style."
One of the reasons for the ready acceptance of borderline values
springs from the powerful effect that the media exerts in shaping
contemporary life-styles.

As a result of interviews with psychiatrists and psychoanalysts
who practice in Beverly Hills and other areas of the entertainment
industry, I've become convinced that the Hollywood community,
particularly its writers and directors, is notoriously overpopulated
with individuals of borderline character structure. Within the entertainment industry, individuals with distinct borderline personalities are presently in positions of prominence and influence.
Their efforts are directed toward the expression of their own life-
style, irrespective of whether or not the vast majority of their audience shares these particular preoccupations. Thus our movie the-
aters are glutted with examples of "adult" entertainment. In most
instances, "adult" is a euphemism for sadomasochistically tinged
hostile, impersonal sexuality, what psychoanalyst Natalie Shainess
refers to as "hostile sex."

"Sex has beome a 'fix' rather than a fulfillment; a 'stroking' or
'snatching,' but not a giving or a sharing . . . there is a growing
new prominence of hostile sex—and this includes in my view
swinging, orgies as part of an ongoing lifestyle, the increase of
rape, the 'gang bang' and 'sport fucking.'"

The rise of "soft porn" coupled with hostilely tinged sexuality,
formerly limited to fictionalized presentations, is now becoming a
life-style. The borderline character structure is increasingly encountered within our novels, movies and plays. Sexual perversion

linked with violence and degradation; sex as a commodity; impersonal and evanescent relationships based on convenience and exploitation—these are the modus operandi of the manipulative borderline personality.

The borderline life-style with its violence, sexual degradation and impersonality is entering the mainstream of American life because we are becoming convinced through the media that this is the way things are in America. As a first step, producers and directors with borderline personality structures succeed in putting forth their distorted versions of reality. From here, the next step involves the public's ready acceptance that this is the way things are and the book or movie is only "telling it like it is." Finally, the values of the characters depicted are assimilated into the culture.

One of the results of this process of indoctrination in borderline values is the lack of distinction which presently exists between reality and fiction. Movies and TV specials based on "real-life events" have become a genre. We read with horror about Jim Jones and then begin wondering who will be selected to play him on the TV special. Someone writes a movie about a terrorist setting off a bomb at the Super Bowl and we sit glued to our TVs on a Sunday afternoon in January to see if it will really happen. The interweaving of the real and the fictional has become such a part of our everyday lives that our sense of reality has become distorted. Further, there are recent trends that indicate that violence and pornography in the media are fusing into sadistically, sexually tinged murderous fantasies which *directly involve the audience.* Because of existing limitations regarding what can be shown on TV, this process is presently most clearly seen in the movies.

Chicago film critic Roger Ebert, writing in *American Film,* called attention to the trend in recent years for horror movies to be presented from the point of view of the killers. Typically, a nameless, faceless, deranged individual stalks his victims (almost invariably women) and eventually murders them with a knife or hatchet or other weapon which makes possible a visually gripping combination of bludgeoning and cutting. Since the killer is only sketchily identified and little effort is made to place his actions within any kind of framework which we can "understand," the killer remains a stick figure, a nonperson.

The purpose of the killer's anonymity, according to Ebert, is to displace the villain from the film and to place him into the audience. The "lust to kill and rape becomes the true subject of the movies and the lust is not placed on the screen where it can be attached to the killer character, but it is placed in the audience. The missing character in so many of these films can be found in the audience; we are all invited to be him," writes Ebert. The danger of these productions stems from their capacity to elicit from the audience the murderous, rageful emotions which accompany the physical mutilation shown on the screen. The victims in these horror films are frequently independent, sexually liberated and self-assertive women. The killer is, in contrast, a sexually frustrated, impotent, inadequate character who strikes out against victims whom he can't understand but nonetheless loathes with a frenzied passion. The overall effect is to invite the audience to *identify with the killer*.

"It is a truism in film strategy, all else being equal, that when the camera takes a point of view, the audience is being directed to adopt the same point of view," writes Ebert. In these instances, the point of view is that of a dangerous, explosively psychopathic killer who dehumanizes his victims and then butchers them in living color. Since we are not given enough background to put their behavior in some kind of framework (a disturbed childhood, perhaps, or earlier 'traumatic experiences' and so on) the murderer eventually becomes none other than *ourselves*.

"The more these movies make the killers into shadowy noncharacters, the more the very acts of killing become the protagonist, and the more the audience is directed to stand in the shoes of the killer," according to Ebert. In the process, the sexual and sadistic fantasy of deeply disturbed, borderline characters are incorporated into visual imagery and presented to the audience with sometimes startling results.

Media commentator Joel Swerdlow believes that television violence serves as a stimulus for certain individuals to engage in violent acts they might ordinarily not carry out. "It is impossible to isolate and quantify entirely the incidence of television-inspired real-life violence, but the bulk of the evidence is alarming." Swerdlow cites the case of a nineteen-year-old boy in San Diego County, California, who chopped his parents and sister to death with an ax. This occurred after viewing a made-for-television movie about Lizzie Borden, who had axed her parents to death in 1892. The boy, a high school honor student and athlete, had discussed the movie with classmates in the days following its showing on television. How many similar episodes have there been in the contemporary United States?

Although there are no statistics on the subject, senseless, brutal crimes are on the increase in most American cities. The idea that these crimes might somehow be related to earlier exposure to video reenactments is a fairly recent hypothesis that needs further exploration. What is not speculative, however, is the eerie correspondence that exists between video reenactments of violent crimes and the descriptions given by real-life killers.

My purpose in bringing up violence and pornography is more than merely to inveigh against their portrayal on television. Rather, I wish to point out the splitting effect that they have upon our personalities. As I have discussed throughout this book, problems having to do with the integration of the self are responsible for wide-ranging pathologies (narcissistic and borderline character disorders, psychopaths, and so on) which I've subsumed under the general term of manipulators. All these different yet strikingly similar character pathologies share a division within the fabric of the self. Furthermore, there are certain conflicting situations having to do with the expression of hostility and affection which is characteristic of these personalities. At the extreme, love and violence are merged into sadomasochistic and narcissistic rage. In milder instances—notably the narcissistic personality—the individual isn't capable of loving at all, but exists in the isolation of a kind of splendid grandiosity. While no one can gauge exactly the number of these manipulators within our society, my research —including interviews with several hundred psychiatrists and a review of the existing literature on the subject—indicates that they are multiplying at an alarming rate. Even more important, however, are the reciprocal relationships which exist between the manipulator and the larger social order. Our society is geared, one could say *designed*, to accommodate the pathology of the manipulator.

Within our culture, narcissistic and borderline issues predominate both in the ways people think about themselves and in the nature of their relationships with each other. The resulting personality characteristics include but aren't by any means limited to:

1. An intense vulnerability to slights, whether openly expressed in behavior or only verbalized. In a culture where guilt is replaced by shame, the severest strain that can be placed on a person's sense of cohesion is to become the object of another's ridicule or derision. The response to slights is sudden, massive and out of all proportion to the seeming triviality of the offense. Thus, narcissistic rage is becoming commonplace. People are increasingly flying off the handle, attacking each other verbally or, in the extreme cases, physically, inflicting brutal and sometimes fatal injuries. This is the basis for "senseless crimes." The offense is not senseless at all to the one who has sustained an attack on his narcissism.

2. A pervasive search for heroes who can replace the missing dimensions of meaning and personal cohesion. When the self is conflicted and fragmented it tends, via splitting, to view complex issues in simplistic ways. Leaders and "heroes" who suggest extreme solutions thus become appealing. Large numbers of people, all of them suffering from a sense of personal fragmentation, can thus unite behind the strength or singleness of purpose of a leader who is able to reduce issues to slogans. This is one explanation of how a Jim Jones can rise to a position of power.

3. A trend toward short-lived interpersonal relationships in which emotional demands and commitments are minimized. Marriages, for instance, are viewed as only temporary "arrangements." Deep friendships give way to superficial relationships based on temporarily shared interests. The feeling

prevails that emotions are too dangerous, too "hot," too encumbering.

4. Pervasive lack of direction and inner purpose coexisting with an extreme monomaniacal "devotion" to work for its own sake. Workaholism, for instance, is presently epidemic while increasing numbers of people are reporting a general lack of direction and inner purpose in their lives. How long and how hard one can work at something becomes a substitute for examining why the job is being done in the first place.

5. A preoccupation with images and the outward display of emotions which aren't felt. After a while, by a strange circularity, people begin to take their cues about how they "feel" from the way they "appear." To be a sucesss, it's only necessary to talk or dress like a success. Eventually a point is reached when projecting the correct image becomes the basis for subjective experience.

This fascination with "images" and "projections" and "scenarios" is, of course, drawn from the world of television and video media. It is also the stock in trade of the psychopathic manipulator. At this point in our history, the two trends of media hype and psychopathy have intersected with inevitable results.

As each new scandal in Congress hits the newspapers, we ask ourselves, "Why are so many of our leaders turning out to be corrupt?" Part of the answer, I would suspect, stems from the fact that manipulators are best equipped to prevail in the media-based campaigns which have become so important as part of the election process. The individual to whom form is more important than substance; rhetoric and appearance more vital than issues; the politician for whom everything is negotiable; the smiling, superficial "nice guy" who covers up his lack of depth with a "show of sincerity"—these are the "leaders" who are emerging within our present society. So enamored have we become of the manipulative style that it is no longer possible to gain any real insight into how our candidates think and feel about issues. Everything is referred to "media consultants" who determine the candidate's position according to public perceptions. Public opinion polls have become the determinants of what is allowable for any politician. In such a milieu, the psychopathic con man, the narcissistic power grabber—these are the personality types most likely to succeed.

The key question is the extent to which manipulation can be controlled. And here the prospects are, unhappily, far from promising. With the development of large, bureaucratic organizations, the leadership emphasis has shifted from individuals with strong personal convictions to group members possessing finely honed social skills. Individual leadership is less important than the ability to "manage" other people. Management is, of course, only another word for manipulation.

In the past, people have sought shelter from such uncertainties in their public lives by investing more of themselves in their personal, private activities. If the work place was uncertain, at least a person could look forward in the evening to returning to a home which was reasonably predictable and controllable. But today, the wife and children are equally caught up in transformations of the self. The open-ended quality of modern marriage; the increase in divorce; the feeling that one is entitled to personal development and fulfillment, however arbitrarily defined—all have placed great strain on modern family life, which in some ways is even more difficult to cope with than the psychological stresses of the workplace.

Radical "life-style changes" have become commonplace as indicators of "maturity" and "personal growth." A man who abandons a wife and three or four young children for a woman twenty years younger than himself is likely to dismiss the whole thing as a necessary action in order for him to "realize himself." He will speak of his gratitude that he has finally found his "real self." Since greater and greater numbers of people are discovering their "real" selves or more "fulfilling" aspects of themselves, the private aspects of one's life have become as precarious as the more public ones. Who can be certain that one's wife is not currently undergoing a crisis of identity, slowly but relentlessly coming to the con-

clusion that she must trade in her life-style like last year's dress
and "find" herself through new relationships?

Due to uncertainty in both the public and the private spheres,
the importance of the "objective" aspects of many people's lives
are becoming less important to them than their own subjective interpretations. Relationships, the marriage relationship in particular, are monitored constantly as to whether or not they're providing development, fulfillment, depth—terms which imply that the
self has become an object of anxious scrutiny and constant attention. In such a world, nothing can be taken for granted. The potential for greater and more varied social and sexual relationships
fixes attention on the "quality" of all existing relationships. But
since the only measure of the "quality" is one's own internal sense
of satisfaction or dissatisfaction, ever more energy must constantly
be expended into further efforts aimed at self-exploration.

One consequence of this is that individual subjectivity becomes
increasingly complex, highly differentiated and, in the final analysis, bewildering. Subjectivity acquires the status of an absolute:
one's responses, what one feels in one's guts, the "vibes" that one
picks up—these are taken as the true measures of "reality." This
is, of course, a complete reversal of traditional attitudes, where "reality" existed relatively independently of anyone's wishes or desires. But in the modern consciousness, subjective interpretation is
taken as "more real." Such a belief engenders a peculiar form of
anxiety in which the individual feels that he must latch on to his
own "feelings," constantly monitoring his "responses" and remain
ever vigilant, lest meaning begin to elude him. The world is thus
experienced through the intermediation of consciousness. The self
thus becomes ever more painfully *self-conscious*.

With changes in subjective meaning and intention, there often
comes a corresponding change in external reality. Relationships
which are no longer experienced as "relevant," are broken off and
the self enters into a new phase of "fulfillment." Life experiences
are thus split off from each other by new "interpretations." One's
biography is ever changing. The self becomes a kind of jigsaw
figure in which the pieces must be constantly rearranged since the
"model" is constantly altering. As with Krapp (p. 334), each inter-

pretation is contradicted by another; aspects of the personality must constantly be denied in order to provide some measure of coherence for the self preeminent at the moment. The saddening paradox of modern life comes from the coexistence of a heightened self-consciousness coupled with an increasingly fragmenting identity.

X

Toward an Integrated Personality

". . . Man is not truly one, but truly two. I say
two, because the state of my knowledge does not
pass beyond that point."

Robert Louis Stevenson,
The Strange Case of Dr. Jekyll and Mr. Hyde

Shuffling of the Self

I am sitting in a booth in a small, out-of-the-way bar in Sacramento, California. On the wall in front of me is a picture taken in 1879 of five men standing in the sunshine outside a Fancy Goods Shop. Each is dressed in the stiff, humorless garb of a nineteenth-century milliner-businessman. They are obviously the owners of the store.

The photographic image has captured all of the pride of ownership and stolid burgherlike solidity of these five men who, in their total identification with their "role," are, in fact, a form of "dry goods" themselves. To think of transporting them into the present is to imagine their identity dissolving like a mist under the assault of the first rays of the sun. For these burghers are totally identified in their own minds with their occupational role.

Today, such a photograph would be difficult to imagine. For one thing, there isn't any code of dress by which a milliner-businessman could be recognized. Even more important, the commitment given to occupational roles is minimal. We live in an age marked by what Kohut refers to as "the shuffling of the self." Today, people won't and can't be so readily identified with their professional persona. We rejoice in the freedom that we have to express ourselves as beyond and quite apart from our professional roles. We can "shop" for our identity the way we shop for our clothes or groceries. We can, in a sense, construct ourselves from the various "models" we come into contact with. With all the advantages that this entails, it also results in some ambiguities and troubling preoccupations.

Carl Schorske, the chronicler of *Fin-de-Siècle Vienna*, describes a society marked by a chaos of conflicting value orientation as "riven and driven" eventuating in a "value vacuum." Speaking of a fictional composer and aristocrat created by the novelist Arthur Schnitzler, Schorske's description might well be applied to each of us who must construct a self out of the vast and variegated social network in which we live.

"The incapacity for commitment paralyzes Wergenthin's existence. He dwells in the sterile marshlands of the conscious life: between work and play, between affirmation and negation of his inner drives, between flirtation and love, between aristocratic wisdom and bourgeois rationality. He makes no choices."

In such a world, choices are not made; rather, events are reacted to according to "whatever pressures, social or instinctual, register most strongly upon his seismographic consciousness."

Today, as in the Vienna described by Schorske, we encounter a society in which all life-styles are proclaimed equally valid, all values of equal pertinence. We are even convinced of the validity of the position that espouses no values at all. As a result, we end up with a kind of smorgasbord of the mind, a desultoriness of the spirit which makes moral and ethical eunuchs of us all. As a consequence, the self is fractionated into separate and noncommunicating realms of experience. Out of this discontinuity emerges the manipulator under his various guises. What makes the whole process so fascinating as well as deeply disturbing is the closeness of fit which exists between this character type and the social milieu from which he emerges. The interpenetration of social values (or lack of them) and the manipulative character disorder is positively uncanny:

The need to maintain a "front" or "image"; the delight in fooling other people; the emphasis on style, verve and wit in outsmarting and outmaneuvering the "competition"; the overdependence on other people's evaluation for the sense of self-esteem or worth; the confirming power of physical possessions as a basis for self-identification—all have become a part of our current life-style. Since these qualities are also peculiarly adapted to narcissistic adjustments, they are now part and parcel of contemporary experience. What makes the whole process so frightening and disturbing is that a society constituted along these lines is playing according to rules which guarantee the success of the manipulator, who can outmaneuver and exploit the competition in ways that aren't even imaginable to individuals whose narcissism is under control. Thus we're now already deeply immersed in life-styles (psychopathy, imposturing, narcissistic grandiosity) which, disturbingly, aren't recognized for what they are: the expressions of severe emotional imbalances and disturbances.

We're becoming accustomed to people with no sense of history, no continuity, no connections, no sense of allegiance or fidelity. We have replaced real accomplishments with tokens of accomplishment. As a result, we wind up with pseudodiplomats like M'Biye or pseudojournalists like Janet Cook, Washington *Post* reporter, who constructed her Pulitzer Prize-winning story on a lie in order to win a prize she hoped would provide the self-confirmation that was missing and unobtainable by honest effort.

We've entered the age of the sham, the hoax, the cosmic clown who pretends to be seer, prophet, soothsayer and reader of tea leaves. Life is all "image," spacing out on ego, a façade, a special game of "tell me who I am," a great "What's My Line?" in which everybody is free to be anybody he wishes if only he learns to act the part with sufficient "credibility."

Amid the grasping for possessions, accomplishment and recognition lurks a chasm of inauthenticity. People are searching for "values," a sense of "commitment" but, most of all, an integrated self. At this point it's clear that disturbances of the self comprise our principal mental health problem. The sheer numbers of people today who experience problems with narcissism, intimacy and the expression of anger are simply astounding. Furthermore, a solution to self disorders expressed in these areas isn't going to be easy to come by, principally because as a culture we're committed to psychopathy or, at the very least, narcissistic life-styles and attitudes. But despite the ominous interpenetration of societal "norms" along psychopathological lines, I think there's hope. What's required is a fundamental alteration in our ideas concerning the nature of the self. Although there can be no simple solution to such a complex problem as contemporary self disorders, a hopeful approach involves an updating of our concept of just what is meant by a self.

An End of Manipulation

It is not always appreciated that concepts no less than things can become obsolete. The term community, for instance, has changed so much in the recent past that it is difficult to know now what is meant when anybody speaks of the "community." "Community" isn't limited to an immediate geographic neighborhood. This ceased years ago when ethnic groups moved out of their "communities" and spread out over the cities. Thanks to rapid international travel, high-speed communication and interdependent international currency exchange, the world has become, in a sense, a "community." As a result, the word community has outgrown its former narrow boundaries and our understanding of "community" has become updated.

The *self*, too, has outgrown its former connotations. The concept of separate and unchanging identities which persists throughout time requires extensive revision. For instance, we must now develop a new vocabulary to adequately portray each of the several selves within us. Our attempt to maintain the fiction that each of us is, in fact, a separate, monolithic, unchanging personality over time serves as an obstacle toward our understanding of our own and other people's behavior. The contemporary personality, partly for reasons having to do with conditions prevailing today, is *many selves*, each of which is clamoring for control at any given moment. Only by coming into contact with these other selves—many of whom we've relegated to the broom closets of our mind—can we enrich our personalities.

In regard to the multiplicity of selves within us, it is uncanny how often other people are more sensitive to what's going on than we are. "Relax, be yourself"; "let yourself go," they enjoin us, as if implying, "Let one of your other selves [the amusing self, the life-of-the-party self] come out."

Recognition of the multiplicity of selves within us doesn't imply a fragmenting of our personality. On the contrary, it's the attempt to shut out and deny our repressed or multiple selves that is responsible for the fragmentation we experience. Rather than producing discomfort, the recognition of a multiplicity of selves within each of us produces a feeling of fulfillment. When it's no longer necessary to maintain the fiction of a singular, relatively unchanging self, we are freer to allow each of the innumerable sub-selves a certain degree of freedom. We are no longer constricted along the lines of constructing and maintaining a "consistent," relatively unchanging self across time. This, of course, will not eliminate conflict within us, but it will allow us to appreciate more clearly what is going on.

As it is now, the pretense of a singular identity results in the disavowal of some motives because of their apparent incompatibility with others. For example, since my self is constructed along the lines of a conscientious performance of "duty," I am likely to deny certain aspects of my own inner reality. "I must go to the hospital and visit my patients this morning and therefore it is impossible that I might wish to skip rounds and go fishing with the neighbor."

By casting such a dilemma in terms of two or more competing selves, I formulate the situation more precisely: "My spontaneous self wants to go fishing, but my professional self wants to go to the hospital." Such a reformulation may not make my decision any easier, but at least the issue is more sharply focused: Each of several subselves is vying for control of my consciousness. The resolution of these competing demands by means of my conscious decision to do one or the other leads to a stronger, more cohesive self.

The recognition of the presence of multiple, competing and often incompatible selves within us makes possible new interpretations of why many people are so unhappy and unfulfilled. They have overinvested in the maintenance of only one or two subselves and refuse to recognize the existence of others. Freud's unconscious; the "minor" hemisphere of modern brain research; the subdivisions of the mind into ego, id and superego—each of these different ways of thinking about personality is a metaphorical attempt to get around the need to recognize a multiplicity of selves.

Since there is an aggressive, lecherous, uncompromising aspect to all of us, we label it our "unconscious" in order to avoid thinking about the possibility of a subself dwelling within each one of us who is not unduly "nice" but, instead, is given to episodes of violence and raw sexuality.

But how do we discover the existence of these multiple subselves? Herein lies the dilemma which has plagued mankind's attempts at self-understanding. "Know thyself" was the Socratic injunction. But how is this self-knowledge to be obtained?

In our age, the attempt to discover the multiplicity of the self has been carried out by the psychoanalyst. But at a certain point, the theory reached a dead end. Not until the comparatively recent formulations on narcissism and character disorders was the framework provided for understanding the splits within the personality which give rise to subselves. Newer developments within analytic theory are taking for granted the existence of a series of subselves even in the most seemingly "normal" people.

"All abnormal personalities, as well as most so called normal personalities, seek generally to exist as split-off selves in various degrees of communicative integration or disruptive disharmony. Each split-off self behaves as though it has a separate agenda or scenario which is as a rule unmodifiable . . . by the agendas of other selves," says Beverly Hills psychoanalyst James S. Grotstein.

"Every ego-dystonic impulse emerges, I believe, from an alien self which has long ago sequestered itself within the framework of the overall personality and has continued to live under a repression which keeps the cohesive self from recognizing it," writes Grotstein.

The subselves within the personality continue to exert a powerful influence, but an influence carried out at a distance since these subselves "seem to be enclosed in nefarious dungeons and time warps and seek to become integrated with the rest of the personality by perforating the precocious closure which, in the past, has separated them off from the rest of the personality."

Only through understanding and acceptance of our multiple selves can we expect to achieve a sense of inner harmony. Mental symptoms can, in fact, be considered, according to Grotstein, "powerful reminders of those lost aspects of our selves which are still entrapped in the nether world and which return to beckon our attention in grotesque pantomimes so as to remind us that we are not yet whole without them."

Our traditional views of personality as a homogeneous, essentially monolithic structure must now give way to a version in which multiplicity forms the basic underpinnings of our humanity. The task is to *unite* these multiple selves, bring these separate and often contradictory aspects of our existence into a coherent whole. To this extent, we *create our self* by permitting the separate subselves within us to interpenetrate and become one.

The first step toward this is to accept the reality of distinct and often conflicting subselves. But to do this, we must accept as natural and inevitable the splits within our personality.

"Splitting is a basic mental mechanism," says James Grotstein. "It is a universal experience of man and originates from the experience of existing in separate subselves or separate personalities which have never been totally unified into a single oneness."

An overvaluation of one aspect of our total personality—one self among the many subselves within us—leads to deeper internal splits as we become further estranged and cut off from our other selves which demand a hearing. Lacking an opportunity within our daily lives, these alternate selves make their appearance in dreams, slips of the tongue and other processes formerly labeled "unconscious." Our emerging familiarity with our multiple selves often comes from these sources. In all instances, the subselves conform to separate agendas or scenarios which often cannot be assimilated into or modified with the agendas of the other selves within us. Oftentimes the agendas can be extremely simple ones: the requirement for courting failure or punishment; the need for controlling other people or, alternatively, being controlled by others. Thus a "controlling" self has no other purpose than exerting control and our familiarity with this fact enables us to break out of self-defeating patterns of behavior. By recognizing that one of our subselves is irrationally committed to a course of action that our other selves don't fancy, we can modify our behavior toward greater integration.

A tendency toward alcohol abuse, for instance, can be viewed as the result of a separate self which has no other purpose than getting a drink. "It" encourages us to drink when we are happy in order to celebrate. When we are depressed "it" suggests a drink in order to "cheer us up." In either case, this self has no other purpose than obtaining alcohol. Once alerted to the presence of this "alcoholic self" we can be on guard against the rationalizations that in the past have encouraged us to drink. We recognize and assimilate into our awareness the existence of a subself (the alcoholic self) which formerly camouflaged its actions behind rationalizations (celebration, cheering up and so on). This is just one example of how the recognition of splits within us and the existence of separate subselves leads toward an integration rather than a fragmentation of our personality.

As another example, consider the individual who cannot maintain an intimate relationship. Marriages break up; friendships deteriorate into arguments and petty antagonisms. By recognizing the existence of a self which is devoted to breaking up long-term relationships, we can begin planning ways of confounding this antisocial self. For instance, we can make up our minds beforehand that our next relationship will be lasting since we're not going to listen to the arguments of our antisocial self, who undoubtedly will begin supplying us with hundreds of reasons for estrangement. In this way we are able to control our lives, wrest power away from the rebellious subselves within us which, over the years, have contributed to our unhappiness. Further, once we are alerted to a subself which cannot abide intimate relationships, we take the first step toward controlling our future. We are no longer under the sway of this antisocial self who formerly was able to grasp power from our other selves and destroy the relationships which we had painstakingly constructed.

The existence of multiple subselves within us lives on in many of our everyday expressions: "He's his own worst enemy," i.e., one of his subselves always manages to ruin everything for him in the end. "She doesn't know her own mind," i.e., the scenario of one of her subselves is to keep her permanently confused about her goals and how to achieve them.

In my own life, the recognition of several subselves has enabled me to achieve significant breakthroughs. For instance, for years I was a flagrant procrastinator. "Never do anything today that you can do tomorrow" was my unspoken policy. By recognizing the existence within me of a "procrastinator" subself who was bent on delay, I've been able to increase my productivity. Now whenever I am tempted to wait until tomorrow, I recognize that this dilatoriness emanates from my procrastinator self, who will do anything to obstruct me. Now I am able instantly to see through rationalizations (perhaps tomorrow will be a nicer day to cut the grass; maybe tomorrow I will be more inspired to do that book review) and get down immediately to the business at hand. Sometimes I even chuckle at the ways I am disrupting my procrastinator self, who, in the past few years, has fared very badly indeed. More important than the gain in productivity, however, is the sense of enrichment which has come from recognizing this subself within me and integrating it into my personality, my personality as I wish it to be.

A frequent criticism that people often bring up to me in response to my suggestion that we all become comfortable with the idea of multiple selves concerns the confusion and dismay they experience when it comes to determining who's in charge? If we really are composed of multiple rather than one self, which is the *real self*? Who am I *really*?

Rather than leading to confusion, the recognition of our multiple selves actually makes possible real autonomy as we gain insight into scenarios which, in the past, have determined our actions but outside of our awareness. For instance, each time we reach for a drink we are free to gauge whether our behavior is part of the scenario of an "alcoholic self," or whether in contrast we merely wish a drink in order to enhance our enjoyment of the moment.

Or each time we are tempted to put something off until tomorrow, the question arises whether we are enacting a scenario of our procrastinator self which, at this time, is out to delay us. This doesn't mean that we stop drinking or never allow ourselves the luxury of an occasional procrastination, but it does mean that we are better able to maintain insight into and control over our actions when we recognize that our behavior emanates from multiple selves rather than a single self. Thus we are able to free ourselves from the fiction that we are one individual self. We are able to do this by operating on a dual track, a form of parallel processing in which we are capable of thinking simultaneously in different modes: actor and observer.

In addition, as we've become more aware of the existence of the subselves, all of them different within each of us (some people have never taken a drink in their lives and therefore by definition can't possess an "alcoholic self"), our personality becomes unified. After a while, we're able to operate on several channels at once. For instance, it's possible to feel anger and yet elect not to express the anger since we're no longer overwhelmed by a state of mind that we recognize as only temporary. In this instance, we can refuse to express the anger of our grandiose self, who responds to imaginary or real "slights" by erupting into a rage. This capacity to experience emotions and yet recognize these emotions as emanating from subselves within us which possess limited perspectives on reality enriches and deepens our experience. In this way, the disparate selves are united and we move toward cohesion and integration. A growing sense of continuity is thus established among previously repudiated or unknown selves who, formerly, acted out their separate scenarios outside of our conscious awareness. In this way, we're able to confront and compare incompatible and contradictory aspects of our thoughts and behavior. We're no longer split into separate "islands" like the individuals described throughout this book. We achieve what psychoanalyst James Grotstein describes as a sense of at-one-ment within our consciousness.

Recognition of the multiplicity of selves is already apparent within our society but, unfortunately, often in ways that lead to further estrangement and fragmentation rather than wholeness.

Public figures who have been caught in compromising and em-

barrassing situations have taken to explaining away their difficulties (drug addiction, bribetaking, alcoholism or any combination
thereof) as due to something beyond their control, something
done in the past which they now totally repudiate. They thus establish a schism between their former actions and their present
selves. In this way, bribetaking, instead of something freely chosen
at a former time, becomes something that "happened" to them.

Instead of owning up to the consequences as the result of
choices which, retrospectively, he now recognizes as foolish or
mistaken, the individual splits his consciousness, refusing to recognize the existence of any self other than the present one, who
"deeply regrets" his past actions. The greatest loss stemming from
this *self-deception* is the lost opportunity for integration. For it's
only by taking responsibility for our past actions that we're able to
come in contact with the subself within us whose scenario is based
on drugs or whatever the "regretted" past behavior may have
been. But if we repudiate the existence of this self by blaming our
actions on "circumstances beyond my control," we lose the opportunity for experiencing and integrating this subself within the
unity of our personality. We remain, in a sense, "split off" from
one aspect of our consciousness; we become a stranger to ourselves, totally unable to assimilate and grow from our past experiences.

Growth never results from adapting a mechanical viewpoint in
which things just "happen" to us. Rather, all of our actions result
from some one or other of our multiple selves, and it's by our actions that we learn about the scenarios and agendas that our various selves are trying to express. All of these disparate selves comprise our identity, which is multifaceted rather than singular: we
are *many selves*, each with its own agenda and scenario. Only by
recognizing and accepting the existence of our multiple selves—
usually expressed through our present and past behaviors—can we
achieve integration, wholeness.

Paradoxically, it's the person who insists on the reality of a singular, once-and-for-all-time self who is the most fragmented. Anything which doesn't fit into the scenario of the self ascendent at
the moment is repudiated as being due to "circumstances" or

"events beyond my control." The scenario isn't recognized for what it is: a segment of behavior emanating from a separate, perhaps vastly different self. As a result of this failure of recognition, one of the multivariate selves is free to work out its scenario outside of awareness. Thus, we lose empathy with our former behavior and, in the present and future, continue to experience failure to "understand" ourselves. The result is further alienation, further difficulties when it comes to self-integration.

Only by understanding the existence of separate conflictual selves, each with its own plans and goals, can we achieve insight. This doesn't mean that we give in to or cooperate with the realization of every scenario. On the contrary, only by recognizing that each of our impulses, each segment of our behavior, comes from one of our multiple selves can we begin to freely choose which scenario we are going to cooperate with. Only after we're aware of our multiple selves and their separate agendas, can we integrate them and—where integration is impossible because of incompatible agendas—choose which self we wish to actualize.

Once we've started on the path toward integration, our need to *manipulate* other people will decrease. Manipulation is a result of confusion and uncertainty about the nature of the self. Our knowledge of the multiple subselves within us, when combined with our attempts at integration, will make manipulation unnecessary. Finally certain of who we "really are," we will no longer have to depend on manipulating others.

From our efforts to recognize and come to terms with our multiple selves, our consciousness is raised as we achieve insight into the reasons we think, feel and behave the way we do. This requires nothing more nor less than the recognition that a single unitary self is an illusion: *the self* is a concept which must now be replaced in our thinking by *multiple alternative selves*, each attempting to work out its destiny within us. It's necessary that we modify the Socratic dictum "Know thyself." Rather, "Know thy multiple selves, and seek to integrate them!"

Notes

The following are the principal sources that provided the background for *The Self Seekers*. Each refers to dozens of additional references, which will introduce the curious reader to what many thinkers have written on the subject of the infinite subtleties of the self.

The R. D. Laing material is from an interview in London, August 29, 1980, and from quotes and material adopted from *The Divided Self* and *Self and Others*.

The Searles material is from "The Effort to Drive the Other Person Crazy—An Element in the Etiology and Psychotherapy of Schizophrenia" and "Concerning the Development of an Identity."

The patient quotes are from Michael Stone's *The Borderline Syndromes: Constitution, Personality and Adaptation* (Pages 79–80).

The cat woman is from Vamik Volkan's *Primitive Internalized Object Relations*. Material was also obtained from an interview in Charlottesville, Virginia, on September 28, 1980 (Page 83).

The story of Freud and the narcissistic cat is from Lou Andreas-Salomé's *The Freud Journal of Lou Andreas-Salomé* (Page 98).

The Kohut material is gathered from several of his many publications as well as an interview on March 28, 1981, in Chicago.

The Otto Kernberg quotes are from an interview on April 24, 1980, in White Plains, New York, and also from the papers listed in the bibliography.

The material on the manipulator in "Natural History of the Narcissist" was developed on the basis of a lecture and interview with Ben Bursten in San Francisco, May 8, 1980.

Jonathan is based on a patient described in *The Psychology of the Self: A Casebook* (Page 136).

The Giovacchini material is from *Treatment of Primitive Mental States*.

Anita is based on a patient described by Samuel Atkin as "A Borderline Case: Ego Synthesis and Cognition."

The Meissner material is from "Narcissistic Personalities and Borderline Conditions: A Differential Diagnosis" and an interview in New York City on December 20, 1980.

The McGlashan quotes are from "The 'We-Self' in Borderline Patients."

The history of our concepts of psychopathy is drawn from Henry Werlinder's *Psychopathy: A History of the Concepts*.

The 1955 Deutsch paper is "The Impostor: Contribution to Ego Psychology of a Type of Psychopath." The 1942 paper is "Some Forms of Emotional Disturbance and Their Relation to Schizophrenia."

The Frank Abagnale, Jr., material is from an interview in New York City on October 10, 1980, and from his book *Catch Me If You Can*.

The McCarthy citation is "Narcissism and the Self in Homicidal Adolescents."

The Kohut quotes are from "Thoughts on Narcissism and Narcissistic Rage."

I'm grateful for the help given in the section on the Parakeet Murder by Washington *Post* reporter Sandra G. Boodman.

The James Grotstein quotes are from *Splitting and Projective Identification* and from discussions in Philadelphia, New York and Beverly Hills, 1981. Dr. Grotstein contributed greatly to the development of the ideas expressed in the concluding section of the book.

Bibliography

ABAGNALE, FRANK W., JR., with Stan Redding
  1980. *Catch Me If You Can*. New York: Grosset & Dunlop.

ADLER, GERALD
  1979. "The Myth of the Alliance with Borderline Patients."
  American Journal of Psychiatry, 136:642–45.

  1981. "The Borderline-Narcissistic Personality Disorder Continuum." *American Journal of Psychiatry*, 138:46–50.

ANDREAS-SALOMÉ, LOU
  1964. *The Freud Journal of Lou Andreas-Salomé*, translated by Stanley A. Leavy. New York: Basic Books, Inc.

ATKIN, SAMUEL
  1974. "A Borderline Case: Ego Synthesis and Cognition." *International Journal of Psychoanalysis*, 55:13–19.

BLACKMAN, NATHAN and WEISS, JAMES, M.A., and LAMBERTI, JOSEPH W.
  1963. "The Sudden Murderer." *Archives of General Psychiatry*, 8:289–94.

BURSTEN, BEN
  1973. "Some Narcissistic Personality Types." *International Journal of Psychoanalysis*, 54:287–300.

  1973. *The Manipulator, A Psychoanalytic View*. New Haven: Yale University Press.

  1978. "A Diagnostic Framework." *International Review of Psychoanalysis*, 5:15–31.

CLECKLEY, HERVEY
    1964. *The Mask of Sanity.* St. Louis: The C. V. Mosby Company.

COLLUM, JULIUS M.
    1972. "Identity Diffusion and the Borderline Maneuver." *Comprehensive Psychiatry,* 13:179–83.

DEUTSCH, HELENE
    1942. "Some Forms of Emotional Disturbance and Their Relation to Schizophrenia." *Neuroses and Character Types.* New York: International Universities Press, Inc. 1965. 262–86.

    1955. "The Impostor: Contribution to Ego Psychology of a Type of Psychopath." *Psychoanalytic Quarterly,* 24:483–505.

DOMASH, L., and BALTER, LAWRENCE
    1979. "Restitution and Revenge: Antisocial Trends in Narcissism." *Journal of the American Academy of Psychoanalysis,* Vol. 7, No. 3, 375–84.

DURRELL, LAWRENCE
    1961. *Justine.* New York: E. P. Dutton.

EBERT, ROGER
    1981. "Why Movie Audiences Aren't Safe Anymore." *American Film,* March, 54–56.

EISNITZ, ALAN J.
    1969. "Narcissistic Object Choice, Self Representation." *International Journal of Psychoanalysis,* 50:15–25.

EYSENCK, H. J., and NIAS, D. K. B.
    1978. *Sex, Violence and the Media.* New York: Harper & Row.

FAST, IRENE
    1974. "Multiple Identities in Borderline Personality Organization." *British Journal of Medical Psychology,* 47:291–300.

GIOVACCHINI, PETER
    1964. "The Submerged Ego." *Journal of the American Academy of Child Psychiatry,* 4:279–92.

    1977. "Alienation: Character Neuroses and Narcissistic Disorders." *Journal of Psychoanalytic Psychotherapy,* 6:289–314.

    1978. *Treatment of Primitive Mental States.* New York: Jason Aronson.

GOFFMAN, ERVING
    1973. *The Presentation of Self in Everyday Life.* Woodstock, New York: The Overlook Press.

GOLDBERG, ARNOLD, editor
    1978. *The Psychology of the Self: A Casebook.* New York: International Universities Press, Inc.

    1980. *Advances in Self Psychology.* New York: International Universities Press, Inc.

GROTSTEIN, JAMES S.
    1981. *Splitting and Projective Identification.* New York: Jason Aronson.

GUNDERSON, JOHN G.
    1978. "Discriminating Features of Borderline Patients." *American Journal of Psychiatry,* 135:792–96.

HÄRING, BERNARD
    1975. *Manipulation: Ethical Boundaries of Medical, Behavioral and Genetic Manipulation.* Slough, England: St. Paul Publications.

    1976. Published in the U.S. as *The Ethics of Manipulation Issues in Medicine, Behavior Control and Genetics.* New York: Seabury.

HARRINGTON, ALAN
    1972. *Psychopaths.* New York: Simon and Schuster.

HORNER, ALTHEA J.
    1979. *Object Relations and the Developing Ego in Therapy.* New York: Jason Aronson.

KERNBERG, OTTO F.
    1966. "Structural Derivatives of Object Relations." *International Journal of Psychoanalysis,* 47:236–53.

    1968. "Factors in the Psychoanalytic Treatment of Narcissistic Personalities." Presented at the 55th Annual Meeting of the American Psychoanalytic Association, Boston.

    1975. *Borderline Conditions and Pathological Narcissism.* New York: Jason Aronson.

    1976. *Object Relations Theory and Clinical Psychoanalysis.* New York: Jason Aronson.

1980. "Contemporary Controversies Regarding the Concept of the Self." 5th Annual Richard L. Scharf Memorial Lecture at Psychoanalytic Institute at New York University, March 1, 1980.

1980. "The Cultural Consequences of Narcissism." Presented at the Symposium on Narcissism at the University of California School of Medicine, San Francisco, March 1980.

1980. "The Psychopathology of Narcissism: Clinical, Theoretical and Therapeutic Aspects." Draft.

1980. "Normal and Pathological Narcissism in Middle Age." Draft.

KHAN, MASUD M. R.
1979. *Alienation in Perversions*. New York: International Universities Press, Inc.

KNIGHT, ROBERT P.
1953. "Borderline Patients." *Bulletin of the Menninger Clinic*, 19:1–12.

KOHUT, HEINZ
1966. "Forms and Transformations of Narcissism." *Journal of the American Psychoanalytic Association*, 14:243–72.

1971. *The Analysis of the Self: A Systematic Approach to the Psychoanalytic Treatment of Narcissistic Personality Disorders*. New York: International Universities Press, Inc.

1972. "Thoughts on Narcissism and Narcissistic Rage." *Psychoanalytic Study of the Child*, 27:360–400.

1977. *The Restoration of the Self*. New York: International Universities Press, Inc.

KOHUT, HEINZ, and WOLF, ERNEST S.
1978. "The Disorders of the Self and Their Treatment: An Outline." *International Journal of Psychoanalysis*, 59:413–25.

KOSINSKI, JERZY
1971. *Being There*. New York: Harcourt Brace Jovanovich, Inc.

LAING, R. D.
1959. *The Divided Self*. New York: Penguin Books.

1961. *Self and Others*. New York: Penguin Books.

LANGBAUM, ROBERT
  1977. *The Mysteries of Identity: A Theme in Modern Literature.*
  New York: Oxford University Press.

LICHTENBERG, JOSEPH D., and SLAP, JOSEPH W.
  1973. "Notes on the Concept of Splitting and the Defense
  Mechanism of the Splitting of Representations." *Journal of
  the American Psychoanalytic Association,* 21:772–87.

MANKIEWICZ, FRANK, and SWERDLOW, JOEL
  1978. *Remote Control: Television and the Manipulation of
  American Life.* New York: Quadrangle/The New York
  Times Book Company, Inc.

MANN, THOMAS
  1955. *Confessions of Felix Krull, Confidence Man (The Early
  Years).* Translated by Denver Lindley. New York: Vintage
  Books.

McCARTHY, JAMES B.
  1978. "Narcissism and the Self in Homicidal Adolescents." *The
  American Journal of Psychoanalysis,* 38:19–29.

McGLASHAN, THOMAS H.
  1980. "The 'We-Self' in Borderline Patients: Manifestations of
  the Symbiotic Self-Object in Psychotherapy." Presented at
  the American Psychiatric Association Meeting, San Francisco, 1980.

MEISSNER, W. W.
  1979. "Narcissistic Personalities and Borderline Conditions: A
  Differential Diagnosis." *The Annual of Psychoanalysis,*
  7:171–202.

MELVILLE, HERMAN
  1857. *The Confidence Man: His Masquerade.* Norton Critical
  Edition, edited by Hershel Parker. New York: W. W. Norton.

MISCHEL, THEODORE, editor
  1977. *The Self: Psychological and Philosophical Issues.* Great
  Britain: Basil Blackwell, Oxford.

MODELL, ARNOLD H.
  1975. "A Narcissistic Defence Against Affects and the Illusion of
  Self-Sufficiency." *International Journal of Psychoanalysis,*
  56:275–82.

NELSON, MARIE COLEMAN
    1977. The Narcissistic Condition: A Fact of Our Lives and
    Times. New York: Human Sciences Press.

NUGENT, JOHN PEER
    1979. White Night: The True Story of What Happened Before—
    and After—Jonestown. New York: Rawson Wade Publishers,
    Inc.

PRUYSER, PAUL W.
    1975. "What Splits in 'Splitting'?" Bulletin of the Menninger
    Clinic, 39:1–46.

PULVER, SIDNEY E.
    1970. "Narcissism, the Term and the Concept." Journal of the
    American Psychoanalytic Association, 18:319–41.

RAY, ISAAC
    1838. A Treatise on the Medical Jurisprudence of Insanity. Bos-
    ton: Charles C. Little and James Brown.

REICH, ANNIE
    1960. "Pathologic Forms of Self-Esteem Regulation." The Psy-
    choanalytic Study of the Child, 15:215–32.

REID, WILLIAM H.
    1978. The Psychopath, A Comprehensive Study of Antisocial
    Disorders and Behaviors. New York: Bruner/Mazel.

RESTON, JAMES, JR.
    1981. Our Father Who Art in Hell. New York: Times Books.

ROSENFELD, HERBERT
    1964. "On the Psychopathology of Narcissism, A Clinical Ap-
    proach." International Journal of Psychoanalysis, 45:332–37.

ROSSNER, JUDITH
    1976. Looking for Mr. Goodbar. New York: Simon and Schuster.

SCHORSKE, CARL E.
    1980. Fin-de-Siècle Vienna: Politics and Culture. New York:
    Alfred A. Knopf, Inc.

SEARLES, HAROLD F.
    1959. "The Effort to Drive the Other Person Crazy—An Element
    in the Etiology and Psychotherapy of Schizophrenia." Brit-
    ish Journal of Medical Psychotherapy, 32:1–18.

1966. "Concerning the Development of an Identity." *Psychoanalytic Review*, 53:507–30.

1977. "Dual and Multiple Identity Processes in Borderline Ego Functioning." *Borderline Personality Disorders: The Concept, the Patient and the Syndrome*. Edited by Peter Horticollis. New York: International Universities Press, Inc.

SHAINESS, NATALIE
1978. "Sexual Ethics in America." *Psychiatric Opinion*, January 13–14.

SMITH, ROBERT J.
1978. *The Psychopath in Society*. New York: Academic Press.

SPITZER, ROBERT L., et al.
1979. "Crossing the Border into Borderline Personality and Borderline Schizophrenia." *Archives of General Psychiatry*, 36:17–24.

SPOTNITZ, H., and RESNICKOFF, P.
1954. "The Myths of Narcissus." *The Psychoanalytic Review*, 41:173–81.

STOLOROW, ROBERT D.
1975. "The Narcissistic Function of Masochism (and Sadism)." *International Journal of Psychoanalysis*, 56:441–48.

STONE, MICHAEL H.
1980. *The Borderline Syndromes: Constitution, Personality and Adaptation*. New York: McGraw-Hill Book Company.

VOLKAN, VAMIK D.
1976. *Primitive Internalized Object Relations: A Clinical Study of Schizophrenic, Borderline, and Narcissistic Patients*. New York: International Universities Press, Inc.

WEISS, PAUL
1980. *You, I, and the Others*. Carbondale and Edwardsville: Southern Illinois University Press.

WERLINDER, HENRY
1978. *Psychopathy: A History of the Concepts, Analysis of the Origin and Development of a Family of Concepts in Psychopathology*. Sweden: Borgströms Tryckeri.

WOODEN, KENNETH, editor
1981. *The Children of Jonestown*. New York: McGraw-Hill Book Company.

Index